A Passion for Theth

A Passion for Theth

Albania's Rugged Shangri-La

Robert Elsie
Gerda Mulder
Herman Zonderland

Second Edition

Skanderbeg Books

Based on the original Dutch version:
Een fascinatie voor Theth: Het Albanese bergdorp van A. den Doolaard.
Skanderbeg Books, 2012, Utrecht | Tirana.
Translated from the Dutch and substantially expanded by Robert Elsie.

© Skanderbeg Books, Utrecht | Tirana 2014, 2016

© Introduction Part I, Texts Part II, Translations: Robert Elsie, Berlin
© Introduction Part I, Texts Part II and III: Gerda Mulder, Rotterdam
© Introduction Part I Herman Zonderland, Delft
© Cartography Jill Seagard, Silverdale, USA
© Cover Photograph Herman Zonderland, Delft

ISBN 978 90 76905 39 6 (black & white edition)

'I think no place where human beings live has given me such an impression of majestic isolation from all the world.'

Edith Durham on Theth (*High Albania*, London 1909, p. 118)

Table of contents

Part I Introduction   9
Albania's Rugged Shangri-La   11
A Passion for Theth   13
A Graduation Project   27

Part II Visions of Theth in Years Past   33
Venturing into an Unknown Land   34
Climbing the Highest Peaks   54
Blood Feuds in Shala   65
The Bajraktar Wants to Marry the American Lady   88
Two English Minstrels in the Mountains   116
The Horseshoe Inn   144
The Burial of Ujk Vuksani   163
The First Agricultural Co-operative   170
Adventures on a Motorcycle   183

Part III Present-Day Theth   197
The Road to Theth   198
The Village of Theth Today   201
Theth and its Inhabitants   209
Tourism in the Shala Valley   223

Bibliography   320
Photo Credits   324

Part I Introduction

Albania's Rugged Shangri-La

Robert Elsie

I have travelled a good deal in Albania over the last thirty years, but I must admit that I had never been to Theth. It was simply too remote and difficult to get to. When Gerda Mulder told me enthusiastically about her trips to Theth, I realised I had to go.

Theth is a tiny settlement in the northern Albanian Alps, northeast of Shkodra. It is situated in the Shala Valley of the mountainous Dukagjin region. Although it is not far from Shkodra as the crow flies, Theth is one of the most isolated regions of Europe. It seems centuries away.

Getting there still involves catching a rather run-down van (one a day at the most) that leaves a backstreet in Shkodra early in the morning and makes its way undauntingly over a high mountain pass on a narrow twisty road that does not seem to have been repaired since it was built in 1936.

Many figures more eminent than I had managed to get to Theth in the past. The Austro-Hungarian writers, Karl Steinmetz and Erich Liebert, reached the valley in 1904 independent of one another on their expeditions through the mountains. In their footsteps followed the noted Hungarian scholar Baron Franz Nopcsa who spent several years in northern Albania. He journeyed to Theth and beyond in order to scale and map the mountains and to investigate the reasons behind the notorious blood-feuding among the Highland tribes. His memoirs leave us with a lucid account of his visit to Theth in 1907. The English traveller and writer, Edith Durham, journeyed through the Albanian Highlands in 1908 and so surprised the natives, as a woman travelling on her own, without a husband, that they were convinced she was the sister of the King of England. Her *High Albania*, London 1909, is perhaps the best book ever written on Albania in English. In 1921, the well-known American journalist Rose Wilder Lane visited the region with her girlfriend Frances Hardy in order to set up schools on behalf of the American Red Cross. The fruits of this journey are recorded in her book *Peaks of Shala*, London 1922, which was widely read at the time and went through several editions. Lastly, mention must be made of the restless Dutch writer, A. den Doolaard, who visited Theth in 1932 while travelling through Albania on foot. This journey inspired one of his best-known novels, *De Herberg met het hoefijzer* (The Horseshoe Inn), Amsterdam 1933, a tale of murder and vendetta that was more real than anyone would have imagined at the time.

For my part, I arrived in Theth in style... on horseback. This was a modest adventure in itself because I had not been on a horse for over forty years. At any rate, my travelling companions and I rode gallantly up the mountains, over a 2,000 metre pass, and then down into the deep and verdant valley of Theth, that distant Shangri La. I, too, had finally made it.

Portrait of Robert Elsie on horseback, 2011.
(Photo: Artur Metani)

Now, those who hear the word Shangri La, will probably conjure up a vision of an isolated mountain kingdom where the inhabitants live long lives in eternal bliss, harmony, prosperity and wisdom. Theth is, let it be said, none of this. Indeed, it is quite the opposite. It is bitterly poor, backward as only northern Albania can be, and certainly not harmonious. The male inhabitants of the Shala tribe still have the unfortunate tendency, on rare occasions, of shooting one another in longstanding blood feuds (for potential tourist, it must be stressed at this juncture that visitors are never shot!). And, eternal bliss? Well, you are more likely to hear the natives grumble bitterly about their situation and ask you why you bothered to go to Theth when you come from much nicer countries. And yet, Theth is indeed something very special. I can now understand Gerda Mulder's enthusiasm, which has become my own.

This book presents Theth as one of the many beautiful and untouched spots in the mountains of northern Albania. It offers the reader a selection of historical texts written by scholars, explorers and adventurers who got to Theth in years past, including a good number of intrepid women, and a presentation of Theth and the Shala Valley in the early years of the twenty-first century as seen and interpreted by Gerda Mulder. The charm of this rugged Shangri-La can be sensed in particular in the captivating pictures of Dutch photographer Herman Zonderland.

It is to be hoped that this book will inspire more people to visit and cherish the pristine and savage beauty of these remote valleys. A certain spirit of adventure is still needed, as it was a hundred years ago. But that is part of the fun.

Robert Elsie travelled to Theth in 2011 and 2013

A Passion for Theth

Gerda Mulder

A passion for a country or region of the globe is nothing unusual if it is somewhere like Japan, Iceland or the Toscana. However, if the object of one's passion is called Albania, as is the case here, some explanation may be needed. Indeed, one is almost obliged to justify oneself. "You are going on holiday to Albania again?" "How did you get along there?" "What is it that attracts you to the country?" "Wasn't Albania that country with the terrible communist dictatorship?" "Isn't Albania known for the mafia, corruption, human trafficking and politicians who are constantly bickering?" "It will probably never get into the European Union, will it?"

I suppose it may all be true, and yet I am still drawn to this curious and very particular land.

My Discovery of Theth

My passion for Albania derives from a Dutch novel written in 1933. It was a bestseller in its time and went through forty editions. Nowadays you can only find it in second-hand bookshops. It was written by an author called A. den Doolaard who was well known in his day and has now been virtually forgotten. A biography about him, published recently by Hans Olink, has now revived some interest in him. The novel in question is set in two locations in northern Albania. One of them is the city of Shkodra and the other is the tiny settlement of Theth which is situated in a mountain valley in northern Albania, east of Shkodra.

My story begins in 1966. I was fifteen at the time and was attending a secondary school in Apeldoorn. As a student there, I had a card that gave me free access to all the museums and, through it one day, I received an invitation to attend the opening of an exhibition at the town's brand new museum of modern art, the Van Reekum Gallery. The exhibition focused on the works of the writer A. den Doolaard and presented all of his books printed by the Querido publishing house. The author was to be present himself and was to give a lecture about modern Dutch literature. Of course I had heard of Den Doolaard from my Dutch literature courses. I knew that he lived in the village of Hoenderloo near Apeldoorn and had been a well-known author in his day. His best-known books, such as *De Herberg met het Hoefijzer* (The Horseshoe Inn), *Oriëntexpres* (Orient Express), *Het land achter Gods rug* (The Country Behind God's Back), and *De Bruiloft der zeven zigeuners* (The Marriage of the Seven Gypsies), were not set in the Netherlands but in the Balkans – in exotic locations such as Albania, Yugoslavia and Bulgaria. In his day, these books were on the lists of compulsory reading for final school exams throughout the Netherlands. I had never actually been to the opening of an exhibition or to such a lecture in my life, but I decided this time to go. None of my schoolmates were interested in coming with me, so I set off by myself, clad in a twin set and pleated skirt – and somewhat timidly, I must admit.

Den Doolaard was an imposing figure, a man in his sixties who smoked a pipe. He was a talented speaker with a loud voice that resounded in the auditorium. His tales were colourful and his opinions unequivocal. He held a passionate plea for realism and vitality in Dutch literature and fumed against the generation of young writers such as Jan Wolkers and Jan Cremer. There was little reaction from his audience.

After the lecture, I had a look at the book exhibition and was impressed by the creative and productive life he had led. What an exciting past! What an adventurer! I waited in admiration until the great writer, accompanied by his wife, had strolled through the exhibition and sat down at a desk to sign copies of new pocket book editions of his works that local salesmen had piled around him.

Cover of the novel "The Horseshoe Inn", edition 1965

It was there that I bought a copy of The Horseshoe Inn which the author signed for me. I began to read it the moment I got home, and was enthralled. It is a small book containing a brief tale, but one with a complex message to it.

Earnest student that I was, I endeavoured to analyse the novel according to the methods taught to us in our Dutch literature teachers: the theme of the book, the characterization of the main figures, descriptions of nature, perspectives. The novel involved various concepts of honour, conscience, ancient laws of the mountains, blood feuding, passion, revenge and adultery. One of the main characters comes to a bad end. It was not your standard fare, certainly different from the other twentieth-century novels on our reading lists at school. I made the following abstract of it for my exams:

"The Horseshoe Inn is about an English geologist in the 1930s who is sent to northern Albania by his company on a secret mission to search for copper ore in the mountains. He stays at an inn in Shkodra, where he meets a young shepherd who has just punished his sister-in-law by killing her lover in accordance with the provisions of the *kanun*, the mediaeval law of the mountains. A blood feud results with more victims, but the subject is dealt with in a balanced manner. Insight is offered into how the feud is interpreted by the four main characters: the geologist Raine, the shepherd Leonard, the wife Katarina, and Father Josef. Locations such as the city of Shkodra, the mountain road over to the Shala Valley, the village of Theth and its surroundings, and a mountain pass called the Sheep Trail Pass play a major role in The Horseshoe Inn."

Up to this point, I had only been to Germany and Belgium, but after reading the book, I began to realize that I had to see that foreign land and the exotic city of Shkodra where the Horseshoe Inn stood. Above all, I wanted to visit the wild, isolated valleys of northern Albania, and especially Theth, where the novel reaches a dramatic climax.

Fifteen-year-olds were considered adults in those mountains (the shepherd Leonard was my age), and there were strict codes of conduct in accordance with ancient rules. This meant taking the law into one's own hands and committing murder. How different our lives and our countries were...

I prepared The Horseshoe Inn for my final exam in Dutch literature, but in the oral part I was not asked a single question about it. Instead, I was only quizzed – and in great detail – about Hildebrand's classic work, *Camera Obscura*.

Theth: So Far and So Near

Four years later, I got very close to the locations mentioned in The Horseshoe Inn. My boyfriend and I were both studying sociology in Utrecht, but we spent much of our time dabbling in politics. We were active on local committees and he was a member of an extreme left-wing party, a splitter faction of Maoist orientation. Much later, this faction transformed itself into the Socialist Party. He went from house to house in the evenings and sold copies of the Red Tribune in working-class neighbourhoods. I was in a group that studied the works of Karl Marx.

As soon as summer arrived, we wanted to go on holidays. But where? We did not want to go to Greece, Spain or Portugal because they were still ruled by the dictators Papadopoulos, Franco and Salazar. As good Maoists, we could not go to Eastern Europe because it was ruled by revisionists. Was there no respectable left-wing country where the masses were in power, and – from a more practical perspective – which we could get to by hitchhiking and which had a nice, sunny climate? My boyfriend decided that Yugoslavia might be acceptable. I suddenly remembered the land of The Horseshoe Inn and proposed Albania. In our circles, Yugoslavia and Albania were considered politically correct. After all, Tito's Yugoslavia had rebelled and broken ties with Moscow, and Enver Hoxha's Albania had done so, too. And Albania was now allied with China.

After hitchhiking for a week through Germany and Austria, and after a long boat trip down the Yugoslav coast to Dubrovnik, we found ourselves with our heavy backpacks in a no-man's land between Montenegro (south of Titograd, now called Podgorica) and Albania. There we sat at the roadside for hours waiting for a lift to the Albanian border. We had consciously taken no camera with us, and were intent on recording every impression in our brains. In fact, years later, I could still remember every detail of the surroundings – an album of photos never taken, with views of gypsies in their tents, marshy landscapes, the gentle waves of an azure-blue lake, the sound of waterfowl, and the fascinating snow-covered mountains in the distance.

An American in a camper who had travelled throughout Europe finally picked us up and we made our way the last few kilometres to the tiny Albanian border post of Han i Hotit. It was stiflingly hot out. The tall gate of the Socialist People's Republic of Albania was shut tight. No one there. Finally, a border guard of the People's Army with a red star on his cap sauntered over the fence, rather dismayed at seeing unexpected visitors. His reply was friendly but definitive. We were not to be allowed in.

Shkodra was forty kilometres away, and it was a mere fifty kilometres to Theth! We were so close to the two locations mentioned in The Horseshoe Inn!

There was nothing to be done, so we turned back and headed for the Yugoslav capital, Belgrade, where we were told we could get an Albanian visa. This was at least what we understood from the laconic border guard: "Belgrade, consulate, visa!"

So that is what we tried. The American fellow drove us to the Albanian consulate in Belgrade, a long journey through a bleak and arid landscape. Alas, the consulate was closed. No visa. From Belgrade, we continued hitchhiking, and got an offer from an Iranian driver to take us all the way to Kabul in Afghanistan. It sounded exotic, but we decided to get out in Istanbul.

Reading about Theth

The atmosphere of hermetic isolation at the Albanian border served to stimulate my determination to get to the land of Den Doolaard's novel. When I got back to the Netherlands, I endeavoured to find books and literature on Albania. This was not easy at the time. There was no internet, and Albania was an extremely isolated communist country that was generally considered xenophobic. It was rarely mentioned in newspapers. Here and there I managed to find some brief articles about it, but the university library in Utrecht did not have a single book on the country. There were no guidebooks either.

I also read all the autobiographical texts written by Den Doolaard to try and learn more about the background of The Horseshoe Inn. The writer was seventy at the time and was in the process of publishing his memoirs. In one of his books, *Het leven van een landloper* (A Vagrant's Life) he discusses in detail how and when he decided to write The Horseshoe Inn. In the spring of 1932, he had embarked on a long journey from Salonika to Sarajevo that took him through Albania, a country that was a *de facto* Italian protectorate at the time. He was on the road for several weeks and had met many *malissors*, Albanian highlanders, by the time he reached northern Albanian Alps. He was fascinated by their tales of vendetta and decided to write a novel about them. The result was The Horseshoe Inn, which was published in 1933 and proved to be a great success.

In January 1971, an issue of the monthly journal *Avenue* included a rare cover story about Albania. I was primarily focused on politics, but was also interested in aesthetics, fashion, art and culture, which is why I had a subscription to *Avenue*, one of the few Dutch glamour magazines of the period. It was noted for its pioneer travelogues by well-known writers, and was illustrated by top photographers.

Two Dutch journalists had managed to get into Albania as part of a tourist group organised by an Austrian travel agency. While we were being turned back at the border in 1970, they had been on a bus touring the country. Their article revealed what a fascinating experience the trip had been, and the colour photos – taken secretly and smuggled out of the country – showcased a land of dramatic mountain ranges, shabbily dressed workers, and womenfolk in local costumes. It reminded us very much of our travels to Yugoslavia, Bulgaria and Turkey.

The photos of huge statues of Stalin, Lenin and of the Communist Party leader Enver Hoxha were new to me, as were the banners with political slogans on them in the various cities, and panegyrics to the party leader written in metre-high letters of white stone on the mountainsides. Most importantly, we now knew that it was possible to get into Albania and kept our eyes out for guidebooks to get more information.

We Finally Get to Albania

In 1973 a tiny advertisement appeared in the weekly newspaper *Vrij Nederland*, that a lot of students had subscriptions to. It offered a tour to Albania for a Dutch group in the summer. The organisers of the tour were a somewhat mysterious bunch calling themselves "The Friends of Albania - Shqiperia", but this was of no importance to us. We applied immediately, even though the tour was not particularly cheap. The group turned out to be a curious mixture: wealthy tourists who had seen it all and been everywhere except that one country, a scholar writing his doctorate on the Dutch Military Mission to Albania in 1913, and students of various Maoist splitter groups fighting with one another. We were in among the latter.

It was a breathtaking moment when our Yugoslav bus approached the Albanian border at Hani i Hotit. There they were again, those distant mountains, that sparkling lake and the gypsies huddled beside the customs office. This time, the high gate was opened for us and we crossed into Albania.

It so happened that a nation-wide campaign against Western decadence was raging in Albania that year, and it was to have certain repercussions for our group. All of the men were immediately dragged off to the barber at the border post to get their mostly shoulder-length hair cut. Beards and moustaches also had to go. The barber was strategically positioned under a portrait of the party leader, Enver Hoxha, and did his work with obvious dedication. When he was finished, the men in our group looked more like members of a military commando. It was a bit hard to get used to then. It was not an age of skinheads.

We had to exchange our bellbottom jeans for more traditional Albanian trousers. Bellbottoms were suspected of being an imperialist ploy. Once we got across the border we were greeted by a German-speaking pharmacist in an old Skoda bus made in Czechoslovakia – with no air conditioning. He was to serve as our interpreter.

The journey from the border to the first Albanian town of Shkodra was spectacular. We were bedazzled by the landscape: miles of rolling fields of corn, tobacco and sunflowers. There were horses and carriages on the road, and not a car or tractor in sight. Toiling in the fields were women in extraordinary red-and-white striped costumes with the scythes and hoes in their hands.

I was once again so close to the northern Albanian mountains, so near to Theth. From the bus window I could see the peaks rising on the left to the heavens. We had passed the first and most important hurdle and were now in Albania. Not only that, we were in the town of Shkodra (known as Scutari under the Italians), the initial setting of The Horseshoe Inn. The state travel agency *Albturist*, accommodated us in a clean but rather dull government hotel called Rozafa, and not in a flea-ridden country inn with a horseshoe over the main door, as I had imagined. I was burning to find out whether the "Grand Hotel London" mentioned in the novel actually existed.

> "Raine arrived in Scutari three days later. All he had with him was a backpack with his drawing tools, geological instruments, a folder of maps, some underwear, a toothbrush and a Steyr revolver. He was enchanted by the oriental-looking town from the first moment, and he dragged his poor porter along with him as he viewed the deep-green islets floating in the lake. It was one-thirty on a baking hot afternoon. All of Scutari was asleep except for the two guards in front of the barracks and three women dressed in white who were sitting on the pavement with their crossed bare feet and selling raw silk cocoons. The Grand Hotel was full. With a sigh of relief, he handed his backpack back to the porter and they continued down the dusty alley. At the corner of a nameless square across from a small mosque with a shabby minaret he espied an attractive inn in the shade. On its pink façade was written "Grand Hotel London'. Raine gave a laugh, paid his porter and went in".[1]

There was no time for exploring. Our schedule in Shkodra was full and involved a series of visits and excursions in which we all had to take part: the copper wire factory of Shkodra, the old Ottoman Bridge of Mes with its many vaults spanning the Kir River, and the ancient fortress of Rozafa rising high above the town. One visit was quite special – the Museum of Atheism (Karl Marx had held the view that religion was the opium of the people, and for this reason all the churches and mosques were closed down in Albania in 1967). Then came the Mao Tse Tung Hydroelectric Power Station where Chinese technicians were running the show, with a high dam and a large reservoir.

The meals for our group of forty people lasted hours in the government hotels. In the evenings we had long lectures followed by fierce political discussions drenched in *raki*, a strong Albanian grappa. There was hardly a free minute and we rarely got out of Hotel Rozafa. At night we were simply too tired and went to bed, which of course was what the authorities intended. The few tourists who managed to escape peer pressure to attend the lectures and when out into town on their own were spotted by the police in civilian clothes within an hour and escorted back to the hotel.

The next day we set off for the south of the country. In the backseat of the bus, I looked back nostalgically at the northern Albanian Alps, with the village of Theth in them somewhere, a vision that was gradually fading behind me.

Fellow Travellers

Back in the Netherlands we soon became "fellow travellers" of the Albanian regime.

---

[1] A. den Doolaard, *The Horseshoe Inn*, Amsterdam 1933.

We had been so fascinated by the country that, together with a couple of other politically active members of the group we joined, we set about lobbying for Albania. We imported Albanian propaganda films that we showed to full houses, prepared pamphlets, and organised readings. We also penned enthusiastic articles about the just political course of little Albania in our magazine *Albanië informatie* (Information on Albania).

Once, when we were preparing an issue about art and culture in Albania, I was reminded of Den Doolaard and The Horseshoe Inn. The communist regime had put an end to blood feuding in the mountains and The Horseshoe Inn was now a mere literary reflection of the distant past. It seemed a good idea to interview some older writers and Balkan experts on their views about modern-day Albania, so I wrote a letter to Den Doolaard and asked him what he thought of the fact that blood feuding had been eradicated under communism, whether he would like to go back to Theth, and whether he would be willing to be interviewed about the current political climate in Albania. I also put an issue of our Albanian magazine in the envelope. This turned out to be a bad idea. The cover of the magazine showed resolute workers with rectangular jaws clutching flags in their fists. He replied immediately on a handwritten postcard making it eminently clear that he wished to have nothing to do with a propaganda magazine promoting socialist realism as a form of art.

My boyfriend and I organised two more trips for political groups to Albania. On our 1974 journey, we witnessed the tens of thousands of concrete bunkers that were being constructed throughout the country. In 1978, we had just arrived in Albania when our interpreter announced solemnly that the country had broken off relations with China. This set off fierce arguments in the bus between the various political factions in our group which ended in the Netherlands with the disintegration of our committee. We lost a number of good friends who had chosen, in our view, an erroneous political course, that of Red China.

Disturbing reports published by Amnesty International about political prisoners in Albania brought our ideals crashing to the ground. Our political fascination with Albania was over. We dissolved the committee and henceforth, like everyone else, went on holiday to Spain, Portugal and Greece, where the dictatorships were now gone.

Old Travel Books

I did not get back to Albania for many years, but I continued to read a lot about it – its history, the fight of its national hero Scanderbeg against the Turks, the Ottoman period, the growth of Albanian nationalism, the struggle for independence, the Balkan Wars, the First World War, the Kosovo issue, the Italian occupation, the Second World War. I bought every novel of the well-known Albanian writer Ismail Kadare that I could find in translation and was interested to discover that the Royal Library in The Hague possessed a substantial collection of old travel books and anthropological studies on Albania. I learned that in the nineteenth and early twentieth centuries, many travellers, journalists, writers, anthropologists, linguists, artists, painters and photographers had visited Albania, or had lived there and published their memoirs.

The English poet Lord Byron was there in 1809, the English *Book of Nonsense* poet and painter Edward Lear visited the country in 1848. The Hungarian palaeontologist, geologist and Albanologist Baron Nopcsa was in Albania in 1903-1914, the English writer Edith Durham in 1908, the American journalist Rose Wilder Lane in 1921, and the Scottish anthropologist Margaret Hasluck in the 1930s.

I devoured all of these old anthropological studies and travel books with growing fascination. My private library of Albanian books was growing, too. On my birthday, a friend of mine who knew of my interest in Albanian lore gave me a large gift and useful reference work – a bilingual (Albanian-English) edition of the *Kanun of Lekë Dukagjini* dating originally from 1933. An Albanian Franciscan priest, Shtjefën Gjeçovi, spent a lifetime collecting these old customary laws of the northern Albanian mountains preserved in oral tradition and dating from the fifteenth century. The Kanun is a unique code of laws with fascinating articles about traditions and the hard life in the mountains where there were no judges or prisons. Yet justice was somehow spoken in those mountains.

Years later, a travel agency in Amsterdam asked me to serve as a travel guide for a group going to Albania. On familiar roads through a picturesque landscape I was once again on a bus, hearing the same stories and information from our interpreter. I decided then that it was high time for a Dutch-language travel guide to Albania, and began writing. In the book, I included a good deal of background information about the particular laws and customs of the northern mountains, with much material about blood feuding, marriage ceremonies and the laws of the mountains.

It was great fun. I spent the whole summer studying the works of Edith Durham, Rose Wilder Lane and Margaret Hasluck who, before the Second World War, had all travelled and lived in the remote recesses of the mountains and had learned the language. These were my heroines and indeed they still are. They were headstrong, emancipated women who were not easily put in their place. Like Den Doolaard, they reached the distant mountain valleys without any official government permits. I greatly admired their courage. They travelled on foot, or by horse and mule, with local guides and under great hardship. And they all got to Theth and stayed with the Franciscan priests in the vicarage. There was no other accommodation to be had.

My sense of awe for Den Doolaard increased. He had been there for but a short time, a couple of weeks, but he gained insight into the essential elements of northern Albanian culture and its laws, and wove them into his novel. In my view, everyone who goes to Albania should read The Horseshoe Inn.

My Albanian travel guide was published in 1984 and reprinted in a second edition in 1988. Nonetheless, after years of travel in the country, I had still not made it to Theth. Even though I now had good contacts in Albania and was the author of a modest guide book, I had still not managed to get to the northern Albanian Alps and visit my original goal of Theth. The state travel agency *Albturist* was implacable on this point – Theth was out of bounds for foreign tourists. Only party leaders and members of foreign political delegations were allowed to go there. Theth began to take on something mythical – it became an obsession.

The End of Communism
Then came the end of communism. The Berlin Wall fell in the early 1990s and the Stalinist regime in Albania, that final bulwark of communism in Europe, collapsed, too. For the first time in their lives – after forty-five years – the Albanians were allowed to cross the border and travel abroad. Thousands of them fled to Italy and Greece.

I followed the dramatic events taking place in the country closely. In 1994, I returned to Albania for the first time in nine years with my former boyfriend, with whom I had organised the bus tours. We both had the impression that it was important for us to take part in what was going on. The German-speaking pharmacist who had served as our interpreter on the first trip invited us to come and stay, and was willing to serve as our guide again. This time he had no more tales of propaganda to spout and could say what he really thought. He showed his old friends around a country that had undergone a radical transformation.

We were bewildered by what we saw. The towns and cities were bursting with energy and entrepreneurial skills. We had the impression that half of the Albanians now owned a restaurant, café or shop. Private initiative abounded. The Albanians who had been working in Italy and Greece were feverously investing their money in land and were constructing new homes. The whole country was abuzz with construction activity. In glaring contract to this were the old government factories, state enterprises and collective farms, not to mention the government hotels that had been plundered, taken apart and now lay in ruins. The windows of public buildings, such as schools and hospitals, were smashed and broken in. The fury of a whole people was focussed on the symbols of communist power. No one wanted the badly paid government jobs anymore, and everybody seemed to be trying his hand at private enterprise.

The next summer, we returned to Albania and, with the same interpreter and a Toyota Pajero and driver, toured northern Albania. In Shkodra we did not stay at the state Hotel Rozafa, our former home-away-from-home that had now been plundered, but in a new little private hotel. The proud owner was a retired dentist who had lived on the site with his parents. He told us what had happened to his home under the communists and how his family had been forced out and quartered in a tiny flat. In a recent land reform, his family had regained its property after forty-five years of state ownership. Something of the one-time grandeur of the building was still to be seen. The family had been well off. At breakfast we had tea in old china cups, slightly cracked but cherished by the family for decades. I looked up at the ceiling and saw a horseshoe nailed to the wall. If that was not sign enough for me! Could this vaguely aristocratic home have once been the Grand Hotel London that Den Doolaard referred to in his novel? I knew that the old bazaar of Shkodra with all the shops and inns had been destroyed in an earthquake in the late 1930s. This time I was finally able to tour the town of Shkodra on my own.

The road to Theth
The next day we decided to continue on to Theth. Nothing could stop me this time. The one-time state travel agency *Albturist* no longer existed so there were no official

impediments. There was nothing to hinder us in practical terms either, because we had a four-wheel-drive! Full of enthusiasm we set out early in the morning for the once so elusive settlement of Theth. The journey on a terrible road over a high mountain pass was not an easy one, but the views were spectacular. There was hardly any traffic at all.

After a five-hour trip from Shkodra through some wild and spectacular countryside, we reached one of the houses on the outskirts of Theth overlooking the valley, and made a stop there. When the communist dictatorship fell, the owners of this house lost no time in converting it into a little café, even before any foreign tourists got there. We were exhausted and starving from the long journey and went in. The café was furnished with simple plastic tables and chairs, and they had beer and water to offer. But there was nothing to eat. We begged the proprietors for something and they eventually came up with a plate of tomatoes and cucumbers with a bit of bread. This was enough to keep us going, and we continued our journey for another quarter of an hour, down to the valley floor. It was stunning. Just as it had been described in The Horseshoe Inn:

> "A long flat valley between high horseshoe-shaped cliffs of granite, with white waterfalls cascading down them. This was Theth. Through rectangular fields, marked off from one another by neat fences, there were straight paths leading to square houses. So wild and rugged were the mountains with their plummeting cascades, dark-bellied promontories and the razor-sharp grooves etched into them that the geometrical display of little gardens seemed a ridiculous last line of defence of man overwhelmed by the forces of nature."[2]

The mountain landscape was stunning. Our driver stopped after our long and spectacular descent at a swift-flowing torrent tumbling down from the cliffs. Here there was a rickety wooden bridge over the river, built as a temporary solution, but passable. On the other side, the road became an increasingly narrow sandy path. After a short distance, our driver stopped the car and got out to smoke a cigarette. We got out, too. It was Theth!

Two hours in Theth
After thirty years, I was finally in the location of Den Doolaard's novel. In the distance, both in the valley itself and on the slopes were the isolated grey stone farmhouses with wooden roofs and a few sheds. The famous church of Theth was nowhere to be seen. Near the river stood the sad remains of various plundered government buildings, some of which were in total ruins. On the roofless and doorless Communist Party building stood an inscription, barely legible, with the words: "Long Live the Albanian Party of Labour!" and "Long Live Enver Hoxha!" It was simply too much work for the populace to efface the slogans. After the fall of communism, the mountain people,

---

2 ibid.

not unlike the town dwellers, manifested their rage at the regime by destroying all the government buildings: the shops, the hotel, the school and, of course, the offices of the Communist Party. It had all had been plundered, dismantled and abandoned. Everything of value had been carried off.

In my imagination over the last thirty years Theth had been a Balkan Shangri-La, something like Ohrid in Macedonia, with narrow alleys, oriental houses with overhanging balconies, bustling workshops, markets filled with peasant women in colourful costumes selling plums and peppers, little shops – all in all, a sort of open-air museum full of life, sound and colour.

It was not very realistic of me. Theth was a different story. I had my picture taken there. In the photo of our short, two-hour visit, I stand somewhat disillusioned on the primitive bridge over the river, with the ruins of government buildings in the background.

We actually wanted to spend the night in Theth and depart the next morning, but as there was no more hotel, we would have to have fended for ourselves and knocked on doors to find a place to stay. And then we would have to have found something to eat. We noticed that the native inhabitants were not too enthusiastic at seeing us. They had no extra provisions and were not prepared for visitors. We looked around at the isolated farmhouses and wondered what to do, realising it would be very difficult and time-consuming to find shelter.

Edith Durham, Rose Wilder Lane, Margaret Hasluck and Den Doolaard had no other choice but to seek shelter in Theth. But we had a vehicle. In the end, we decided to return to Shkodra, another five-hour journey. Indeed we had to hurry to get over the

Gerda Mulder visiting Theth, 1995 (Photo: Richard van den Brink)

pass on the pot-holed road before it got dark. Thus ended my first encounter with the village of Theth. For years I had been unable to visit it and, now that I was there, everything was different from what I had imagined and there was no more time to explore the valley. As we drove up the mountain side on our way back, I was frustrated and filled with a feeling of regret. It was a spectacular site, no doubt about it. But would I ever get another opportunity to see the Sheep Trail Pass, the church, the school and the farmhouses of Theth? A couple of hours later, it was getting dark on the pass. The barren mountain peaks cast their menacing shadows, plunging the valley into night.

Theth Revisited
About ten years later, an occasion arose for me to take a longer trip to Theth and spend several days there. Food and accommodation were no longer a problem. A tourism project had given rise to a number of houses that offered bed-and-breakfast accommodation. There were many reasons for me to want to go back to Theth, and, of course, they all had to do with Den Doolaard and his novel.

The inhabitants of Theth had asked the Dutch Embassy in Albania whether it would be willing to finance the restoration of a 150-year-old *kulla*, a stone tower used over the years to hide and protect victims of blood feuds. It was an important historical monument in the valley. They were not able to do it themselves and there was a good chance that the building would collapse. A *kulla* is a fortified building, and this one was used by families who were targeted by feuds and who could take shelter there for months on end. According to the customary law of the mountains, men who killed someone in a blood feud were outlaws and could be shot by anyone. They thus took shelter in this *kulla* with their family members. The *kulla* in Theth was duly restored and was to be officially opened at the end of September 2007 by the Dutch Ambassador and the Albanian Minister of Tourism. The Embassy wished to send a delegation to Theth for the opening. It also intended to organise a little exhibition in the *kulla* on blood feuding and the involvement of the Dutch writer Den Doolaard.

The novel itself, The Horseshoe Inn, was translated into Albanian and printed by the Dutch-Albanian publishing house Skanderbeg Books in Tirana. The Albanian title is *Bujtina me patkua*. A Dutch travel guide who visited Albania quite often bought a number of copies for distribution among the people of Theth, and the books were to be ceremoniously presented to the mayor of the village.

So I was off to Theth again. This time I travelled with some friends of mine, the Dutch photographer Herman Zonderland and the Albanian publisher of The Horseshoe Inn, Flutura Açka. After the opening we intended to spend a few days in Theth to get to know the inhabitants and take photographs.

We set off from Tirana at the end of September in a convoy of three four-wheel-drives. The convoy included members of the Dutch Embassy and some representatives of the German development organisation GIZ that had financed the tourism project in the valley. Taking a 4WD is an absolute must because the road over the mountains and down into the valley is still not paved. Autumn was fast approaching and heavy clouds hung over the mountains north of Shkodra as a storm rolled in.

On our way, the creek at the side of the road suddenly swelled, transforming itself into a deluge, and it washed away a substantial stretch of the mountain road, such as it was. After two hours of going nowhere, we were obliged to turn back. Was this to be the end of our expedition? Was I to be stopped once again from getting to Theth? Fortunately there was another route that led us through the village of Bzheta and, with much delay, we were able to get back onto the main road leading from Boga over the mountains to Theth. It took us five and a half hours to travel seventy kilometres. Now and then we gave lifts to some drenched natives who were out on foot from one village to the next and were more than grateful for the ride. Up at the pass, we made a stop at jet-black mountain lake. It was beginning to get dark and the peaks seemed to scowl at us. On the other side, we passed the sign saying "Theth National Park" and from there, it was only half an hour to our accommodation in Theth, a farmhouse owned by the brothers Prek and Gjergj Harusha.

This time I was better informed and knew that Theth was not really a village but a string of tiny hamlets. I had the impression of being at the end of the world.

Why this Book?

It has been more than seven years since that time, and this edition with stories and photos from the past and present of Theth has now made its appearance. Why this book?

First of all, I prepared it to be a posthumous homage to the writer Den Doolaard who introduced me to the inhabitants of another world when I was at school – a bitterly poor yet proud valley in the Balkans. I would also like to acquaint people visiting Albania with the writings of intrepid scholars and explorers as Steinmetz and Nopcsa, those fearless pioneer women, Edith Durham and Rose Wilder Lane, who made their way at their own peril over the snow-covered passes long before Den Doolaard and who published what they learned from the Albanian highlanders in their eminently readable and anthropological fascinating works. I also wish to introduce readers to Kurt Seliger who had the courage to explore the country in the 1950s, and to Nina Rasmussen who, following in the footsteps of Durham and Wilder Lane, got to Theth all by herself on a motorcycle in 1994 after the fall of the communist regime.

They all experienced the primitive world and unique culture of the Albanian highlands and wrote about it with such clarity. Their travelogues are difficult to find nowadays, and this is why I decided to gather them here. I have illustrated their journeys with some original black-and-white photos taken by the noted Albanian photographers Pjetër and Kel Marubi, and Shan Pici of Shkodra, but also with some of the pictures they took themselves. Edith Durham and Den Doolaard took photos on their travels. A year after her gruelling journey, on which no photos were taken, Rose Wilder Lane sent her friend, the photographer Annette Marquis, back to the Shala Valley to take some pictures for her book, *Peaks of Shala*, that the publisher wished to include.

I sincerely hope that travellers who visit Theth in the coming years to go hiking in the mountains, to stay with local families and to get to know the region, will appreciate the texts and photographs.

Gerda Mulder reading Edith Durham, 2010 (Photo: Herman Zonderland)

At the same time, this book is intended to serve as a photo reportage of my visits to Theth and of its inhabitants, as they appeared in the first years of the twenty-first century. Theth and the surrounding region is overwhelmingly beautiful. It is a savage and pristine land, and I hope it will remain so for a long time. I am glad that tourism has now prevented Theth from becoming a ghost town, or a place where only foreigners come and buy houses, as they have in many parts of Spain, Italy or France. I am concerned about the construction activities currently underway. The wonderful old grey roofs made of wood must be preserved and not replaced by roof tiles of ugly red plastic. I hope that the cultural heritage division of the Ministry of Tourism will ban them, but this is probably in vain. More and more shiny red roofs are appearing in the region. The local inhabitants of Theth have increasingly begun renting out rooms and, unfortunately, the additions they have made to their old farmhouses have not been constructed in traditional style.

The homemade "moonshine" *raki* and the fresh butter churned in the kitchen before your eyes are rapidly disappearing from local menus. Herman Zonderland was able to get pictures of them, but it won't be long before they are a thing of the past. So go and see for yourself before it is too late. Discover Theth!

Gerda Mulder travelled to Theth in 1995, 2007, 2010, 2011 and 2013

A Graduation Project

Herman Zonderland

In 1994, when I was a student of documentary photography at the Royal Academy of Fine Arts in The Hague, I chose to do my graduation project in a foreign country. What I wanted to do was let the world see how a team of doctors from Médecins sans Frontières lived behind the scenes. I was not primarily interested in the reasons that led to the emergency assistance they were providing in the field, but in how these people coped and held up in the midst of human tragedy. With this idea in mind, I approached Médecins sans Frontières in Amsterdam, and their response was enthusiastic. It may have been somewhat naïve on my part to start with, because a catastrophe is not something you can plan for in advance. Yet, on the other hand, my graduation project had to be ready by the end of April for the final exams. Fortunately, three opportunities arose. Médecins sans Frontières was not only involved in emergency assistance but also in longer term development projects. I therefore had the choice of Brazil, Liberia or Albania. To be honest, I did not really care which. Since I would be intruding in the private lives of the doctors, I thought it would be a good idea to ask for their permission in advance. They would have to agree and be willing to have me around. I sent out letters of request and in no time at all received a positive reply from Tirana.

As such, at the end of March 1994, I set off for Albania where I was to spend three and a half weeks. I did not know much about the country. Once, in 1980, I had wanted to travel through the country on a motorcycle trip with some friends on our way to Greece, but this proved impossible. We had no choice but to take another route and skirt around Albania, via Skopje, on our long road to Athens.

I needed to find out more about the country. I had received some basic information from Médecins sans Frontières and had also now read a few novels about Albania. One of them was The Horseshoe Inn by A. den Doolaard. At that time, the only Albanian author who had been translated into Dutch was Ismail Kadare. I read several of his historical novels, including The Three-Arched Bridge, The Niche of Shame, The Palace of Dreams, and Broken April. I was particularly impressed by The Palace of Dreams, in which the author provided a very clear picture of what it was like to live in a dictatorship.

Den Doolaard's The Horseshoe Inn and Kadare's Broken April both focused on the subject of blood feuding in Albania, but each in a different way. Nonetheless, they were fascinating books. I had many occasions to discuss the subject with the doctors of Médecins sans Frontières and with our Albanian interpreters and drivers. They all knew Kadare's works.

Blood feuding is particularly prevalent in the north of Albania, so this is where I wanted to go. Unfortunately, after a week and a half in Albania, I was sent to accompany a team going to the south of the country.

Off to the South

The reason for the presence of the medical teams of Médecins sans Frontières in Albania was the fury of the Albanian population after the fall of the dictatorship – they had vented their raged upon the country's public health system. It had occurred to the populace that the authorities had been using these services to keep a check on the people. Much of the public health infrastructure was attacked and demolished. Subsidized by the European Union, Médecins sans Frontières was now endeavouring to help restore basic health services by vaccinating babies, disinfecting needles, etc. As a first step, hospital directors and well-trained healthcare providers in Tirana were instructed by Médecins sans Frontières employees in the use of new equipment being delivered to the country by Médecins sans Frontières. When these initial training sessions were over, Médecins sans Frontières sent the equipment and the instructors out to the various hospitals and health clinics around the country. Under the supervision of Dutch and Belgian specialists from Médecins sans Frontières, Albanian instructors would then transmit their knowledge to local staff at the healthcare centres. Once the necessary information and training had been carried out, the equipment was installed.

I intended to photograph the private lives of the Médecins sans Frontières staff members, but I also wanted to get some pictures of them at work. The training sessions were carried out in a disciplined fashion, however the distribution of the equipment was pretty chaotic. During and after the sessions we were all invited to meals by local public figures and the hospitality was overwhelming – food galore, raki, music and endless conversation.

My plan of photographing the Médecins sans Frontières staff members behind the scenes soon became illusory. They were put up in three different houses in Tirana, though not far from one another. Their office hours varied, with different shifts and different locales, and on top of this, a conflict had broken out among the team members. I spent much of the first week in Tirana with the fellow who was at the centre of the conflict, and it was only with time that I realised what was going on. He was not particularly dedicated to his job and was more or less waiting around until his time was up and he could get back to the Netherlands. Nevertheless, he was a great guide while I was with him, and together, and with some other people, we made some wonderful discoveries. In due course, I had taken enough photographs of the training sessions. My plan gradually shifted towards capturing life, Albanian society as it was at that moment in time. My motto became: "If things don't go as planned, then change the plan". Apart from attending the training sessions organised by Médecins sans Frontières, I had all the time I wanted to go out and photograph whatever caught my eye. Eventually, with the vast amount of material I gathered, it became virtually impossible to select and arrange it as originally planned for my final exam. The period leading to my graduation thus turned out to be quite stressful. I knew it would take some doing to convince my professor that I was coming back with a totally different project than what I had originally planned. He was not too thrilled, but I managed.

Nomination for a Dutch Silver Camera Award

One of the subjects I focused on in Albania was dentistry. I wandered around a dental clinic in Delvina while the *Médecins sans Frontières* staff were conducting their training courses. At one point, I found myself in a large room with all sorts of doors to it. It was a sort of collective waiting room and the doors led into the offices where the dentists saw and treated their patients. There was one specific office for each type of treatment. I managed to get into one of them where a patient was being seen. Two dentists, one of whom was smoking a cigarette, were glaring into his mouth. I caught them on camera before they noticed me. The man who was smoking turned out to be the director of the polyclinic. When he saw me with my camera he shrugged. I wanted to capture everything and show the world under what pitiful circumstances the dentists were working there. They only had forty needles left and used them for injections until they were quite blunt. For this reason, there was no more anaesthesia for children, which turned dentistry there into a particularly unpleasant affair. The dental spittoon served as an ashtray, the toilets did not function, and the atmosphere in the waiting room was punctuated by screams from neighbouring rooms. I still do not understand why people attended that clinic under such conditions, but of course, if you are in pain, you have no choice. Perhaps I was looking at things from a Western perspective. It was nonetheless a pretty repulsive site. The photos received much publicity after my graduation. They were also nominated for the Dutch Silver Camera award for best foreign documentary series.

Gerda Mulder had somehow heard of my visit to Albania and gave me a call. She and Richard van den Brink wanted to see all of the photos I had taken. We had never

At the dentist in Delvina, 1994. (Photo: Herman Zonderland)

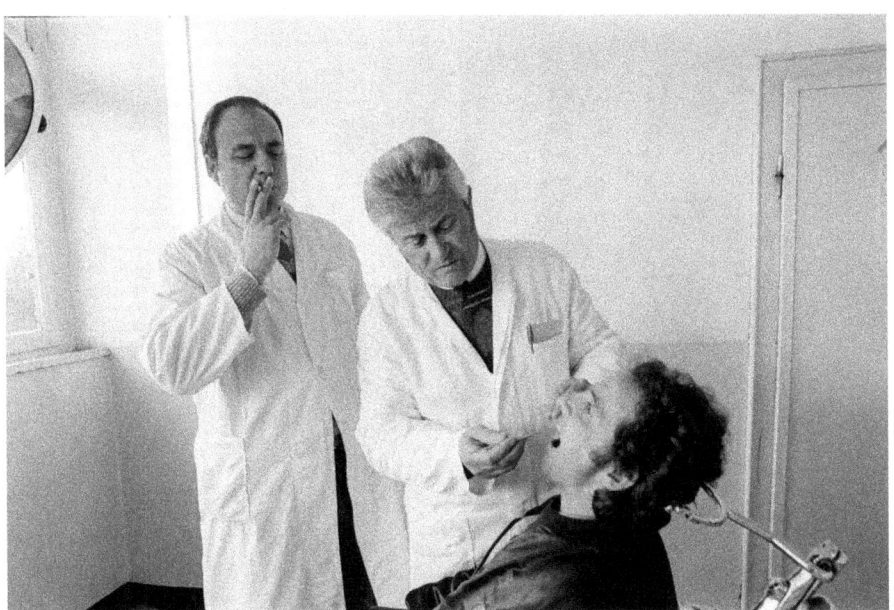

A family caught up in blood feuding. In the background are photos of family members who have been shot dead, Shkodra 2009. (Photo: Herman Zonderland)

Two brothers of a family in a blood feud. They are both in danger and must stay indoors, Shkodra 2009. (Photo: Herman Zonderland)

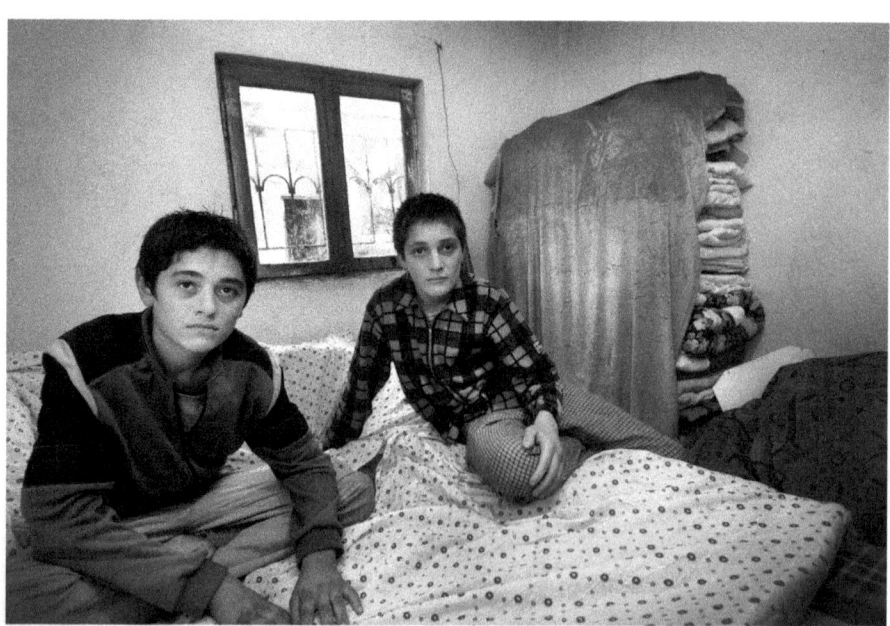

Herman Zonderland reading A. den Doolaard, 2011. (Photo: Roger Sorel)

met before, but got along splendidly and had a great evening together.

It was customary with the *Médecins sans Frontières* people that, whenever anyone had a birthday or when someone departed and left the mission, they would be given a present, something they didn't have. I was never particularly fond of raki, but when I left Albania, I was given a large bottle of the stuff – a litre and a half of homemade raki in a plastic coke bottle sealed with medicinal tape. When I visited Gerda and Richard, I took the raki bottle with me and it made the rounds that evening. I almost began to enjoy drinking it myself.

Richard and Gerda were both active in promoting a twinning project between the towns of Utrecht in the Netherlands and Elbasan in Albania, and I was able to use my photos for a number of their advertising campaigns. The pictures I took at the dental clinic were used to collect money for dental chairs. I have been in close contact with them since that time. I participated as a photographer in a number of symposia on Albania and exhibited my pictures when the first Albanian consul arrived in the Netherlands.

A den Doolaard Museum in Theth?

Several years passed before I returned to Albania. It was 2007. I was busy with my growing family and with my career as a professional photographer, but northern Albania was still present, somewhere in the back of my mind.

One day I heard something that caught my attention. A museum was to be constructed in northern Albania, in Theth, to the honour of A. den Doolaard. Gerda and I talked and decided to go. It was too great an opportunity to miss, a once-in-a-lifetime occasion. Before we knew it, we were there in the midst of a verdant valley in northern Albanian Alps. In the centre of the village was the said *kulla* that was closely associated with the curious phenomenon of blood feuding, about which I had read. Together with the Albanian writer and publisher Flutura Açka, who was now Richard's wife, we spent several days there to get to know the region and its inhabitants, and of course to take pictures. During this trip, the idea gradually emerged of writing a book about Theth and the valley.

In my return to Theth in 2011 I took part in a strenuous trek over a mountain pass to the village of Valbona in a neighbouring valley. This time, my partner went with me to that crazy country.

I was fascinated by the phenomenon of blood feuding. In 2009, I took part in a documentary made about it in Albania and visited several families in the Shkodra region who were more or less imprisoned in their own homes as a result of feuds. One family made a particular grim impression upon me. They had six children and a foster child who all stared blankly at me. I often wonder what happened to them.

Herman Zonderland travelled to Theth in 2007, 2010, 2011 and 2013

Part II Visions of Theth in Years Past

Robert Elsie & Gerda Mulder

Venturing into an Unknown Land

Karl Steinmetz in Theth (1904)

Woman with basket, 1870. (Photo: Pjetër Marubi)

Who was Karl Steinmetz?
The Austro-Hungarian explorer and travel writer, Karl Steinmetz, was an engineer by profession. After an extensive trip to South America, he journeyed several times through the Ottoman Empire before venturing into its wildest part, the mountains of northern Albania. In August 1903, he set off on an expedition through the mountains from Shkodra to Gjakova and Prizren in the summer heat. Soon after his arrival in Skopje, he sailed right back to Albania by steamer from Salonika to San Giovanni di Medua (Shëngjin) where he arrived on 12 September, to begin a second expedition which took him through Mirdita for two weeks and back down the Drin Valley to Shkodra.

Why Theth?
In August 1904, he returned to Albania to explore the northern mountains once again. This journey took him though similar territory, but slightly to the north, through the high mountains of Shkreli, Theth, Shala and Merturi on to Gjakova. A third expedition in 1908 took him once again through the northern mountains, this time in the direction of Mat and the valley of the Black Drin in Dibra country. Steinmetz's travels are described in his three German-language books: *Eine Reise durch die Hochländergaue Nordalbaniens* (A Trip through the Highlands of Northern Albania), Vienna 1904; *Ein Vorstoß in die nordalbanischen Alpen* (A Venture into the Northern Albanian Alps), Vienna 1905; and *Von der Adria zum Schwarzen Drin* (From the Adriatic to the Black Drin), Sarajevo 1908. Together with Baron Nopcsa and Edith Durham, he was regarded as one of the best informed foreign travellers of northern Albania in his day. Karl Steinmetz learned Albanian and was also the author of an Albanian grammar and dictionary: *Albanische Grammatik: nordalbanische Mundart* (Albanian Grammar: Northern Albanian Dialect), Sarajevo 1913; and *Deutsch-albanesisches Feldwörterbuch* (German-Albanian Field Dictionary), Sarajevo 1913.

Travelling to Theth
It was in the heat of August 1904 that Karl Steinmetz set off from Shkodra. His goal was the forbidden Muslim town of Gusinje (Gucia), now in southeastern Montenegro. Having arrived in Theth (Nrejaj), however, a dispute between the native tribesmen forced him to change his plans.

"By their behaviour, the people who were supposed to take me to Gusinje, forced me to continue my journey southwards to Shala and then on to Nikaj in the east, i.e. to travel through country that I already knew." Shkodra is not an attractive town to spend much time in. For this reason, as soon as I arrived, I applied to the Austro-Hungarian Consulate General for the permit I needed to travel in Turkey, the *yol-teskere*. On the following day, I was informed that the governor was not allowing travel in Albania pursuant to a directive that had reached him from Constantinople a few weeks earlier. They thus refused to issue the travel permit despite the fact that Consul Rémi von Kwiatkovsky did his best to support me, and I am very grateful to him for this. I therefore had no choice but to set off without permission. The *teskere* is not needed in the mountains at all, and once I got across them, into the Vilayet of Kosovo, I would just have to see how to deal with the authorities.

I left Shkodra at the break of dawn on August 9th in the company of two men from the town, taking back roads to avoid the Turkish guard posts checking the main roads. Since we had good horses, we were able to ride in a trot almost all the way across the plain – interspersed with meadows, fields and groves of trees, that stretches between the mountains and Lake Shkodra. The countryside only changed when we reached the trail leading to Kastrati and Hoti, near Hani i Çesmës, and turned right. On our right side were barren stony hills and on the left, a flat, slightly sloping plain covered in rocks as big as fists or heads. We crossed the dry bed of the Benushi River, carved deep into the landscape, which in the rainy season discharges its water into the lake, and stopped for a short while at Hani Koder Ars, where there is a little shop among the tall trees. The shop offered coffee and was always abuzz with activity because it had the only well within an hour's walk. Around noon, we reached the Proni i thatë creek at the point where it emerges from the gorge. We crossed its bed, stony and completely dried out, and climbed up towards the church of the Shkreli tribe at the settlement of Bërzheta, about 40 m. in elevation above the valley. It is a simple building but somewhat larger than most of the churches one encounters in Albania. Beside it was a large, two-storey vicarage belonging to the missionary, a diocesan priest. On the steep slopes around it were a number of farmhouses, trees and small fields carved out of the rocky soil.

The missionary was not there and had been gone for several weeks. I did, however, manage to meet his representative, a young priest, as well as the missionary of Boga, Dom Noci, who was there for a short visit. Dom Noci intended to return home that afternoon, so I decided to join him. I dismissed my guides and we set off for Boga late in the afternoon.

The trail took us up the narrow valley of the Proni i thatë creek. Initially the slopes were covered in bushes but higher up, there were imposing cliffs with steep embankments, some of which were covered in shrubs. Our surroundings were bleak and desolate indeed. Neither grass nor water. Proni i thatë (Dry Creek) was the perfect name for the valley. It is the stoniest and most arid region in all of the Highlands and, for this reason, the Shkreli tribe that lives here does not do any farming but only herding. In the summer, they drive their animals up into the lush mountain pastures, and in the wintertime they keep them in the lowlands and feed them on hay they bring down from the mountains and on cobs of corn. Only a few families move south to the warmer coastal region in the winter. In this sense, the Shkreli are different from their northern neighbours, the Kelmendi, almost all of whom spend the winter on the coast south of Shkodra.

The Shkreli are a comparatively wealthy tribe consisting of about 600 families, of whom most (about 500) are Catholic. The rest are Muslim. The largest settlement in Shkreli is Vrizi at the foot of Mount Veleçik where the *bajraktar*, Vat Marshi, lives. The

Man from Dukagjin, 1890-1919. (Photo: Kel Marubi)

other settlements are – according to size – Bërzheta, Dusej, Dedaj, Stërkuja, Pojica, Grizhaj, Stillo and Zagora.

After crossing the meagre flow of a spring, about two hours northeast of Bërzheta, we came to a small, flat plain with some corn fields and a few houses here and there.

This was the settlement of Dusej where the northeastern direction of the valley makes a turn northwards. At this spot, the trail enters a ravine, only about 2 m. wide, and proceeds for some time up the narrow gorge that also serves as the bed of the creek. Thereafter it opens up into a pleasant valley with gentle slopes covered in meadows, fields and houses here and there. On this side of the gorge, the region is called Gryka e Dusejt (The Gorge of Dusej).

Spending the night in Preçaj
On the other side of the creek, one comes upon a gushing spring of ice-cold water with a trough for animals to drink in a grove of lofty beech trees. It was a perfect spot for a rest. We had a *kahvexhi* (coffee man), who had taken up residence here in a primitive hut, make us a steaming cup of coffee. Night was approaching so we were soon back on the trail up the left side of the valley, stumbling over stones. At the point where the valley turns eastward, one leaves Shkreli territory and enters the region of the Boga tribe. We reached Preçaj in the dark a quarter of an hour later, where this tribe's church is located. In accordance with northern Albanian tradition, the church is named after the tribal territory it is in, and is thus simply called the church of Boga.

The Boga actually belong to the Kelmendi tribe and constitute one of its four *bajraks*. In actual fact, they have very little contact with the Kelmendi because the latter live in the valley of the Cem, from which the Boga are separated by a 2000 m. high mountain range. The Boga are made up of about 75 families that, with one exception, are all Catholic and live in the following nine villages: Gjokaj, Preçaj, Malej, Gegaj, Mihaj, Leshaj, Mikaj, Ulgjekaj and Nrej. The *bajraktar*, Llesh Sokoli, does not live on tribal territory but on the plain of Shkodra and only visits Boga for a couple of weeks each year. The rest of the time he is represented by Zejf Prenka. The Boga, too, are primarily herdsmen because there is very little farmland, only around Preçaj.

As we arrived late in Preçaj, I was only able to have a good look at the surroundings the next morning (August 10th). Here, too, the fields rise gradually up the slopes until they change into steep rocky cliffs. Most of the houses are on the right side of the valley, whereas the church is on the left.

Although one has the impression on the trail from Bërzheta to Preçaj that there is no particular difference in elevation, Preçaj is actually rather high. The measurement for Bërzheta was 580, whereas for Preçaj it was 920.

At my request, the missionary there got me a young man to take me to Theth. In contrast to my experience the year before in Dushmani, Toplana and Nikaj, where my guides never even mentioned the issue of remuneration, this fellow wanted to know how much he would get, and indeed demanded quite a hefty sum.

The same thing occurred in Theth (and later in Raja), but this is due to the fact that Theth and Raja are situated on the most frequented trails leading from Gusinje and Peja to Shkodra. Accordingly, the population here has had more contact with the outside world. Albanians are endowed with great natural intelligence and learn quickly

Young man from Dukagjin, 1929 (Photo: Shan Pici)

how to take advantage of situations. In dealing with foreigners, they are convinced that everyone from abroad is immeasurably rich because they have come all the way to visit the mountains just for fun. Half a *medjid* (two crowns) per person and day is usually considered a good wage.

Having reached an agreement with my guide in Preçaj, we set off on foot because the path from here on is unsuitable for horses. Just past the church, one crosses a gushing spring of water near which there are two shops (*dugoj*) run by men from Shkodra. They are both exceptionally primitive and have only very basic provisions such as salt, coffee, scarves, needles and thread, etc. Beyond Preçaj, the valley narrows

39

to a gorge with cliffs. The farmland ends here and one proceeds up a wild ravine in which one is forced to clamber over rocks and boulders. Shrubs and tall beech trees grow in the ravine, too, above which are massive cliffs. It is one of the most romantic landscapes in all of the Highlands. The path, if one can call it such, continues up to the end of the valley and rises up into a splendid forest of tall beeches in stony soil. We climbed higher and higher. The beech trees were now replaced by conifers until the forest came to an end in a small barren basin just below the pass. The basin, called Gropa e Borës, is surrounded by cliffs covered in deep snowdrifts. In the middle of the basin, we came across a poor soul in a primitive stone hut who was busy brewing coffee there for passers-by. There is no water to be had at this elevation so, to make the coffee, the fellow used snow which he melted in a wooden vessel.

Crossing the Sheep Trail Pass

The trail divides near the hut. To the left was a difficult path up over the Maja e Vijavet directly towards the valley of Gusinje. To the right was another trail, suitable for pack-horses. It ascended the slope over scree and a large patch of snow to the pass. I chose this trail and in twenty minutes I was on the Qafa e Shtegut të Dhenvjet, meaning Sheep Trail Pass, the highest pass in the northern Albanian Alps. The aneroid showed that we were at 1770 m. in elevation. The pass is only a few metres wide. To its right looms a lofty cliff.

Northern Albanian Alps, 1933.
(Photo: Shan Pici).

Rocky landscape, *Valley of Theth*, 1940. (Photo: Giuseppe Massani)

When I got to the other side of the pass, I had the impression that curtains had suddenly been drawn open before me. An extraordinary view presented itself. At my feet was a rock face that descended almost vertically. Far below me, at the bottom of the valley, I could see verdant fields and meadows, the Valley of Theth, through which a river meandered. To my right and left were snow-covered mountains, jagged ridges and awesome cliffs rising into the blue sky. Only in the southern part of the valley are

41

there slopes covered in brush and woodlands. To the north, there were only barren cliffs in hues of white and grey. The scene was majestic but somehow intimidating as well, because the many of the precipices before me plunged 500 m. right into an abyss. Not a blade of grass grew there. [...]

Having enjoyed the panoramic view from the top of the Sheep Trail Pass, I began to make my descent. The path was steep and extremely arduous. [...] After clambering down over the rocks and scree for several hundred metres, I eventually reached a part of the mountainside that was covered in grass, bushes and trees. Here there was a juncture in the trail - one path to the left followed down into the valley for another half an hour and then up again to the Peja Pass. This is the trail to Gusinje. The path to the right continued steeply down the mountainside through the bushes until one reached the first fields and pastures. I passed several farmhouses until I got to two watermills beside the swiftly flowing crystal-clear waters of the Shala River. Even when it is hot out, the river is freezing cold all the way down to the end of the valley where it flows into the Drin. This is because it is fed directly by the snow up in the surrounding mountains. It makes excellent drinking water.

Arrival in Theth
I crossed the little (1 m. wide) bridge over the river and, continuing along the left bank for a quarter of an hour, I reached the church of Theth in Nrejaj. It is quite a large building. The main floor comprised the church, or rather the chapel, itself and two storage rooms. The upper floor consisted of three rooms and a kitchen that were used by the missionary. The building is situated on flatland and is surrounded by cornfields. There are also a few other houses around it.

When my guide and I got to the church, we found the door locked, and there was no one there to answer our calls. From a passer-by, we learned that the priest had gone to Abata to visit a colleague for a few days. While I was wondering what we should do, a young man came around and introduced himself as the church custodian and representative of the missionary. When I explained that I had come to see the missionary, he let us in, stating that the priest would certainly have no objections. I dismissed my guide and gave myself to the care of the custodian, Pjetër Gjoni. Pjetër was a crafty devil. One should not be led to believe that, by inviting me in, he was acting out of Christian charity. He was already calculating how much more he could make out of me than by slaving away in the fields.

Theth is marked on the maps as a settlement, but this is not completely accurate. It is more of a region. The valley of the Shala River from its source southwards down to the Qafa e Boshit (Bosh Pass) is the territory of the Shala tribe. At Ndërlysa, the valley is interrupted by a ravine several kilometres long through which the river makes its way. The area north of the ravine, the region of the river's source, is called Theth, and the area to the south is known as Shala e Madhe (Greater Shala), or simply Shala. Although both areas belong the Shala tribe, they live more or less separated from one another and do not regard one another as relatives. Marriages between the two halves

Cin N. Deda and his wife in highland costume, 1897-1903.
(Photo: Pjetër Marubi)

of the tribe are thus allowed. Each of the areas has its own missionary. The one in Theth resides in Nrejaj and the one in Shala resides in Abata.

Theth comprises the following seven hamlets, 90 houses in all: Nrejaj, Markdedaj, Gjeçaj, Nikgjonaj, Okol, Leçaj and Ndërlysa. One is wont to calculate seven souls per household, but for some villages and areas this gives erroneous results because, due to the patriarchal customs of the Highlanders, whole extended families can live under one roof. Even if there are several married sons in the family, none of them leave home to build a house of their own. They all continue to live together. In some cases, fifty people can be found living under one roof. It is obvious that such circumstances do not promote proper sanitary conditions. Syphilis is particularly prevalent. Until quite recently, this dreadful scourge was unknown in the Highlands. It was brought in from Shkodra five or six years ago and spread rapidly, promoted by the customs and living conditions of the Highlanders but also by a lack of knowledge about the way the disease is spread. Nowhere have any precautionary measures been taken, not even the simplest.

The people of Theth are active in herding and farming but the proceeds of the latter activity are not sufficient since there is too little farmland available. The crops consist almost entirely of corn, which is processed at the watermills, of which there are several in the valley. The main food staple is corn flour, and what is lacking is brought in from Peja because it is cheaper there than in Shkodra. Every week a group of villagers from Theth and Shala sets off to get flour which they carry on pack animals or on their own backs. Because of the difficult mountain terrain, the only pack animals used in the valley are mules. They are astoundingly sure-footed and can clamber up difficult rocky slopes like chamois. There are no horses to be found in the Shala Valley, or in the neighbouring areas to the east and south.

With Pjetër's assistance, I was put up at the home of the missionary. Theth makes a very pleasant stay in the summer as opposed to most other parts of northern Albania. The heat is not so intense because of the high elevation (780 m.) and the surrounding snow-covered mountains.

The next morning (August 11th), the *bajraktar* of Theth, Sokol i Marash Nikës, came around to see me. He was about fifty years old and had a friendly expression on his face, that was marked by the years. We had a very interesting conversation, during which Pjetër made lunch in the adjoining kitchen. Pjetër suddenly came back into the room, informing us that he had slaughtered a chicken but had no idea how to cook it. I went into the kitchen, followed by the *bajraktar*, and altogether, we manage to make a palatable meal out of the poor bird. As compensation, I invited the *bajraktar* to join us and we had a splendid time of it. Pjetër had found plates, knives and forks in the missionary's cupboard, not only for me, but also for himself and for the *bajraktar*. I was highly amused to observe the difficulties my companions had with the utensils with which they were not familiar. After some time, the *bajraktar* threw the knife and fork aside in a huff and used his fingers, as his forefathers had done.

Life of women in the mountains

After lunch a woman and a girl came in to speak with the priest. The woman must have been quite beautiful in her day and her girl was quite attractive, too. In fact, one encounters many a fair maiden among the Highland women. Coarse peasant faces that we are used to seeing in our country are extremely rare in Albania in both sexes. We invited the women to sit down for a while, and such a warm-hearted conversation arose that I felt quite at home, as if I were in an Austrian farmhouse. The bajraktar and Pjetër took advantage of the occasion to consume great amounts of the tobacco that I had brought with me from Shkodra. The Highlanders love to smoke. Even the women smoke.

The life of women in the mountains is radically different from that of women in town. They are all treated with great severity. Once they are fourteen years old, girls in town are almost never allowed to leave the house. In the Highlands things are different. No one stops them from taking long walks alone in the mountains. Marriages in town are almost always arranged by the parents, and the couple often only see one another on the day of their wedding. Because contact is not impeded in the Highlands, couples sometimes get married because they are in love. If a boy is attracted to a girl from a neighbouring tribe - the Highlanders do not marry those whom they regard as their blood relatives – he visits the house in question on numerous occasions. Then, he sends his mother or another relative with a present for the girl's father. If the father accepts the gift, it means that he has agreed to the engagement. If the father refused, but the girl wants to marry him, the boy will abduct her with the help of his friends, but he then becomes the object of a blood feud. Women are quite often abducted with their consent.

Brides have no dowry. What is more, before the marriage, the bridegroom must pay the bride's family a sum of 1,100 to 1,500 piastres, according to his financial situation, 3,000 piastres at the most.

The Missionary of Theth, Father Ludovico and his household, 1904.
(Photo: Kurt Steinmetz)

45

Despite the efforts of the missionaries, polygamy is quite common in the Highlands. In some cases it is required by custom. If one of two married brothers dies, the other brother is required to take the widow as a concubine. This also applies to an uncle's wife.

In the afternoon, Pjetër and I visited the open graveyard beside the church which is full of big wooden crosses in the shade of large trees. We were sitting around on the grass with several men who came around, smoking and talking all the time, when someone approached with a spade and began digging a shallow grave next to us. He then fit the grave, half a metre deep, with boards and made a sign to several women who were waiting in the distance. One of them carried a little cradle with a dead baby in it. She took the baby out and gave it to the man. He lay the small corpse in the grave, placed a board upon it, and covered it all with soil. The mother then placed the cradle upside down on the grave as a sign that there was no more need for it. The whole event took place in silence without any sign of emotion, with the exception of a few tears that welled in mother's eyes when the soil was thrown onto the improvised coffin. All the time, we were sitting just a metre away, talking and laughing, and even the gravedigger joined in on our conversation [...].

[Two days later] in Nrejaj we finally met the missionary, a Franciscan, together with his mother and two sisters who had come to the vicarage to keep house for him. The reverend gentleman was still quite young, just over twenty, and was not well versed in the customs of the Highlands. He had only been transferred here from his native Shkodra six week ago. His inexperience was a major reason why my travel plans were thwarted. His name was actually Father Lodovico, but the Highlanders prefer very short names. The names they are baptized with are all monosyllabic, such as Kin, Kol, Lek, Nou, etc. He was thus informed when he arrived that they did not like his name and that they would call him Father Gjon. The people of Theth put up with no contradiction in such matters. The priest of Abata had to undergo a similar metamorphosis, too. Father Cyrill became Father Deda.

The two sisters, fourteen and seventeen years old, were the first girls from Shkodra that I had occasion to meet. Their names were Age and Leze and they were both pretty, indeed the elder one was quite attractive. Initially, they were rather shy in the company of men they did not know and only opened up a couple of days later. In my presence, even when we ate together, with me being the guest of honour, they did not dare to say a word. On one occasion, when I got up to get the bottle of water at the other end of the table, there were cries of consternation. It was unheard of that I, as a man and thus a lord and master of creation, should deign to do something that was the job of the girls. Whenever I lit a cigarette, one of them was always on the spot with a burning matchstick in her hand. From these examples alone one can see the subordinate role that women play, even in better urban families.

Troubles around the church of Theth

The next evening I told the priest where I intended to go next on my journey and asked him to find some reliable men to take me to Peja. As most reliable he suggested Pjetër, whom I already knew, as well as Zogu, the son of the *bajraktar*, and two other men that I did not know - Sokol i Marash Ukës and Sadri Luka. The first three lived in Nrejaj and the latter in Okol. He offered to discuss the matter with them. He did so the next morning and informed me that the first three were willing to take me to Peja for an appropriate wage. The fourth, Sadri Luka, was unavailable but would be back the following day. Since the priest told me that Sadri Luka was the most intelligent of them all and was feared because of his dauntlessness and temerity, I resolved to talk to him before making a final decision. Another aspect of my decision was the fact that Pjetër and Zogu had said that they would not take me over the trail to Gusinje but would try another side route through the mountains. Gusinje, isolated and surrounded by high mountains, was notorious for its xenophobia and insolent behaviour, Aside from this, the area was up in arms because the Turkish government was trying to introduce taxation. Even Albanians from Shkodra who had business there had been threatened and could only move about in Gusinje in the company of respected local men. There was thus good reason for their suggestion to take me on a different route. However, I was particularly keen to visit this area that few Europeans had ever seen and did not want to give up my original plan.

The next morning I discussed the issue with Sadri Luka who was an intelligent and agile fellow. He sat smoking his cigarette and said nothing for a while. Then he replied: "The tour involves certain danger, and the more people involved, the more danger there would be. The attention that a group would cause would inevitably lead to violence. It would be better to try and get there with one guide." He stated that he would get me there and would take me right through the middle of the bazaar of Gusinje and Plava.

This was the man I was looking for! The serenity with which he spoke and the carefully considered remarks made about my trip gave me the impression that, with his support, my project could more likely be brought to fruition than with the other three, i.e. the triumvirate. The others were no less sly and daring, but seemed not to have thought the project through and seemed to rely on brute force alone. As payment for his services Sadri Luka demanded the wage that I had promised to the other three men together, and I agreed. We arranged that I would go to meet him in Okol in the afternoon to discuss the details. Pjetër and his companions were not to be informed because they would be up in arms when they discovered that they had been left out of the deal.

But they were not to be deceived. They were suspicious at the long talks I held with Sadri, all the more so when Sadri had departed, when I gave an evasive answer to their question about the journey. Pjetër declared that they would in no way accept being sidelined. When I countered that I had not come to a final agreement with anyone and that, at any rate, I was the one to decide who accompanied me, he seized a crucifix on the missionary's table and swore that I would never reach Gusinje alive with Sadri.

This was not simply bravado. His companions and Sadri had long been on bad terms, and Pjetër himself was in a difficult financial situation that he hoped to overcome with the help of my wallet. To get out of an earlier blood feud, he had sold all of his Martini rifles and now only possessed one muzzle-loader. He desperately needed to buy a new Martini. I had lent him mine on our excursion up to Maja e Drenit.

The issue was becoming more and more complicated and I was curious to see what Sadri would say about the new turn of events. However, before I could go and see him

Two women from Dukagjin, 1892 (Photo: Pjetër Marubi)

in Okol, I was obliged to accept an invitation, with the missionary, for lunch with the *bajraktar* at his summer cottage. His house was situated on a slope of the Maja e Lisit, three-quarters of an hour from the church. The cottage was built of twigs and branches and was inhabited by the whole family. When I arrived with the missionary around lunchtime, preparations for the meal were already underway. We first sat down on a

Lule Demja and her friend in Dukagjin costumes, 1897-1903. (Photo: Pjetër Marubi).

heap of leaves and the *bajraktar* made us the usual coffee and invited us to partake of his fresh green tobacco. Lunch was served on a low round table as is custom throughout the Orient and we sat around it cross-legged. There were no individual plates. We all ate out of the same bowl. Boiled mutton stew was the first course that was served with delicious cornbread. The second and final course consisted of *mazë*, a speciality of the Highlands that is only served on exceptional occasions. This is a corn-flour porridge made with water over which cream is poured.

If this was a festive meal offered by one of the leading men in Theth, one wonders what it would be like eating with the average Highlander. The staple food they consume are crusts of cornbread boiled in saltwater and then eaten dry. The better-off can afford cheese or sour milk diluted with water. What a miserable state of affairs! When will the time come for this highly intelligent people to be able to live a decent life?

The *bajraktar* accompanied me a ways down the trail when we left the cottage and the conversation turned to my coming departure. He, too, insisted that he would not allow me to be guided by Sadri and declared that I would never make it to Gusinje with him. The matter was now very serious because the *bajraktar* was an elderly gentleman, and everything he said was well considered in advance. He appealed to me to talk to Sadri so I hastened to Okol with the missionary and a young boy who was with us. We arrived at Sadri's house an hour later. It was one of the largest buildings in the valley, which showed just how prosperous its owner was. When I explained to Sadri what had occurred and mentioned the oath that the other side had taken, he gave a contemptuous laugh and stated that this was no problem whatsoever. "We are all armed, so they will be just as intimidated by us as we are by them." I decided that, if Sadri were willing to risk his head, then so was I. We agreed to set off the next morning at dawn and decided what Albanian clothing I should wear. It would have been far too dangerous for me to try and get to Gusinje in my European clothes. The young boy who was with us agreed to take me to Okol before sunrise where Sadri would be waiting for me.

We returned to Nrejaj with a sense of relief and chuckled at the thought of how surprised the other side would be when they discovered that the bird had flow the cage. I prepared my small pack, the boy spent the night at the house, and we went to bed. I am wont to sleep in the cool night air and, as such, I had the bedroom window open. About an hour after midnight I was awakened from my sleep, light as it was before a journey. "Father!" I heard from outside the window. "Father Gjon!" I recognised the voice of Zogu, the son of the *bajraktar*. No one answered. The missionary was sound asleep. This was followed by some whispering and then more calls. I got out of bed without making a noise and woke the missionary up who was sleeping in the next room. He was petrified. It was very unusual for one of his parishioners to come by at night and risk being shot by a Nikaj from over the border who might be prowling around in Theth or Shala with a loaded rifle. In view of the wild temperament of the people of Nrejaj, I feared violence was imminent. Initially, the missionary wanted to ring the church bell to inform everyone that there was an emergency. After consideration, however, we decided to talk to the men outside first. The missionary went over to the window and asked who they were and what they wanted. It was the triumvirate of the opposite party who asked if they could come in. They could not stand outside for long because of the Nikaj. Neither he nor I had anything to worry about, they added. After a long discussion, we agreed to let them in but not before they gave up their weapons. Each of them handed his Martini through a little window near the door. The missionary carried the rifles into his mother's bedroom and then opened the door. A great dispute ensued. They had found out about my visit to Okol and surrounded the vicarage that night, observing me make preparations for an imminent departure, and concluded that Sadri would be picking me up that night. They had been observing the house all night, intent on killing both Sadri and me, should we attempt to leave. They also stressed that they had taken leave of their families so as to flee from tribal territory right after the deed, and escape any blood revenge. Since Sadri had not turned up and they were in constant danger from the Nikaj outside, they decided that they had to get into the house to keep a better eye on me.

There was no more question of me departing now. My satisfaction had been premature.

The next morning (August 16th), the church looked like it was under siege. Armed supporters of the triumvirate were pacing around and agitated talks were being conducted here and there. The whole valley was up in arms. The prevailing opinion was that both the missionary and I should be shot so as to put an end to the problem. On top of this, later in the day, Sadri informed us that he was waiting in a house a quarter of an hour away to talk to us. He could not approach the church because this would have resulted in an unbridled exchange of fire. I took the missionary with me and left to go and see him. The men let us through after first ensuring that I had left all my belongings in the vicarage.

We explained to Sadri that the trip to Peja was impossible under the circumstances. He understood what we were getting at, but then put forth his stance in no uncertain terms. It was now a matter of honour for him and he would have to take me to Peja whether I want to go or not! I would certainly have gone with him, had there been any way of smuggling my belongings through the *cordon sanitaire*, but even if this had been possible and we had gotten over the Qafa e Pejës despite all the uproar in the valley, we would never have reached Peja. Word spreads fast in the Highlands and a barrier would have been thrown up at Gusinje at which not only the trip would have reached an abrupt end. We went back home, pretending that we would do our best to convince the other side and calm them down.

I thus found myself between the flames of two roaring bonfires. Father Gjon advised me to return to Shkodra, but I was not too keen on this because it would have put an end to all my travels in the mountains. I resolved to set out for Abata and get over to Nikaj, and informed all of the men mulling around the church of my decision. Some on them under the influence of the *bajraktar* consented. Others stated that they would not let me depart for Abata or even for Shkodra because they suspected I would meet up with Sadri on the way.

The missionary, who did not want to damage his relations with his parishioners

Highlander from Shala, 1934. (Photo: Shan Pici)

bent one way and then the other like grass in the wind, agreeing with everyone. I secretly asked the sixteen-year-old boy who was to take me to Okol, if he would accompany me to Abata at dawn the next morning and he agreed.

I had a last look through the window before I went to bed and could see some shadowy figures lurking under the trees. The house was still under observation.

At the crack of dawn the next morning I looked out. There was no one to be seen. I woke the missionary up and said a quick good-bye to him and his family. The brave young lad was already at my side, with a rifle over his shoulder and a cartridge belt around his waist. Unnoticed, we snuck out through the nearby fields and, half an hour later, left the valley of Theth.[3]

---

3 Karl Steinmetz (1905), *Ein Vorstosz in die nordalbanischen Alpen*, p. 1-32. Vienna & Leizpig: A. Hartleben.

Climbing the Highest Peaks

Franz Nopcsa in Theth (1907)

Who was Franz Nopcsa?
Baron Franz Nopcsa (1877-1933) was born into a family of Hungarian aristocrats from Transylvania and finished his schooling in Vienna with the support of his uncle and godfather, Franz von Nopcsa, who was headmaster of the court of the Empress Elisabeth. He developed quickly into a talented scholar. Nopcsa travelled extensively in the Balkans and lived in Shkodra for some time in the early years of the twentieth century. Later, aside from his noted work in palaeontology and geography, he became one of the leading Albania specialists of his times and was even a candidate for the Albanian throne in 1913.

Baron Nopcsa's German-language publications in the field of Albanian studies from 1907 to 1932 were concentrated primarily in the fields of prehistory, early Balkan history, ethnology, geography, modern history and Albanian customary law, i.e., the kanun.

Suffering from depression, Baron Nopcsa committed suicide at his home in Vienna on 25 April 1933 and killed his long-term Albanian secretary and lover, Bajazid Elmaz Doda (ca. 1888-1933). His memoirs, *Reisen in den Balkan: die Lebenserinnerungen des Franz Baron Nopcsa* [Travels in the Balkans: The Memoirs of Baron Franz Nopcsa], Peja 2001, were published posthumously.

Why Theth?
Baron Nopcsa was an extraordinarily courageous explorer for his day. In 1907, he had a house in Shkodra, which served as a base camp, so to speak, for his expeditions into the northern Albanian mountains. Nopcsa was fascinated by this region of the Balkans for two reasons. Firstly it provided him with an opportunity of exploring a landscape which few westerners had ever seen. In this connection, he scaled several peaks and carried out survey measurements. As a geologist, he was also interested in the tectonic structures of these mountains.

Secondly, Nopcsa was able to study the life and customs of the northern Albanian tribes that, in view of the difficult terrain, had very little contact with the outside world and, as such, had preserved a time-old heroic culture of their own making. This pristine culture was soon to disintegrate under pressure from the outside world. In later years, he noted: "In general, I must say that the highlanders of northern Albania have become very demoralised over the last few years. The noble savages I so loved, who clung unswervingly to their code of honour – a code that did not correspond at all to ours – are gone, and in their place, with a very few exceptions, are men who are greedy for money, timid and apprehensive, and thoroughly unreliable [...]. Even if my

Portrait of Baron Franz Nopcsa, ca 1928 (Photographer unknown).

Baron Franz Nopcsa in northern Albanian costume, in about 1905-1907, courtesy of Derzsi Elekes Andor, Budapest. (Photo: Carl Pietzner)

research takes me back there, it will never be the same. I doubt if I will ever encounter the noble savages I once loved. Part of my world has vanished."[4]

The following extract from Baron Nopcsa's memoirs is an account of his expedition through the mountains of northern Albania, including the Shala Valley and Theth, in the summer of 1907.

Travelling to Theth

From Trabojna in Kastrati territory I continued the next day (10 August 1907) on to Brixha on Hoti tribal land. I arrived in Brixha just in time to attend mass and was able to take part in a luncheon given by the priest after the service. He found me a guide with whom I hiked from Fushë Rrapsha, that I already knew, to the group of huts known as Gropa e Ahut in the high pastures of the Veleçik region. It was here that I spent my first night outdoors with the shepherds of the Albanian mountains. That we were not in a proper settlement but among nomads was evident from the fact that we drank melted firn ice instead of water and a mixture of firn ice and sheep milk instead of coffee. Otherwise, the appearance of the alpine huts and the hovels in the villages is more or less the same.

As the alpine huts at Bun i Thorës were about half way between Okol i Bogës and Theth, they made a perfect spot for a midday rest. It was hard to decide which hut to choose. All of the shepherds insisted on being our hosts. I left it to my travelling companions to choose. At any rate, we were warmly received. After lunch, consisting of maize bread, yoghurt and a mixture of butter, cheese and corn flour called *mazë*, my companions lay down for a snooze. I chose to have a look around the area that had never been visited by a 'European.'

Thunder clouds caused me to interrupt my inspection of the area and to take shelter in the hut. The storm passed and we were able to go out again. As the hut was filthy and thus not too appealing to spend the night, I decided to continue on to Theth and stay at the home of the parish priest who would be my host for my excursions in the coming days. Aside from comfortable accommodation, Theth had the advantage of being centrally located. I also knew several people there from my earlier trips. The unpleasant part was the greed and avarice of the inhabitants.

One major impediment to further travel was the fact that, while I was there, the Shala tribe, to which the Shoshi belong, were not only, as always, in blood with their eastern neighbours, the Nikaj, but were also at that moment feuding with the Shkreli because both tribes were laying claim to the same pastureland on Mount Troshan. As I learned on my arrival at the priest's house, it was unadvisable to climb the Kakinja summit and impossible to get to Mount Troshan.

---

4 *Traveler, Scholar, Political Adventurer: The Memoirs of Franz Nopcsa* (2014). Edited by and translated from the German by Robert Elsie. Central European University Press, Budapest.

Young fighters of Shala, 1900-1915. (Photo: Kel Marubi).

Arrival in Theth
My first climb from the church of Theth, that is 780 m. above sea level, was to Maja e Boshit in the accompaniment of Zog Sokoli and Lek Curri.

We had a pleasant experience during this hike when we got to the alpine hut called

Kurt i Dudavet at 1230 m. which was made entirely of wicker. The shepherd's mule would not budge and this was regarded by all the natives as a bad omen for any further travel. "Had we known that the mule was ill, we would not have set out in the first place," was the excuse given to me by my very disappointed companions. The prophecy almost became true when we were approaching the Qafa e Dnelit pass (ca. 2000 m.). An old shepherd of the Shala tribe took us for marauding Nikaj and was aiming his rifle at us to shoot, attack being the best defence. No *besa e çobanit* [shepherds' truce] which the shepherds all strictly observe, was in force at that time. It was not easy to persuade him of his error and shield ourselves from his bullets. We remained demonstratively calm and this did the trick. Dod Prela i Prel Marashit later told me that he had been so petrified that he was still shaken. My companions, unaware of the fear that had seized Dod Prela, found no better solution than to make fun of the old man. Dod Prela had enough reason to be frightened because of quite a number of unsolved blood feuds he was involved in.

When we got to Maja e Drenit, I realised that we would not be able to enter Nikaj territory from Shala and that I would have to give up my plan of crossing the Valbona pass via Shala and Curraj. In Shala I learned that the *bajraktar* of Shoshi, on orders from the Turkish authorities, had been laying in wait for me for three days to kill me. His plan only failed because I arrived four hours after he had departed. It was the parish priest who informed me of the danger I had been in.

I made use of my stay in Shala to learn something of the past of this tribe. Having recorded what I could of the stories of their ancestors, I returned to Shesh. On 19 August, I started out from here and climbed the peak Maja Praça, which is only 1630 m. high, and visited the one-time and now forgotten village of Kapreja in the Nerlumza Valley. Then, accompanied by Zog Sokoli and Lek Curri, I set off for the first time for Gusinje [Gucia], having cleverly gotten rid of a whole bunch of nosy companions.

Climbing Mount Jezerca

Since an expedition to the valley of Ropojani-Vruja seemed fraught with difficulty, my plan was now to visit the alpine huts of Bun i Jezercës where a number of unknown alpine lakes were said to be located.

The path was not dangerous but was difficult enough. On numerous occasions we had to crawl hand and knee over avalanche rocks. Rubber shoes, known as *opankas*, which the intrepid Steinmetz used on his recent tours, are excellent for this type of terrain. Aside from a small patch of snow near Qafa e Pejës, there was no snow until we got to the northwestern face of Mali i Shorës, which forms the southern boundary of the Qafa e Jezercës at 1820 m.

The light on the Qafa e Jezercës was amazing, but as it was late in the day, I was not able to stay long and admire the wild and imposing massif – no sign of vegetation, only snow and rock. The sun set and all the higher peaks glowed in a gentle rose red that contrasted with the deep blues and purples rising from the valleys. Despite the overwhelming beauty of it all, there was no point in photographing it.

At dusk we hastened back to the Jezerca huts below us, announcing our arrival with cries and shots. Rifles were discharged in the dark of night to welcome us back. We then had certainty that the inhabitants of the huts of Mark Kola and Zef Toma knew we were coming and that they would get a hut ready for us, make coffee and wait for our arrival.

Before we reached our destination for the night, an opportunity for hunting arose. We were at 1800 m. in complete darkness when, as we crossed a patch of snow, our presence stirred a group of mountain goat creatures who galloped off. I had the impression they were chamois. I dropped my notebook and instinctively seized my loaded rifle, as did my companions, though somewhat more slowly. We were on the point of discharging a volley of fire at them, when at the last moment our hunting instinct failed us. This was fortunate because, as it turned out, they were just long-haired domestic goats that had strayed from the main herd. The error would have caused us much trouble with the owner of the 'chamois'. The episode was, however, not without its advantage. My reputation among the natives had grown because I had raised my rifle at the right moment, ready to shoot. In the eyes of the Albanian highlanders, only those who know how to use their rifles are real men. *Tamam shqiptar* "a real Albanian", this was the highest praise one could aspire to.

It was very late by the time we got to Bun i Jezerzës, which I calculated to be about 1710 m. above sea level.

The arrival of a foreigner in Jezerca, the part of Kelmendi territory where no European had ever set foot, caused great excitement. They were fascinated at me as a person and at my clothes, but there were two other objects that caught their attention particularly: the scope on my hunting rifle and the thick rubber soles of my shoes. I would recommend these to anyone planning such a trip. They raise one's prestige among the locals enormously.

There was enough to eat at Jezerca. My first dinner there consisted of meat, *mazë*, cornbread, milk, cheese, *kos* [yoghurt] and onions. There were plenty of these staples to be had throughout my stay. The only thing that was lacking was water. The Albanians all insisted that the water in the ponds around the alpine huts was not good, so there was nothing to be done. We had to adapt to local ways and drink melted snow, which was not too appetizing. Here as in other alpine settlements in Kelmendi and Kastrati, large blocks of snow are melted in wooden troughs. As the huts have no chimneys, the snow and, consequently, the water is usually contaminated with smoke, rust and ash particles. The snow blocks are brought in by the women only.

After an excellent dinner to welcome us, my hosts at Bun i Jezercës exchanged the latest news, both political and non-political. It was interesting to see that they were actually more interested in the health and appetite of their sheep than anything else. Considering their situation, this was quite normal. We went to bed at four o'clock Turkish time, which is the equivalent of about 11 o'clock in the evening. They spread a mattress out for me and I used by coat as a cover. Although I was comfortable enough, I could not get to sleep for quite a while. The cold in the room and my novel situation among the so-called savage Kelmendi kept me awake for many hours. I had no idea that I had been asleep at all when the inhabitants of the hut began to stir and awak-

Albanian Highlanders from Raja in Merturi, 1907. (Photo: Franz Nopcsa)

ened me at the crack of dawn.

The trip to Bun i Jezercës was worth all the effort. There were new topographical discoveries wherever I looked, with many things to change and add to the current maps I had with me.

On 22 August we were kept indoors by an uninterrupted downpour, but this gave me an opportunity at Bun i Jezercës to meet some of the men of the Muslim tribe of Krasniqi who were spending the night at our hut. A large part of the Valbona Valley belongs to Krasniqi. My well-meaning Kelmendi friends introduced me as an Italian, and I was obliged to expound at length on the wonders of Rome and Italy, even on the recent earthquake in Calabria. The pro-Italian sympathies of my audience were more than evident.

In the night from 22 to 23 August fresh snow fell on the mountains south of Bun i Jezercës and it was in the sparkling frosty weather that I departed with Zog Sokoli, Lek Curri and Zef Toma to explore the upper Valbona Valley. We soon readied ourselves for an unplanned hunt when we heard that there were chamois in the Lugu i Gradës basin. Lek Curri climbed up to Qafa e Paplukës and Zog Sokoli clambered up the Maja e Lisit slope. A çoban [shepherd] was sent around the back of the Qafa e Gradës pass and I advanced from the west towards Lugu i Gradës. There were chamois there but we did not get a shot at any of them. From what I have heard, the chamois have all but disappeared from this part of Albania because of the good rifles the men now have. In a few years time, they will only be known from legends in the treeless expanses of the Prokletije. They seem to have survived better in the woodlands of Cukal and Munella.

From Qafa e Gradës we advanced over large patches of snow on a slop of Maja e

Jezercës towards the salient though the small twin peaks of Maja e Rragamit. A few hundred metres below us there were three depressions full of snow that led, further down, into the fork towards the Valbona Valley.

I spent the night of 23-24 August at the source of the Valbona in Bun i Valbonës (2550 m.). On the 24th I crossed Zog Sokoli's pastures to Ndreaj, which was not far from the source of the Valbona. On 25 August I gave Zog Sokoli his well-earned wages as he was getting tired from the strenuous hiking and continued on with the robust and ever-mirthful Lek Curri. I also hired Sadri Luka from nearby Okol who was well-known for his intelligence and dauntless courage. He was recommended to me for the coming tours in view of his many contacts with the Kelmendi. Zog Sokoli and Sadri Luka detested one another and had once, as a result of their enmity, endangered the life of Steinmetz. I had to be wary because, like Steinmetz before me, I was now letting Zog Sokoli go and hiring Sadri Luka to accompany me. I had to make sure not to compromise Zog Sokoli's reputation in front of his tribe and to prevent any occurrence of rage on his part. Things worked out well with a good tip and on 26 August I was in a position to begin climbing the Maja e Kozhnjes, known on my map as Maja e Radohimës, that forms the highest point of the Prokletije range.

Climbing Mount Radohima

The tour took place without incident although it was very strenuous from Okol onwards. At about 1750 m. I climbed up the narrow path that both Steinmetz and Liebert had taken from Qafa e Pejës to Qafa e Shteguqenës. The last leg of the climb on the southern side of the massive mountain face was particularly perilous because we were confronted with an almost vertical wall indented here and there only by a few deep grooves of water. Lek Curri was excellent in this situation as he was amazingly dextrous. He seemed to cling to the rocks like a fly. He climbed the slipperiest parts first and then hauled our equipment, me and Sadri Luka up after him. I was not the only one of the three of us to be relieved when we reached the top of the frightening cliff face in the late afternoon and got to the narrow ridge rising lonesome in the sky. We were hungry and exhausted.

We stopped here for a short rest. My companions pulled out some of the cornbread and sheep cheese that we had been nibbling on since morning. We devoured the rest of it and drank some water from a dent in the cliff. I then took out my notebook.

The thermometer showed 10 C. in the shade. The aneroid barometer showed to my amazement only 2430 m. In 1906, I had guessed the altitude to be 2800 m. and regarded it as the highest point in northern Albania. The climb proved to us that it was not as high as the Maja e Jezercës. I was frustrated that I had not climbed the latter when I was but a few hundred meters from the top a few days earlier. If I had only known that Jezerca was the highest of all! Dr Liebert told me he thought it was about 2600 m.

We descended initially down a steep and narrow slope on the northeast side until we got to the Qafa e Radohimës, a 2310 m. high pass, where we had to cross a steep ice field. We slid down it at great speed by using all three of my loden coats put together

Baron Nopcsa in northern Albanian Costume, 1916 (Photographer unknown)

as a sleigh. Fun of this sort is not rare in the Malësia e Shkodrës. Lek Curri told me at any rate of many such instances of slithering down the mountainside. Snow tires and crampons exist here, too.

On 26 August I was unable to investigate the geological structure of the stretch between Maja e Radohimës and Bun i Livadhit because of the darkness. I was obliged to wait until the next day, when I climbed to the top of Radohima again, this time from the northeast side. I also investigated the Gropa e Livadhit të Bogës made of Jurassic-Cretaceous limestone.

From Bun i Livadhit të Bogës, I continued northwards with the intention of reaching Gusinje along the western side of the Ropojani Valley, as far as possible. I did not intend to enter the town itself in order to avoid a confrontation with the Muslims there and to avoid creating problems for the Ottoman government, our consular officials and thus for myself.

My companions and I decided to spend the night in Rreth i Vukoçës. The first refreshment that we were offered was, as usual, snow and milk. This time, the mixture proved too much for my stomach and I had to put off the excursions planned for the following days. Dinner was the same as always: *mazë*, *kos*, cornbread and black coffee, and this did not help. As I was carrying little medication with me, I decided to limit my food intake on the following days, as far as I was able, to warm milk coffee. The people were most kind in helping me although it was difficult for them to prepare this unaccustomed drink because they did not have any pots suitable for heating a large amount of milk. My hosts decided to use the frying pan which was black with soot inside and out and dripping with oil from the *mazë* it usually contained. To drink, I had the little bowl that was usually reserved for black coffee. As a result, mixing coffee and milk and then filling the bowl was a complicated procedure which became the focus of much attention and the object of amusement for the mountain people.[5]

5 *ibid.*

Blood Feuds in Shala

Edith Durham in Theth (1908)

Who was Edith Durham?
The intrepid Balkan traveller, journalist, writer, photographer and artist, Mary Edith Durham (1863–1944) stemmed from a prosperous family. She was the eldest daughter of a well-known surgeon in London, where she was born and where she died.

As a woman at that time, she was not allowed to study at the university and instead attended art courses in drawing and painting at the Royal Academy School.

Durham was subsequently active as a book illustrator and exhibited some of her works. Her drawings of reptiles were published in the Cambridge National History series. When her father died of a chronic illness and her mother became an invalid, she, as the eldest unmarried daughter, was forced to remain at home and tend to her aging mother. Her seven younger brothers and sisters all received a good education and embarked upon professional careers.

Tied to the house, Durham soon became depressed. As she notes in her book, Twenty Years of Balkan Tangle (1920): "The future stretched before me as endless years of grey monotony, and escape seemed hopeless."

Her physician advised her to take a trip and get away to another country ever summer for a couple of months, anywhere. A change of surrounding would do her good. Her choice fell upon Dalmatia and Montenegro and, in the summer of 1900, she set off for Trieste by train with a female travelling companion. There she boarded an Austrian Lloyd steamer that took her down the Dalmatian coast to the port of Cattaro (now Kotor). She noted: "Threading the maze of mauve islets set in that incomparably blue and dazzling sea; touching every day at ancient towns where strange tongues were spoken and yet stranger garments worn, I began to feel that life after all might be worth living and the fascination of the near East took hold of me."

At the age of thirty-six, Edith Durham had not only found a sudden escape, but embarked upon a new phase of her life. Fascinated by the people she met and by the history of the Balkans, she came to life in the new environment. Her first trip to the Balkans ended in Cetinje, the capital of the little principality of Montenegro. From this time on, she travelled to Montenegro and Serbia every year, two countries that had recently become independent. Enthralled by the beauty of the countryside, she later took several excursions up into the mountains of Montenegro with her sister Nellie.

In 1903 Durham visited Albania for the first time, entering thus Turkish territory because Albania was still a part of the mighty Ottoman Empire. She reported to the customs office in Shkodra and was told that she did not need a passport. She was welcome. The town was delighted to have her. Without an escort, Durham wandered

Edith Durham. Portrait, about 1895. (Photographer unknown)

through the bazaar up to the foot of the fortress, which was an endless source of inspiration.

Why Theth?
Edith Durham's first book on the Balkans was called Through the Lands of the Serb (1904) and recounted her journey to Montenegro, Serbia, northern Albania and Old Serbia (Kosovo). It is imbued with all her romantic love of the Albanian mountains. Here she found herself in a region that had endured centuries of suffering, but she also among a people that preferred freedom in the barren highlands to servitude in the fertile lowlands.

The political situation in the region was changing quickly. Turkish authority was in a state of rapid decay and there were more and more uprisings against it. In August 1903, there occurred a major revolt of Macedonian freedom-fighters (the so-called Ilinden Uprising), but it was swiftly suppressed. Her stay in the Balkans that year, 1904, was focussed almost entirely on helping Macedonian families whose homes had been burnt down by the Turks. Her mother had now passed away, so she was able to stay in the Balkans longer. She also devoted her time to learning Serbian and to studying Balkan history. In Macedonia, Durham visited hundreds of refugee families housing in the remains of their looted villages, and worked as a nurse and surgery assistant at the hospital in Ohrid.

When her work in Macedonia was over, Edith Durham resolved to explore Ottoman Albania, from south to north. She set off with an agent of the British and Foreign Bible Society of Monastir (now Bitola in Macedonia) called Konstantin Sinas. It was an arduous journey on horseback through Korça, Leskovik, Postenan, Përmet and Tepelena to Berat. Her experience with the refugees in Macedonia and the long trek through Albania are described in the book The Burden of the Balkans (1905), a highly political treatise.

Durham was then able to realise a dream she had earlier had, that of visiting the inaccessible mountains of northern Albania that had long intrigued her. While staying in Shkodra in 1908, she met Marko Shantoya, his wife Teresi and their family. Marko could speak German. She asked him to be her guide and to accompany her on a trip into the northern Albanian mountains. She used Marko as her guide, interpreter and trusted companion on several longer journeys through the mountains that started in Shkodra. Edith and Marko usually set off in the dead of night on mules, without asking permission of the Turkish authorities. She remained a friend of the Shantoya family for the rest of her life.

High Albania
Edith Durham's best-known book, High Albania, was published in 1909, an enthralling tale of adventure in the mountains of northern Albania. It is generally considered to be the best source of information about traditional customs, values, and ways of life in the isolated mountain valleys of northern Albania and Kosovo at the start of the twentieth century. Her experience in the mountains resulted in a love affair with the Albanian people that lasted her whole life long. The highlanders called her the

The Durham family in London with Edith on the left, 1889 (Photographer unknown)

"Queen of the Mountain Peoples." The Norwegian linguist Anka Ryall devotes much attention to her and her book High Albania in her Norwegian-language study on female travellers, Odysseus i skjørt (Ulysses in a Skirt), published in 2004, in which she notes:

High Albania is the first detailed study of the northern Albanian clan system written in English. Durham's anthropological observations are woven into the vivid descriptions she made of her four journeys through the mountains – on foot and on horseback – each beginning in Shkodra. Together with her guide Marko Shantoya, and often with local guides, too, she travelled from village to village. The accounts she gave of these journeys focus on how the people lived, how she got into contact with them and what they told her. "In the wilderness I never want books. They are all dull compared to the life stories that are daily enacted among the bare grey rocks."

As a traveller, Edith Durham was keen on listening to what the people she met on her journeys had to say. But she also reproduces dialogues in which she herself was subjected to many a prying question about English customs and her situation as an unmarried woman, and even about the straw hat she used to protect herself from the strong rays of the southern sun: "Do you wear it in the house? Do you sleep in it? Do you wear it to show you are married? To show you are not married? Did you make it? Are all the women in your vilayet (province) obliged to wear wheat on their heads? Is there a law about it?"

Wherever they went, Marko and Edith were privy to legendary Albanian hospitality. By tradition, a family's home belonged to God and their guests. In some locations, they stayed in local inns, but usually they found shelter with Franciscan priests or local families.

Whether the village in question was Muslim or Christian made no difference. Both groups were hospitable, and even in the poorest regions, they were always invited in to spend the night. "We are poor. Bread, salt, and our hearts is all we can offer," said an old man in a miserable one-roomed hut with a mud floor, and windowless, "but you are welcome to stay as long as you wish."

In her book *High Albania*, she stresses that the Albanians are never lawless, as many observers thought. On the contrary, no other people in Europe was so oppressed by the tyranny of laws. The ancient *kanun*, inherited in oral tradition from the fifteenth-century prince Lek Dukagjini, regulated every aspect of daily life in northern Albania.

The *kanun* took priority over religion both for Muslims and Christians. Whenever Edith Durham's informants defended their customs, rules and traditions, their explanations were always the same: "Lek said so."

Of particular notoriety were the laws on blood feuding. Although they made up but a small part of the *kanun*, they left their imprint on life in the areas through which Edith Durham travelled. "The most important fact in North Albania is blood-vengeance, which is indeed the old, old idea of purification by blood," she wrote. She noted that blood feuding was not to be equated with murder because it followed strict rules. Because individuals did not have an existence outside their clan, it was the duty of the family to restore its honour by killing any male member of the opposing family that had attacked it. "The law is carried out to the last letter. It crushes the innocent along with the guilty; it is remorseless, relentless. But it is the Canon and must be obeyed." Although she unambiguously condemned blood feuding and clearly de-

The family of Edith Durham's guide Marko Shantoya and his wife Teresa (2nd and 3rd from the left), 1908. (Photo: Edith Durham).

scribed the tragic consequences it had, she also endeavoured to understand the logic behind it. She reminded her readers that there was in actual fact not much difference between the blood feuding practised in northern Albania and modern warfare: "And lest you that read this book should cry out at the 'Customs of Savages,' I would remind you that we play the same game on a much larger scale and call it war."[6]

Edith Durham had taken drawing courses and now filled her notebooks with sketches of buildings, interiors, ornaments and people in local costumes. She also took photographs. Her training in the visual arts enabled her to portray what she saw with accuracy. Edith Durham was not a professional anthropologist, but in her books she provides detailed observations of a society that had up to then been unknown to the outside world.

Writing *High Albania* gave her an opportunity to understand local culture. She regarded the isolated mountains of northern Albania as a "land of the living past" where time stood still. The men with their shiny new rifles were the only thing that reminded her that she was living in the twentieth century. In the summary of Albanian history provides in the introduction to *High Albania*, she paints a portrait of the arduous and isolated life of the highland tribes who for centuries had been under pressure from foreign powers – in particular the Serbs, the Turks, the Austrians, the Italians and the Greek – that endeavoured to suppress the native culture of the mountains, a culture that had remained virtually unchanged since the Middle Ages.

All the tribes that Edith Durham visited in northern Albania and Kosovo had one thing in common – they were rigorously patriarchal, which meant a strict separation of the sexes. All men could own land and bear arms, whereas women were the property of men, and could be bought and sold like an ox, a mule or a rifle. For this reason, women were not victims of blood feuds.

"I roused the greatest horror by saying that a woman who commits a murder in England is by law liable to the same punishment as a man." On the other hand, a woman could be the cause of a blood feud, in particular if she refused to marry the man she was promised to or ran away from him. "Not a woman, but a devil for the mischief she has caused, said the narrator. My suggestion that the blame attached to those that had bought and sold her was incomprehensible and quite new."

Albanian Sworn Virgins

As a foreign visitor, Edith Durham enjoyed a privileged position in relation to the local women. She could, for example, take her meals with the men while other women ate humbly in another room, after serving the food they had cooked for the men. She ran with the 'buck crowd,' as she noted herself.

Although she was a perspicacious observer of her own sex, all of her informants were men. Women rarely have a voice of their own in her writings. Being a woman in the northern Albanian mountains was equivalent to being submissive. One excep-

---

[6] Anka Ryall (2004). *Odysseus i skjørt: kvinners erobring av reiselitteraturen*, pp. 215-217. Oslo: Pax.

A Sworn Virgin in northern Albania, 1908. (Photo: Edith Durham).

tion, however, was a group of women known as Sworn Virgins. These women, who swore an oath of chastity, and lived and enjoyed the same privileges as men had. In her book, Durham informs the reader about several conversations she had with Sworn Virgins who had taken the oath. Perhaps, as a woman of a certain age, she had the impression that she was in fact one of them. There is little doubt at any rate that she used these encounters with the Sworn Virgins to find out more about something of vital importance to her – what it was like for women in society to live outside social norms.

Differences between the independent-minded Englishwoman and her Albanian counterparts were more than obvious. Edith Durham noted herself that the phenomenon of Sworn Virgins had to do with the total lack of self-determination for Albanian women. Marriages were arranged in advance by the heads of households, with girls being engaged to their prospective husbands as children, as babies or even before they were born. A man who wished to conclude an alliance with another family would say to his counterpart: "If your wife has a daughter, I want her as a wife for my son." Wives were almost always purchased, and children were destined for someone from the moment they were born, with part of the bride-price being paid in advance. A girl could thus not marry anyone else and was dispatched to her prospective husband, whom she had never met, as soon as she was old enough. The remainder of the bride-price was then paid and the man promised to marry her – whether he liked her or not. Otherwise, a blood feud would arise between the two families. In rare cases, a girl could refuse to marry the man she was promised to, but this demanded much courage. She was obliged to take an oath in the presence of witnesses that she would remain a virgin, and if she ever broke it, much blood would be spilled as a result.

The oath of chastity saved the honour of both parties to the prospective marriage. For many northern Albanian women, becoming a Sworn Virgin was the only acceptable alternative to a forced marriage. Edith Durham noted that only women who had taken an oath of eternal chastity enjoyed the same rights and privileges as men. In other words, a change of status required women to disavow their sexuality. The examples Durham gives, however, reveal much regional variation. In some locations Sworn Virgins could inherit property and hold the functions of a head of household if they had no brothers. They usually dressed as men, but not in all cases. Many of them also bore weapons.

One of Edith Durham's hosts told her that he knew of a Sworn Virgin who was now forty-years-old. "Her only brother had been shot when she was ten. Since that she had always worn male garb. She had a house and a good deal of land. I asked if the men ate with her. He slapped his thigh and said: 'Of course! She has breeches on just like mine and a revolver'."

Edith Durham provided several examples of Sword Virgins who dressed in male attire and indeed had many of the physical features of men. They behaved as men and were treated as such. From a social perspective, they were male, even though everyone knew that they were biologically female.

The Balkan Wars

Edith Durham spent much time in Albania in the years preceding the First World War. The situation in the country was growing increasingly chaotic in the struggle against Ottoman rule. The land was inextricably embroiled in what she called the "Balkan Tangle". The Young Turks kept none of their promises o reform the Empire and did whatever they could to sap the Albanian national movement. The Albanians responded with a series of more or less major regional uprisings that were all brutally suppressed. Houses and harvests were burnt to the ground and dozens of families were driven out of their homes. In the summer of 1911, the situation in the north was precarious. Refugees fled in great number to Shkodra, and, for the civilian population, the situation got even worse after the two Balkan Wars of 1912-1913.

From her previous travels in northern Albania, Edith Durham knew many of the victims personally. She used her own money to provide them with relief in the form of food, medicine and textiles to make clothing with. "There is but one thing more terrible than war," she wrote in her book *The Struggle for Scutari* (1914), "and that is the time that follows immediately afterwards; it is then that the war's innocent victims – those who have escaped sudden and merciful death by shot and shell – crawl back to the blackened ruins of their homes to face a slow and cruel death from cold and starvation."

It was imperative for her to help the Albanians. According to the left-wing journalist Henry Nevinson (1856-1941), who was also in Albania to provide relief, her dedication had little to do with sentimental charity. She saw it as a matter of course to help the people who had opened their homes to her.

In his memoirs, Nevinson records that she was called a queen and that the Albanians had great faith in her absolute power and endless wealth. Edith Durham explained

Edith Durham on horseback while distributing relief in northern Albania. On the right is Henry Nevinson, June 1913. (Photo D. Loch)

her status among the highlanders as follows: "The mere fact that I could read and write, and so communicate with the outer world, was a marvel. I protested vainly that I had no political influence; that a little help for the wives and children was all I could promise." Nonetheless, she did her very best to persuade the British authorities to engage more actively in the situation in Albania. She wanted to use diplomatic channels to put Albania on the map because Great Britain, as part of the Entente, was allied with Russia, a major player in the events of the Balkan Wars and the First World War.

Edith Durham was obliged to return to England when the First World War broke out in 1914, and thereafter, she only travelled to Albania once, in 1921. But from London, she continued her courageous and uncompromising campaign on behalf of the Albanians and Albanian independence. She participated in the founding of the Anglo-Albanian Association that provided important stimulus to Albania's accession to the League of Nations.

Later in life, she suffered increasingly from bad health, but she never lost any of her combative energy. In April 1939, when at the age of seventy-six she heard that Mussolini's armed forces had invaded Albania, she went out into the streets of London wearing a sign saying "Hands off Albania!" During the Second World War she was in contact with Albanian refugees in London. A few months before she died, she wrote that she hoped the Albanians who had fought the Germans and Italians would finally gain their freedom when peace came and would be able to choose their own government because they knew best what the country needed. In November 1944, two weeks after her death, Enver Hoxha seized power and, instead of democratic elections, the Albanians got almost fifty years of tyranny.

Edith Durham wrote a total of seven books on her travels in the Balkans. In addition, she was active as a journalist and known for her obstinate "letters to the editor" that appeared in daily newspapers. She also wrote articles for Man, the Journal of the Royal Anthropological Society.

In all of her books she stressed the need to understand Balkan history. "The events seen by the casual traveller are meaningless if he knows not what went before," as she noted in Twenty Years of Balkan Tangle (1920). "They are mere sentences from the middle of a book he has not read."

Travelling to Theth

As recounted in her book High Albania, Edith Durham left the village of Plani for Theth with Marko Shantoya and two other men who were given to her by the Franciscan priest in Plani. After a bloodcurdling journey, slipping and sliding over the rocks and down the chasms – "Luckily I am never giddy or I should have gone overboard long ago." – she arrived in the Shala Valley where Theth is located.

Extracts from High Albania:

"Time was flying. I wanted to see all High Albania. It was time to move on. The kirijee then said he had a bad foot and was tired of the journey, so the Padre kindly lent me his own man to take me to Thethi. We had a second as escort. The way, said the Padre, was good, but after sitting my reeling, struggling beast for some ten minutes over large rocks, to shrieks of "Jesus, Maria, Joseph!" which were supposed to encourage it, I dismounted, and was in for another roasting tramp.

The ever-rising track swung round the head of the valley, above the source of the Kiri, and over the Chafa Bashit (some 4000 feet), into Shala. Once up and over, all Shala lay before us and below us, a long, lorn wall of huge, jagged mountains, still snow-capped, with the Lumi Shalit flowing in the valley at their feet.

I daresay you have never heard of Shala. I have looked towards Shala and the beyond for years – the wild heart of a wild land.

Do you know the charm of such a land? It has the charm of childhood. It has infinite possibilities – if it would but grow up the right way. It has crimes and vices; I know them all (that is to say, I trust there are not any more). But it has primitive virtues, without many of the meannesses of what is called civilisation. It is uncorrupted by luxury. It is cruel – but so is Nature. It is generous as a child that gives you its sweets. It can be trusting and faithful. And it plays its own mysterious games, that no grown-ups can hope to understand.

I hurried forward. There was grass underfoot, and – always a joy – we were to go down-hill for hours and hours. Our two men were not so inspired. They said they wished to call on a friend, and left us under a tree with a Martini, saying that any one who passed would recognise the weapon (decked with silver filagree), and consider us properly introduced.

And sure enough the first-comers recognised it at once, and were most friendly. The glee with which they learnt how many brothers I possess – married or single, how old – c., their pressing invitations that we would at least come and have a cup of coffee or rakia, or stay the night at any of their respective houses and accept "bread, salt, and my heart," whiled away the time pleasantly till our two men returned.

We descended to the river's bank by Gimaj, a village of Shala, and followed up the valley. The river became a torrent, leaping from rock to rock – the pine-clad mountains towered on either hand, and the houses were all *kulas* – tall stone towers, loop-holed for rifles.

A final ascent brought us to the plain of Thethi, a grandly wild spot where the valley opens out. The ground is cultivated, and well watered by cunning little canals. Great isolated boulders are scattered over it, on which stand *kulas*.

The eyes, some one has said, are the windows of the soul. In extreme wrath, at fighting-point, when a man goes white and strikes, the pupils of his eyes contract to black specks. So do the blank, windowless walls of the *kulas*, with their tiny loopholes, stand ever threatening.

I think no place where human beings live has given me such an impression of majestic isolation from all the world. It is a spot where the centuries shrivel; the river might be the world's well-spring, its banks the fit home of elemental instincts – passions that are red and rapid.

A great square-topped cliff on the left was covered with broken fir trunks, torn down by a heavy snow-slide in the winter. Bleached and white in the sun, they lay scattered like the bones of the dead. Others stood erect and gaunt. "It is the altar of God, with candles upon it!" cried one of the men who was with me.

At the very end of the valley rises the range of mountains called the Prokletija (the Accursed Mountains), so named, I was told in Shala and Lower Pulati, because it was over them that the Turk came into High Albania. Other routes seem more possible; but for my own part I believe in local tradition. And the bitter truth remains that over all the land is still the curse of Turkish influence.

Arrival in Theth
Thethi is a bariak of Shala. The church and church-house of Thethi stand in the midst

of the plain – a solid, shingle-roofed building, with a bell tower. It is largely due to the personal influence of the young Franciscan in charge that Thethi is almost free from blood. In rather more than four years but two cases have occurred.

We arrived at a moment of wild excitement; crowds of mountain men hurrying up, shouting, yelling, talking at the full pitch of their throats – a regular hurry-scurry, with the little Franciscan buzzing about, commanding, entreating, gesticulating, at once. All the heads of Shala were met *me ban medjliss* (to hold a parliament), nearly a hundred of them. They crowded into a large empty room on the ground floor. The President of Council here is elected by the people (the hereditary Bariaktar in Thethi has no rights as head except in battle; this system is spreading – a big dark man, not at all prepossessing, who looked an ugly customer to tackle. The window was iron-barred; a woman outside, her face pressed close to the grating, listened eagerly. It was a most important meeting on home and foreign affairs. The noise was terrific, and deafened us even in the room above. The Padre came panting upstairs with his arms full of pistols, flintlocks heavily mounted in silver. "Thank God, I got these from them!" he said, as he stowed them in the cupboard with the cups and plates; "they are dreadfully excited to-day!" The room was already stacked with Martinis, deposited in sign of good faith. The question under debate was peace or war.

Shala and the other Christian tribes that border on Moslem ones are always making and repelling raids. Recently the position had become acute. In the previous autumn the Moslems near Djakova captured and imprisoned a Franciscan for many weeks. At the same time the whole of the Moslem tribes were mysteriously supplied with Mausers and quantities of ammunition, it was said by the Turkish Government. Exultant and boasting, the Moslems had just sent in an ultimatum to the Christians that all who had not turned Moslem by Ramazan would be massacred. Krasnich, the next-door Moslem tribe, boasted 350 Mausers, Gasi 300, and Vuthaj 80; Christian Shala but some six or eight, and these only smuggled in with difficulty.

Nevertheless, filled with rage, Shala swore *besa* of peace with its Christian neighbours, Shoshi and Merturi, and passed a resolution to warn the Vuthaj and Gusinje Moslems that in seven days from receiving notice, Shala, Shoshi and Merturi would be on a war footing with them. The decision was arrived at in a wild clamour, and the Franciscan fetched to record it; which he did, when he had vainly talked himself tired in favour of peace. The local priest, being the only man who can write, always has to act as Chief Secretary for State at a *medjliss*, and must write its decision whether he approve or not, and preserve the document for future reference.

The exhausted and excited *medjliss* then started again on local grazing rights, and finally broke up shouting, having decided nothing further. The wary Franciscan retained the pistols of the five most influential men till the morrow, when all was to be concluded.

The *medjliss* met early next morning, and this time in a great circle out of doors. I meant to photograph it, but was dragged away by Marko and the Franciscan and sent indoors, as they feared firing at any minute. Four of the five chief "heads" had agreed the day before to the decision of the majority. The fifth stood out furious and vowed neither he nor his *mehala* would accept it. As he was head of fourteen houses and ruled sixty-four individuals, his agreement was necessary to any grazing right changes. After a most stormy hour or two on the perilous brink of blood, he was talked round. The motion was carried, and the heads came upstairs for their pistols, but the affair had been touch-and-go.

"I am afraid they find it dreadfully boring," said the Franciscan. "They say no one has been shot for two whole years! We nearly had a row at a *medjliss* a little while ago – (that was why I got the five chief pistols this time) – I heard a fearful noise, and as I ran out a lot of them all got up into a bunch like bees, and raised their rifles. They were just going to fire. They would not listen to me. I rushed into the church and rang the bell as hard as I could. It had a splendid effect. As soon as they heard the bell, from habit they all shoved their pistols in their belts and took their guns in their left hands, and began to cross themselves. No one knew what had happened. They poured into the church to see. By the time we came out again and had had a talk they were quieted."

Such was my coming to Thethi. I stayed some time, and came back to it, and hope to go again.

Shala, Shoshi, and Mirdita, says tradition, descend from three brothers, who came from Rashia to escape Turkish oppression, shortly after that district was occupied by the Turks.

One of the brethren possessed a saddle *(shala)*; the second a winnowing sieve *(shosh)*; the third had nothing, so he said "good-day"*(mir dit)* and withdrew. The tale as it stands is doubtless fabulous, but the fact that to this day Mirdita does not intermarry with either Shala or Shoshi is, to my mind, conclusive proof of original close consanguinity.

When Shala and Shoshi settled, they found inhabitants already in the land, who, they tell, were small and dark. In Shala, eight families are still recognised as of this other blood. The rest, a very large number, migrated "a long time ago" (probably when the Serbs evacuated the district), to Dechani and its neighbourhood, and are now all Moslem.

I remember in 1903, when at Dechani, being much struck with the small, dark-eyed Albanians there, for then I was familiar only with the fair, grey-eyed type.

As the Turks overcame Rashia earlier than they did Bosnia, it is likely that the emigration of Shala-Shoshi's forefathers from Rashia was earlier than the Bosnian migrations into Maltsia e madhe, already noted.

It may even have been at the end of the fourteenth or beginning of the fifteenth century. Local tradition in Shala tells that three hundred and seventy-six years ago (i.e. in 1532) the bariak of Shala had sufficiently increased in numbers to be divided into three main "houses" – Petsaj, Lothaj, and Lekaj – which, as separate bariaks, still exist. This is evidence that at that date they must have been settled for some time. Lothaj and Lekaj have recently decided that they are sufficiently far removed to be intermarriageable. But Petsaj still refuses on the ground of consanguinity.

The bariak of Thethi consists of 180 houses, of which 80 form the village of Okolo at the extreme end of the valley.

Thethi can, and does, grow enough corn for its own support, and has passed a law strictly forbidding the export of any, as has all Shala. The only near corn-supply is the Moslem Gusinje, and in case of that being cut off by "blood" or war, there is no nearer supply than Scutari, a dear and distant market.

Life at Thethi was of absorbing interest. I forgot all about the rest of the world, and having paid off and dismissed the *kirijee* and horses, there seemed no reason why I should ever return.

It was the time of ploughing and harrowing. The harrow is a large bundle of brushwood, on which some one squats to weight it down.

All day long folk came and hollowed under the window, "Oy Padre," and received spiritual consolation, or doses of Epsom salts. Often they came merely to see me, in which case their curiosity was satisfied.

The relations of a parish to its priest are amusing. They refuse to call him by his name, if they do not like it; hold a *medjliss*, and solemnly decide on a better one, by which he is henceforth known. I came across no less than four of the mountain priests thus renamed.

Numbers of sick came for help. In spite of the magnificent air, the death-rate is appallingly high. Thethi had been devastated four years ago by smallpox, which rages every few years through the unvaccinated Turkish Empire, while vaccinated Montenegro next door goes scot-free. No medical assistance came to the wretched people, who died in great numbers. Only the plucky Franciscan trudged from one deathbed to another, and kept up the courage of the survivors. And this they have never forgotten.

Under the awful conditions of life all epidemics – cholera, typhus, smallpox, even influenza – assume terrible proportions whenever they occur in the mountains. Neither isolation (in a house with one dwelling-room, where perhaps thirty people sleep together), diet, or nursing are possible. The children die off like flies in autumn. Helpless and powerless, the people wait for the storm to pass over. *Eghel* – "It is written."

But apart from epidemics the death-rate in the mountains is high. The blood-feud system accounts for the death of many men, some in feud within the tribe, more in feuds with neighbour tribes.

Baron Nopcsa, a most careful observer, after collecting the list of killed in a large number of tribes, estimates the average in the Christian tribes as 19 per cent. of the total male deaths. This list includes the wildest of the Christian tribes, and does not include some of the quieter ones, so that the average for the whole is probably rather lower. Shala-Shoshi and Mirdita stand high on the list – Toplana, highest of all. Of the Moslem tribes no statistics have been taken. Matija has the worst reputation. The Moslem average probably does not differ from the Christian one; religion does not affect national custom.

As for the statement recently published by a self-styled "Observer," that many people are daily shot in Scutari, I can only say that some one had been "pulling the poor gentleman's leg" very badly, and not on that subject only.

In spite of the shooting, there are more men than women. People say it is because God in His infinite wisdom sends an extra supply to Albania, where He knows they are needed.

It is more probably because there is a very high death-rate of women. The very young age at which girls are married – often at thirteen – and ignorant treatment causes great mortality at childbirth; also much evil arises from working too soon afterwards.

Shala is one of the tribes that suffers much from a form of syphilis said to have been recently introduced, as do all the tribes with which it intermarries. In some places I was told that there are scarcely any healthy married women. Mirdita, on the other hand, which is consanguineous, is said to be quite free.

When a blood feud is compounded in Thethi with a family not consanguineous, it is usual to cement the friendship by a marriage – not always successfully. A man some years ago, when laying a feud, sold his daughter to a Gusinje Moslem in spite of her protests. She managed, when fetching water, to induce her companions to go into a house. She then find and hid, and by night got over into a Christian tribe, where the Padre helped her to get to Scutari. A blood feud was the result.

The border Moslems will pay high prices for Christian girls, ten napoleons even above the Christian rate. Moslems rarely sell girls to Christians, but both Moslems

Woman and child in Theth, 1908. (Photo: Edith Durham)

and Christians abduct one another's girls freely. Hence much blood.

The lot of a woman who wishes to escape from a Christian husband is even harder. Recently a Christian woman – married into a Christian tribe – who lived most unhappily with her husband, ran away from him, meaning to go to a Moslem at Ipek and turn Turk.

Passing through Thethi, she was recognised and stopped. The tribe she had fled from was informed. Six men of her own tribe and five from her husband's came and took her back to her husband. It was far better for her, said Thethi, to be unhappy with a Christian than happy with a Moslem.

Should a woman be very badly used by her husband and fly for protection to her family, they may, if they think her flight justified, refuse to give her up. In this case they may summon a *medjliss* which, in extreme cases, permits her to remain at home. Should the family keep her without permission from the *medjliss*, a blood feud with her husband arises.

This custom prevailed also in Montenegro till fairly recent times. I was told of a case in which thirty men were shot in a fight that ensued when a family refused to give up a refugee daughter to the husband who had ill-treated her.

Trouble, as the Franciscans were never tired of impressing on me, was brought into the world by woman. Thethi had lately been much upset by a fair widow. Married very young in Thethi, her husband was killed within the year. As she was childless, she was the property of her own family. The *xoti i shpis* (lord of the house), her nephew, sold her again at once at an enhanced price. The second husband also came to an untimely end almost at once. She had now a great reputation for beauty, and was in much demand. Her nephew had an immediate bid of five purses (22 napoleons) for her and accepted it. Followed a second bid of rather more. He threw over the first and accepted this; but there came a third, of no less than eight purses. His aunt was indeed a gold mine. He jumped at the eight-purse man. A terrible quarrel ensued. The five-purse man took his money back and was appeased, and the second also was talked round. Then a fourth man appeared and said the widow had promised herself to him, and she confirmed his statement.

Eight-purses insisted she was his. The nephew, too, was highly in his favour. The matter was laid before the priest. He, finding the woman was quite decided for number four, supported her choice, for, as he philosophically remarked, "It is really no use marrying them to the ones they don't want; they only run away." The nephew said he would be satisfied with a fair price, so the couple hooked their little fingers together, exchanged rings before the priest, and were pronounced properly betrothed.

Eight-purses arrived in a fury, and forbade the banns on the grounds of consanguinity. A relative of the bridegroom had been *kumar i floksh* (head-shaving godfather) to a relative of the bride. They were head-shaving second cousins, and not intermarriageable. The Padre briefly said "Rubbish," and married them. Eight-purses and all his house flew in wrath to the Bishop and accused the Padre of celebrating an incestuous wedding, demanding his immediate expulsion. His Grace told them to "be off!" Vowing vengeance, they went to Scutari for Government help against both Bishop and priest, but, obtaining none, they finally dropped the matter.

The Upper Pulati tribes are greatly given to the custom of taking a deceased relative's widow as concubine. Against this the Padre was waging active war. One man gave as his reason for taking his sister-in-law that he was a poor man and could thus get a wife for nothing. Nine weeks, Sunday after Sunday, was the pair excommunicated. Then the man said he would leave her if the Padre would find him a cheap wife. An Albanian Franciscan will undertake any job to assist his flock. In a neighbour tribe he saw a likely-looking widow, found she was going cheap, and sent for his strayed sheep to have a look at her. The man was delighted. Her owner "swopped" her for an old Martini, the triumphant Padre married them and received him back to the bosom of Mother Church.

In the wilderness I never want books. They are all dull compared to the life stories that are daily enacted among the bare grey rocks.

A father and mother came sorely anxious to the Padre. Some time ago they had sold their daughter and received the purchase-money. Now, when it was time to send her, they found he had taken his uncle's widow and also his cousin's as "wives," and wished to add their daughter as a legal one to the family circle.

They did not wish her to be one of three, and said he must first dismiss the other two. He refused, said he had bought the girl, and she was his and must live as he chose. They said the deal was "off," and offered to return the purchase-money. He swore vengeance. They were terrified lest the girl should be forcibly abducted, and begged help. The Padre put the girl in charge of his mother, and hurried off to find a respectable man who would marry her and take her to a distance. This he quickly succeeded in doing, and she was safely smuggled away.

Very slowly does tribe usage yield to Church law. Some customs one cannot wish to preserve. Others, that are denounced as Pagan, one regrets. Some years ago it was the common custom to burn a Yule log at Christmas, and with it corn, maize, beans – samples of all the land yields – and to pour wine and *rakia* on the flames as offerings, doubtless to a half-forgotten God. The ashes were scattered on the fields to make them fertile. But an energetic Franciscan argued, "Why waste good food and imperil your souls by Pagan rites, when you might save both by behaving as Christians?" And the picturesque and harmless custom is fast dying out. (It is still practised in Montenegro.)

The belief in what is *eghel* wars with Christianity and sometimes conquers. An old, old man lay mortally ill. The Padre hastened to him, but he refused to confess and did not want absolution. "I cannot die," he said, "it is not *eghel*. Never before have I had such a flock of goats, nor such store of corn and dried meat. I cannot die with all that food to eat." But he had misread the Book of Fate, and died *sine sacramento*.

Thethi is one of the few places in North Albania that has not lost the old art of chip-carving. The graveyard is stately with big wooden crosses, well carved, the arms ending in circles adorned with a rayed sun. A little child died in the night, and hither next morning came the funeral party, bearing the little corpse in its wooden cradle.

It was beautifully dressed, and had been washed quite clean, probably for the first

Deciding on grazing rights (part of large group). Theth, Shala 1908. (Photo: Edith Durham).

time, poor little thing. On its breast lay three green apples. The women sat round and sang death-wails while two men dug the very shallow grave. This was because the child's head had not yet been shaved. After that ceremony it would rank as an adult, and the grave must be dug breast-deep. No coffin was used, but the grave roughly lined with planks.

The wild wailing of the women and long-drawn sobs of the father, while one woman sang a death-chant, were painful in the extreme. But just as I was feeling broken-hearted the song ended, and the party began to chatter and laugh as though nothing were the matter. Some people, on the way to Gusinje to buy maize, stopped to look at the corpse, and all were talking cheerfully when, suddenly, a woman began another death-chant, and at once the sobbing began again.

They then cut a lock of the child's hair, and laid the body in the grave with the three apples on its breast. The Padre arrived, and they asked him if the apples were necessary. He said not, and they were removed and tied in a handkerchief with the hair.

The funeral service was quite drowned by an old man who stood at the head of the grave with his rosary in his hand and shouted a hotchpotch of every scrap of Latin he could remember from any service, at the top of his voice. A plank was laid on as lid, the earth hoed over. No one displayed the least emotion, and the party trailed away carrying the empty cradle. Both in Montenegro and Albania the cradle is often broken and left on the grave, a most pathetic monument. Of the apples I could only learn it was an old custom to put them in the grave. It prevailed till lately in Montenegro also.

The days passed. I visited dark *kulas* perched on rocks, and met everywhere the same frank hospitality and courtesy, though it weighed on my soul that I was receiving it under false pretences; for, in spite of my frequent and emphatic denials, all Thethi persisted in believing me to be the sister of the King of England come to free them, and addressing me always as Kralitse (Queen).

But though happy at Thethi my soul hankered ever after Gusinje. Gusinje, said every one, was impossible. I had tried for it in 1903 from Andrijevica, in Montenegro, but no one would take the risk of piloting me. The Turkish Government gave no permission – the natives would admit no stranger. In former days a consul or two had visited it with an escort. Lately it had become the Lhassa of Europe, closed to all; though several had tried.

The longer I stayed at Thethi, the more I thought of Gusinje. Marko would not hear of it. I gave it up at last, and ordered mules to take us to Lower Shala, and went for a walk with the Padre up the valley to Okolo. It is a wonderful valley – wide grass meadows with a crystal-clear river through them, fed by countless bubbling springs.

Okolo is well-to-do. Many of its eighty kulas are large and fine, and some quite new. Were it not for the curse of blood, Okolo should flourish. In land, wood, and water it has all that a village needs. But though it has been at peace within, for four years, a field full of graves, but a few years older, shows that it is not for nothing that Shala is reputed a fighting tribe.

On a summer evening a party of men strolled down the valley, sat upon the ground lazily, and watched the stars come out.

Then, pointing to a certain star, one said: "That is the biggest," and another said: "No, that one there is bigger." A fierce dispute took place; some took one side, some the other; rifles cracked, bullets sang. When the smoke cleared and the first excitement was over, there lay seventeen dead men – slain for a star – and eleven wounded. Their comrades buried the dead where they fell – for they died in sin – *sine sacramento*.

At the very end of the valley towered Mal Radoina, said to be the highest of the Prokletija range, and Mal Harapit thrust up a sharp pinnacle to the sky with a deep square-cut pass an its shoulder – Chafa Pes – the pass that leads to Gusinje. Beyond that mountain wall lay the Promised Land, and I had ordered the mules for Lower Shala to-morrow.

A headman of Okolo invited us to his kula. We followed him, and then wonders began to happen. At his door was tethered a beautiful little grey saddle-horse. It was the horse of one of the headmen of Vuthaj, a large Moslem village but an hour from Gusinje, and he was guest at the house. My spirits rose; there by the hearth sat a long, lean Moslem, smartly dressed, armed with a new Mauser – a man of means evidently. He greeted the Padre heartily – for the Padre had once visited Vuthaj, and prescribed successfully for some sick – was much interested in my travels, and told of the beauties of Vuthaj. Vuthaj, if not the rose, was next it. Anxiously I asked if it could be visited; the Moslem promptly invited us. He belonged to one of the two chief houses, and said he could guarantee our safety.

But as he was bound for Scutari he could not escort us. I was ready "to see Gusinje and die" – the Padre had friends and would be safe – but Marko said it was impos-

Shala highlander in the graveyard in Theth, 1908. (Photo: Edith Durham).

sible, and he had a wife and children to consider. I was torn betwixt a desire to go and a fear of getting any of my men into trouble. But a few days before, Thethi had sworn to declare war against this very district – the land of Mausers. After much talk, sheep-

The men of Shala sitting among wooden crosses in the graveyard of Theth, 1908. (Photo: Edith Durham)

cheese and rakia, we said adieu with the matter undecided.

As we turned the bend of the valley, and the square-cut pass was lost to sight, I felt I had lost all I cared about. So near, and yet so far. The sporting Padre returned to the charge: "What about to-morrow?" He enlarged upon the ease and safety of the expedition; he suggested that he and I should go and Marko wait for us. Marko refused this absolutely; he had sworn to bring me back safely, his honour was concerned in it; if I died, he meant to die too. God would protect his wife and orphans.

"Nothing will happen," said the Padre firmly. "I will go," said I. No sooner said than arranged. Our host at Okolo volunteered to be escort and provide two mules. He had to go, or send some one, at any rate, as he had promised to send the Moslem's grey horse back. The Padre's servant was to come with a rifle; we were to take no luggage of any sort, and only food enough for the outward track. It took six hours, if you went fast, said the Padre. We were off before six next morning. I fondly believing we should arrive by one o'clock, and return next morning – which, after eight years' experience of the Near East, was extremely foolish of me.[7]

(The next morning at 6 am she set off in her leather opankas with the priest of Theth and her guide Marko Shantoja on the long and gruelling journey of some fourteen hours through the snow up and over the mountain pass to reach Vuthaj in the middle of the night. In the distance she could see Gusinje and took a picture of it the next day, but for political reasons she could not go any further. Otherwise, she would have put her travelling companions in danger...)

7 Edith Durham (1909). *High Albania*, pp. 118-133. London: Edward Arnold.

Father Ludwig Kiri of Theth, 1908. (Photo: Edith Durham).

Church of Theth, 1908. (Photo: Edith Durham).

Kulla of Theth, 1908. (Photo: Edith Durham).

Men who guided me from Plani to Theth, 1908. (Photo: Edith Durham).

The Bajraktar Wants to Marry the American Lady

Rose Wilder Lane in Theth (1921)

Who was Rose Wilder Lane?
The American writer Rose Wilder Lane was born in De Smet, South Dakota, in 1886 and died in Mansfield, Missouri, in 1968. She was the eldest daughter of Laura Ingalls Wilder and Almanzo Wilder and is remembered by posterity as a versatile and active journalist, a political activist, a world-traveller and a novelist.

When Rose was seven-years-old, she set off with her parents on a gruelling, six-week journey over the plains on horse and wagon to exchange the arid Dakotas for the fertile Ozarks. She left home when she was seventeen and got a job. She was an ambitious young woman who studied hard in the evenings and made a career for herself as a telegraph assistant for Western Union in Kansas City and as a journalist. In 1909, she married the merchant and occasional newspaperman Gillette Lane, got pregnant and had a miscarriage or stillbirth thereafter. The couple divorced in 1918 and she never remarried.

Rose Wilder Lane's career as a writer began some time around 1910 when she was working as a journalist for the San Francisco Bulletin. She was extremely productive and published books, articles and short stories. Her most important books were: *Henry Ford's Own Story* (1917), *Diverging Roads* (1919), *Peaks of Shala* (1923), and *Discovery of Freedom* (1943).

Why Theth?
After her divorce, Rose Wilder Lane moved to Europe where, based in Paris, she visited war-afflicted regions on behalf of the Red Cross and reported about them. In 1921 she travelled from Montenegro to visit a refugee camp in Scutari (now Shkodra). Albania had declared its independence in 1912 but was then caught up in the Balkans Wars and Great War. Serbia and Montenegro invaded the new country, a one-time part of the Ottoman Empire. Albania had no central government at the time, and the authorities had enormous difficulty keeping the semi-autonomous regions of the north under control. The political situation was unstable for quite some time.

After visiting the refugee camp, Rose intended to carry on to Constantinople (now Istanbul), but a chance meeting in Scutari with another American Red Cross worker, Frances Hardy, changed her plans.

The American Red Cross wanted to open three village schools in remote areas of northern Albania in which instruction would be given in Albanian. Frances Hardy had collected the requisite funds in America and invited Rose to accompany her on the

Rose Wilder Lane, 1922 (Photographer unknown).

Rrok Perolli, the Albanian companion and interpreter of Rose Wilder Lane, 1922.
(Photo: Annette Marquis)

expedition. In *Peaks of Shala*, she tells us how Frances Hardy convinced her to go:

> "Constantinople's nothing. Everyone goes to Constantinople. But if you don't see Albania, you're wasting the chance of a lifetime. Up in those mountains – right up there in those mountains, a day's journey from here – the people are living as they lived twenty centuries ago, before the Greek or the Roman or the Slav was

ever known. There are prehistoric cities up there, old legends, songs, customs that no one knows anything about. No stranger's ever even seen them. Great Scott, woman! And you sit there and talk about Constantinople!"

"But if nobody goes there, how can we do so?" I said.

"How does anyone ever do anything? Simply do it. Hire horses, get on them, and go."

"Carrying our own guns?"

"Oh, we'll be safe enough! We may run into a blood feud or two, and get our guides shot up, but nobody ever harms a woman. Nobody even shoots a man in her presence."

Travelling to Theth

Rose Wilder Lane abruptly changed her plans and set off with Frances Hardy and Margaret (Alex) Alexander. Also of the party was Rexh Meta, a twelve-year-old refugee from Kosovo who had lost his parents and had walked miles to Scutari with other children to reach the refugee camp. There he had learned English. With them in addition was Rrok Perolli, an employee of the Albanian ministry of the interior as their interpreter. A year before that, Rrok Perolli had been in a Serbian prison and had been sentenced to death. He escaped and, at great risk, had managed to get over the border to Albania. He was afraid that the mountain tribes would hand him over to the Serbs.

Rose, her four travelling companions and two gendarmes set off from Scutari on an April morning in 1921 and reached the mountain pass of Chafa e Bishkasit [Qafa e Bishkasit]. She housed in local homes and vicarages in Pult, Gjoanni, Pog and Plan. Travelling in these mountains was no easy venture. They had mules and horses with them, but much of the time they had to alight and hike up the steep mountain paths on foot, often in the pouring rain. They were all drenched to the skin. In her book, Rose describes how the rivers were mostly swollen and the men would carry the three women on their shoulders over to the other side, as if they were packages. The distances to be covered every day were considerable and were calculated in hours of walking (she omits to mention that the calculation was based on time needed by well-trained highlanders). They would set off early in the morning and spend the whole day hiking and climbing. At dusk they would find a village where they could take shelter. Here they were confronted by new customs and rituals. The travellers were exhausted, drenched and chilled to the bone. What they needed was a warm fire, something to eat and a warm bed. However, northern Albanian hospitality required that they sit in their wet clothes, with empty stomachs, and discuss the affairs of the world with the men of the house, while the women slowly began making dinner.

This took hours and it was only at one or two in the night that dinner was served. By this time, the guests were too exhausted to eat but it was considered bad taste to let their hosts notice.

Meals were always a problem because no one in the mountains had enough food to feed visitors. In one of the houses she stayed at there was a lamb, a goat and a chicken.

The animals were shown to the guests who admired them. They were used to humans because the children loved to play with them. Later, the animals were taken outside, slaughtered and skinned. Several hours later they were in the pot, being cooked or roasted for the hungry guests.

Early the next morning, at about 4 am, the visitors were shaken from their sleep after a very short night, given a cup of strong coffee and sent off on their way without any further breakfast. Before them lay another long and arduous trek to the next village, but Rose and her travelling companions eventually reached Theth (Thethis as she calls it). There they stayed with the local priest at the vicarage.

In Theth, Rose got to know many of the local people and visited several homes. She was forced to interrupt a further journey down the Shala Valley when she caught a lung infection and had to return to Scutari alone with Rexh Meta and a local guide.

Back in Paris she used the notes she had made to write the book, *Peaks of Shala*, that Harper & Brothers published with many of the photos from the mountains of Albania. In actual fact, she had not taken any pictures during the 1921 trek so when she was back in Albania the following year, she had a photographer, Annette (Peggy) Marquis and two guides do the same trip she had taken the year before. This time, the weather was better and the journey was not quite as arduous. After much adventure, Annette got back safe and sound, but the camera had fallen into the water and the negatives only narrowly survived. Back in Tirana, the two women were present during a coup d'état, during which Ahmet bey Zogu seized power.

Rose Wilder Lane's book, *Peaks of Shala*, was published in 1923.

Back to Albania

This journey marked the real beginning of Rose's lifelong attachment to Albania. She had travelled for the Red Cross and Near East Relief through many lands: Italy, Greece, Yugoslavia, Egypt, Armenia, Arabia and Persia, but she eventually returned to Albania. She also learned Albanian, read as much as she could about the country and, in 1926, even decided to move there for a few years. With her new girlfriend, Helen Boylston, she set off for Tirana in a Model T Ford. The account of her trip from Paris to Tirana in the Model T Ford was published posthumously in the volume *Travels with Zenobia* (1983). In Tirana, the two women bought a house and lived there for a year and a half. Thereafter, a family emergency forced Rose to return to America and take care of her parents in Missouri. She also took care of her young interpreter and guide, Rexh Meta, who received a good education at an English university. After his studies, Rexh returned to Albania to get married, as custom demanded.

In the 1930s, Rose worked as a journalist for various dailies, weeklies and monthlies. Many an anecdote from her Albanian travels is to be found in her writings published in *Harper's Magazine* and in the *Ladies' Home Journal* (among them are Padre Luigi of Kiri, Edelweiss on Chafa Shalit, Blue Bead, Nice Old Lady and Song Without Words).

Inspired by the literary success of her daughter, Rose's mother, Laura Ingalls Wilder, began to write when she was in her sixties. Her memories of the trek across the

Inhabitants of the village of Pult, 1922. (Photo: Annette Marquis)

plains in a horse and carriage were recorded in the nine-volume series of children's books called *Little House on the Prairie* (1932). The series was later filmed and made her mother world-famous. Rose Wilder Lane's role in this achievement has been somewhat overshadowed, but there is no doubt that she played a major role in the writing of the books, at least as co-author.

After her mother's death in 1957, and in addition to her work as a war correspondent, Rose Wilder Lane devoted her energy to remodelling the family home and to promoting a Laura Ingalls Wilder Museum in Walnut Grove, Missouri. In later years, she was active as a war reporter, even during the Vietnam War. Rose Wilder Lane died at the age of eighty-one, just a few days before she planned to set off on a trip around the world.

Extracts from *Peaks of Shala*:

Arrival in Theth
"Then the trail turned the shoulder of the cliff, climbed up a gorge so narrow that the two-foot stream covered its bottom, turned again and came out on a little plateau. There was a wide stream running across the flat space; its water was milky green with melted limestone, and it was strewn with large, smooth, round bowlders. Some of the bowlders were pure white marble, others were bright rose pink, others were black as ebony, and one great one was green as jade.

A bridge of two logs, with railing of twisted branches, ran from bowlder to bowlder across this incredible river, and we stood on it, gazing at these colors and at a cliff that rose before us, striped rose and green and gray and white in long jagged lines, as though it had been painted, when we heard overhead an outburst of cries, like a hundred sea gulls shrieking in a storm. We looked higher, and there on the top of the cliff we saw a score of boys, naked except for bright loin cloths, engaged in acrobatics.

They made pyramids of their wet white bodies; four, three, two, one, they stood on one another's shoulders, and the four who upheld the pyramid ran swiftly along the edge of the cliff, passing and circling about a similar pyramid; from top to top of the pyramids the top youths swung, passing each other in the air, landing on other shoulders, balancing, taking flight again. The pyramids melted, as though dissolved in the rain, and formed again, while all along the edge of the precipice other boys made a frieze of living bodies, turning cart wheels, somersaulting over one another, walking on their hands.

We stood paralyzed. What did it mean? Then there was an explosion of shots; the cliffs around us crackled like giant firecrackers, the air seemed to fall in fragments around us, and through the din came multiplied shouts. Four tall chiefs appeared on the cliff trail, gorgeous in black and white and red and blue and green and silver. We were being welcomed to Thethis.

The shouts redoubled, rifles cracked from every rock, the church bell wildly rung, and through the clamor, deafened and a little dizzy, we came into the village of Thethis. The four chiefs, having greeted us ("Long life to you! Glory to your feet! Glory to the trails that brought you!" they said) preceded us up the last breathless quarter of a mile of trail, and all along the way the boys turned handsprings on the cliff tops.

The village of Thethis is built on the plateau that tops the gigantic, ship-like rock wedged in the narrow head of Shala Valley. All around it rise the mountains, snow capped, seamed with white waterfalls like rich quartz with streaks of silver; the shadows of them lie almost all day long across the village. Thethis itself is perhaps thirty large, oblong stone houses scattered at wide intervals on the flat land, and all the land is divided neatly into squares by stone fences – some fields for corn, some for grain, some for meadow. In the midst stands the church, two stories, oblong and gray like the houses, and a network of trodden paths leads to it.

It seemed a quiet, peaceful place. But on the mountains above it to the north the Serbian armies lay; their mountain-trained eyes were doubtless watching us as we crossed the sodden fields. This is the village, these are the chiefs, whose houses were destroyed by a company of soldiers sent from the struggling Albanian government in Tirana. The Serbs held the Albanian cities where the men of Thethis have always gone to market; the grazing lands where they have always fed their sheep lie in the grasp of Serbian armies. Scutari, the nearest free Albanian market place, is a hundred miles away across two mountain ranges. Therefore it was said that Thethis was friendly to the Serbs; it was said that her men still went to market in the Albanian cities that are now clutched by Serbia, that spies came and went across the border, that the chiefs listened to the clink of Serbian gold. And Alex and I remembered that in Thethis we were not to address Rrok Perolli, secretary of the Albanian Minister of the Interior, by his real name.

Bayraktar Lulash Keq Boshi (left), the priest of Theth, Padre Marjan and two inhabitants, 1922. (Photo: Annette Marquis).

Meeting the Priest of Theth

He came barefooted and bareheaded across the fields to welcome us, a thin, ascetic-looking man in the brown robes of the Franciscan friar. Large brown eyes burned in his face that seemed made of bones and stretched skin, the grasp of his thin hand was hot and nervous. He spoke to us in Albanian, Italian, and German, ushering us with apologies into the bleak rooms above the church.

The Serbians and Montenegrins, in their drive down toward Scutari, had looted the church, he said. He had come into Thethis two months ago, and found not even a wooden stool left. He was doing his best, but it took time.

The rickety broken stairway led upward to a long hall; from this, a door let us into the living room. It was bare; rain-stained wooden walls and a floor that clattered beneath our feet. The one window was shattered; fragments of glass held together by pasted paper. There were a long wooden table and a bench, nothing more. No fire. Our soaked garments were suddenly cold on us, and a chill entered our very bones.

The only fire in the house, he said, was in the kitchen. We begged him to take us to it, and in a moment we were sitting on a bench before a crackling fire in a big stone fireplace. The tiny room was crowded with villagers, the floor was muddy with their trampling, and more arrived every moment. Padre Marjan had no servant, but all were eager to help him. Some took off our shoes, others heated water over the fire, a handsome youth who looked Serbian and talked German anxiously beat eggs and sugar together while Padre Marjan made coffee. The warmth and the genuine welcome they all gave thawed us and made us happy, and we sat drinking the heartening mixture of eggs and coffee, while clouds of steam rose from us all and a babble of talk went on.

One tall, handsome chief – Lulash, his name was, and beyond doubt he was the handsomest man we had yet seen – brought us a lamb as a gift. Dripping beside him

95

stood a ragged boy, barefooted and blue with chill, who had come down the valley to bring us three eggs, which he carried tied around his waist in a pouch of goat's skin. He put them carefully into our hands, and we tried to return the gift with some pieces of hoarded candy. But he gazed in dismay at the strange things, and nothing would persuade him to taste them. A colored handkerchief, however, was accepted in an ecstasy that made him dumb; he could only lay it upon his heart and touch our hands to his forehead. Another chief came with a fat hen, others with eggs; all were eager to roll cigarettes for us, all were smiling, and in a hundred beautiful phrases they overwhelmed us with thanks for our coming, for our presence, for the school that Alex and Frances had promised Thethis. For this was to be the first of the mountain schools, and Alex, who had come into the mountains to decide where to put the other two, was delighted to learn that already, before the school building was begun, Padre Marjan had started the school, and Lulash had promised a hundred trees to be burned to make lime for the building.

We sat talking of these things while Padre Marjan set pots of soup to boiling in the fireplace, broke eggs, unlocked his box of precious flour, busied himself with all preparations for dinner, climbing over and around the tangle of lounging bodies, until another outbreak of echoing noises announced the arrival of Frances and Perolli and Rexh and our men with the packs. We felt a little tension with Perolli's arrival, seeing the keen eyes of the men fixed on his English clothes and swarthy, intelligent face. He is as tall as most Europeans, but he was small among those giants, and the neat leather-holstered revolver and dagger that hung from his belt looked inadequate among all those long, bristling rifles.

But Padre Marjan, unaware of our apprehensions, was altogether the happy welcoming host. He greeted the dripping Frances warmly, anxious only to make her comfortable – she who was also responsible for the hope of a school in Thethis. He welcomed Perolli also, calling him by his first name. "How does he know that Perolli's name is Rrok?" we girls asked one another with startled eyes – and then, turning to the chiefs with a radiant smile. "This guest," said Padre Marjan, with pleasure, "is Rrok Perolli, the secretary of the Minister of the Interior in Tirana."

You read of such things calmly. Nothing that one reads is real to him. Therefore you can never know what Padre Marjan's innocent words meant to us as he spoke them in his crowded kitchen in Thethis, at the headwaters of the Lumi Shala, a hundred miles and twenty centuries from anything you know.

The wildness, the savagery and isolation of those mountains seemed to come into the room. A hundred miles to Scutari, a hundred miles of almost impassable mountains between us and any kind of help. There we were, three girls and a boy, alone in the narrow valley beneath the eyes of the Serbs, the Serbs who six months earlier had caught Perolli and condemned him to death.

A chill wind seemed to blow through the room; it was not imagined. Every wide, friendly eye about us had narrowed, every lip tightened a trifle. A thousand currents of antagonism, of distrust, of intrigue, seemed like tangible things in the air; only Padre Marjan remained warm, innocent and smiling.

A Chief of Thethi, 1921 (Photo: American Red Cross)

None of us four, certainly not Perolli, doubted that we had just heard his death sentence spoken.[8]

(Fortunately, the tribal elders held long talks with one another the results, of which were that Rrok Perolli was to enjoy their protection in Theth and was not to be surrendered to the Serbs. Everyone was extremely relieved...)

Lulash Thanks the American Women

Perolli translated at length. When he had finished, Lulash rose, and he was very splendid in his six feet of height, a snowy turban with folds beneath the chin outlining his strong, sensitive, sun-browned face, silver chains clinking against the jewel-studded silver pistols in his orange-and-red sash, and he made a beautiful speech, graceful with a hundred flowery metaphors, thanking us and, beyond us, America, in the name of his village, his tribe, and all his people, for the school and the hope it brought.

"I," he said, "am a great chief; I have a great house and large flocks and much silver, and all that I have I would give if I could read. I am a chief of Thethis, and my people look to me, and many things are happening outside our mountains that mean much to my people, and I cannot learn what they are and what they mean, because I cannot read. Every night I come to Padre Marjan and study the little black marks, and long afterward I lie awake in my house and am shamed before myself for the ignorance of my whole life. But you have brought learning into my village; our children will know more than we. Our hope is in the children; they will be little torches leading us out of the darkness. You have lighted these torches, and I say to you, for Thethis, for Shala, and for the Land of the Eagle, our hearts are yours to walk upon. Long may you live!"[9]

In the Kitchen of the Vicarage

Padre Marjan sat with us, but did not eat, as it was a fast day. An apparently endless succession of dishes – soup, lamb, omelettes, pork chops, chicken – was brought in by Cheremi and served by Rexh in his red fez. Poor little Rexh! He ate nothing but a bit of corn bread; he said the pork chops had been broiled in the fireplace, and he feared that some of the fat had spattered into the cooking pots. He was not sure, but he feared so, and he thought it safer not to eat anything prepared in them.

The lamb's head, skinned but otherwise intact, was served separately, boiled, and the delicacy of the meal was its brains, which we got at by cutting through the skull. When the chicken came, Cheremi presented it with awe in his eyes, and after we had eaten he whispered behind his hand to Perolli. In the kitchen, he said, they were talking of the chicken; it was not of Padre Marjan's raising, but it had been hatched and brought up in the village, and they were sure that its breastbone would foretell the immediate future of Thethis. Would we let him have it?

Perolli took up the thin bone and very carefully cleaned it of every clinging bit of

---

8 Rose Wilder Lane (1923). *Peaks of Shala*, pp. 118-125. New York: Harper & Brothers.
9 ibid., pp. 127-128.

flesh. Then, with an apology to Padre Marjan, he held it up to the light from the window. Through the translucent bone the marrow, clouded with clotted blood, showed clearly, and Perolli read it with serious eyes, pointing out to us its meaning. There was a clot that meant a battle, a battle to the north, and there was a widening red line running from a dark spot; the signs were clear. The government would grow more powerful, and there would be war to the north, war with the Serbs.

He gave the bone to Cheremi, who tiptoed toward the kitchen with it. I strained my ears to hear how it was received; I thought that the portent of strong government might make the people think it unwise to hand Perolli over to the Serbs; they must know that in any case his death would be avenged by soldiers from Tirana. But would it, since he was traveling "on a vacation"? Governments do not usually back up their secret-service men who fail on the job. There was no sound from the kitchen, and we entertained Padre Marjan by showing him how, in America, we use the wishbone to foretell a part of the future. But any wishbone will do that for us, while in Albania only the breastbone of a hen that has lived all her life in the family will foretell that family's future.

Outside, it continued to rain, if that state of the air when it is surely half water can be called rain. We were glad to get back to the kitchen fire. The chiefs and older men of the village did not return, but many women and children came in to talk to the strangers, and it was evident that the padre's kitchen was the village clubhouse; they were all at home and happy there. The padre himself washed the dishes and swept the floor with a pine bough, chatting with them all as he did so; one saw, in the atmosphere of intimacy and democracy and respect around him what the Church used to be to the people long ago.[10]

School Children at Thethi, 1921. (Photo: American Red Cross)

10 ibid., pp. 131-133.

At Night in the Vicarage
Then he set pans of water to heating for our baths, and when they were warm he lighted the way with a candle to his bedroom, which he had loaned to us. Another large, bare room with wooden unpainted walls, a bedstead of rough boards with a mattress laid on them, and sheets and pillow cases of red-and-white-plaided cotton, hand woven; in one corner an office desk, and on the wall beside the bed a rosary.

At midnight Perolli and Padre Marjan retired to the cold, wet living room, to roll themselves in blankets and sleep on the floor. We three girls sat shivering on the mattress and wished we knew what the chiefs were deciding.

But, oh! it was good to take off the clothes, so many times soaked with rain, in which we had walked and climbed and slept for three days and nights. And forks may be idle luxuries, but there is no question that a thin mattress filled with straw and laid on raised boards is one of the greatest comforts in life!

We were awakened in the damp chill of a watery gray dawn, and with surprise found ourselves on its unfamiliar softness, in the bleak room of unpainted boards. Padre Marjan was knocking at the door. In a moment he entered, barefooted, in his long brown robe girded with cord, and, going to the incongruous office desk, he carefully unlocked a lower drawer and took out a box of soap. There were twenty small cakes of soap in the box. He took out one, carefully, put the box back in the drawer, locked it.

He had been followed by a small boy, a very serious child, and visibly nervous. About eleven years old, he wore the long, tight, black-braided white trousers, colored sash, and woolly, fringed short black jacket of his people, but they were all soaking wet and very old, mended and mended again until hardly any of the original fabric was left. His bare feet were blue with cold, and so were his bare arms, for the Scanderbeg jacket has no sleeves, and he did not wear a shirt. He stood very straight, and swallowed hard, keeping his face impassive.

Padre Marjan turned to him, holding the cake of soap. He spoke earnestly and at some little length. He then presented the cake of soap to the child, who bent a knee to receive it, and kissed the padre's hand and then the soap. An impressive little ceremonial, which we witnessed, wide eyed, from the mattress where we sat huddled among the blankets. Rain was still sluicing against the windows, so that the water on them was surely as thick as the glass.

We looked inquiringly at Frances, who understood Albanian. Her eyes shone, she was so excited. "It's a school prize!" she said, and, listening, "He's the best scholar in school; already he can read and write. Isn't it splendid!" The boy saluted us gravely; one saw that he had just gone through a profound emotional experience. "Long may you live!" said he, and went out.[11]

Mass at the Church of Theth
The next morning was Sunday, and we were awakened by the church bell. It hung in a belfry over the padre's kitchen, and the padre pulled the rope himself. Then tucking

---

11 ibid., pp. 133-135.

his brown robe about his bare ankles, he descended the broken, draughty stairs to the church, and we followed him through blasts of cold rain that the wind drove through holes that had been made in the walls by the invading Serbs.

The church itself was bleak and cold; a bare room, whitewashed, with the stations of the Cross represented by crudely colored lithographs stained by the damp. A railing separated the body of the church from the altar, where a very brightly colored picture of the Virgin hung, surrounded by wreaths of paper flowers, above a rough table with a bit of brocade spread carefully upon it. We girls were given a bench inside the railing, and sat there in a row, in our many-times-water-soaked sweaters and trousers. Outside the railing all the women and children and half the men of the village knelt on the cold floor, and their rain-drenched garments, threadbare and patched, made pools of water about their knees. The rain was still pouring down, as undiminished as a river, and the sound of it and of the waterfalls filled the chill place.

Padre Marjan began the mass, his high Albanian voice chanting the Latin, and the congregation made the responses in the same tongue. A ragged, barefooted man came to swing the censer for the padre, and Perolli, in his neat English tweeds, revolver and knife swinging at the belt, also assisted, going behind the altar with the padre to help him put a brocaded robe over the brown one, and reverently handing the cup and the wine. Rexh, in his red Mohammedan fez, watched it all with serious eyes, his head around the edge of the doorway.

After mass the padre dashed upstairs to look at our cooking dinner, and hastened down again for a christening. I am not familiar with Catholic ceremonial, but nothing could have been more touching than Padre Marjan, thin, worn by fasting and work, barefooted, the edge of his brown robe showing below the front hem of a white cotton garment, bringing into the arms of the Church the tiny, wrinkled infant strapped in its painted cradle. The woman who held it looked at him with a sort of apprehensive anxiety; the crowd pressed informally around them. Every time the padre turned to fetch the little glass bottle of oil, or the tin can of holy water, or the square of crocheted cotton lace that he laid over the cradle, the packed bodies gave way for him, and one child or another picked up the end of his trailing robe to keep it from beneath muddy, bare feet.

At the end, "Is it a boy or a girl?" he asked.

"A girl," the woman whispered. And the padre ended his solemn words with the name, "Regina."

The woman sighed and her tenseness relaxed. It must have been a great moment for the mother, I thought; some one said that she had carried the cradle forty miles over the mountains for this christening. We did want to give the baby something; for the hundredth time we regretted not having brought presents, and a hurried ransacking of all our possessions produced only a little colored sport handkerchief. But when we gave it to the baby it was as though we had presented a golden bowl; the excitement, the passing from hand to hand, the reverent marveling over such weaving, such color!

We found Perolli upstairs in the kitchen, grinning to himself, and when we asked

Sugarja spinning in Dukagjin, 1912 (Photo: Kel Marubi)

him why, he said the christening was a joke on the padre. The woman was not the child's mother; the real mother, married by Albanian custom, had not yet got around to having the church ceremony, and the priest in the village forty miles away had refused to christen the child until the parents were married by the Church. But the devout neighbor, knowing that the infant was in danger of hell fire, had brought it over the mountains and had it christened as her own, and Padre Marjan, all unsuspecting, had performed the ceremony.

Not half an hour later an almost naked man, streaming with rain as though he had swum the forty miles, appeared, breathless, with a water-soaked note from the other priest, and Padre Marjan read it aghast. "Merely parochial business," he said, tucking it in his belt and bending over the bubbling pots in the fireplace to taste and season. But his brown face remained wrinkled with worry.[12]

A Visit to the Home of Lulash Keq Boshi

I went across the flat, wet fields with Perolli to drink coffee in the house of Lulash.

The house of Lulash was different from any of the others we had seen. It stood on a castlelike rock; we went up to it by a stairway cut in the side of a cliff that rose almost sheer for so far that the waterfall pouring down it looked like a motionless streak of snow near the top. A natural bridge of rock crossed the little space between the cliff and the rock on which the house of Lulash was built; a furious little stream roared beneath us as we crossed the bridge, and then there was another stairway leading up to the house.

Lulash and a dozen men and women of his household stood outside his door to receive us. No rifles were fired. We passed through a double line of salutes and greetings and into a high-arched stone doorway. There was a little hall, floored and walled with stone, and a massive stone stair leading upward. This we climbed, and were in a large whitewashed room, lighted by a window and furnished with beautifully painted chests and a few hand-woven rugs. But this was not the only room; there were others, and, leading us through several arched stone doorways, Lulash brought us into the living room, where I exclaimed, "My house in San Francisco!"

It was exactly the same – long, wide, with the large gray stone fireplace in the center of one wall, folded blankets of goats' wool piled like cushions around it; the alcove where my bookshelves used to be was there – an old carved chest stood in it; and there were my windows, where the nasturtiums used to grow and the orange curtains frame the blues of San Francisco Bay and the Berkeley hills and the sky. I went to those windows at once. But, no, the magic departed; there was only the flat wet Lands of Thethis below me, the stone houses and stone fences, and beyond them the blue and purple and white and black and rose color of the snow-crested mountains with a hundred waterfalls. Beautiful, but like the stranger's face that shatters the wild, irrational expectation of having found a friend in an impossible place. I turned my back upon those windows.

12 ibid., pp. 203-206.

But it was, it was the living room that I remembered! The gray walls – but these were of plaster; the black floor; the huge gray stone fireplace. Even the rug on the wall, where my treasured shawl used to be. "It is my house!" I said, while Perolli looked as though I had suddenly gone mad, and all the others stood concealing their amazement. "Tell them that it is exactly like my house at home, far away on the other side of the world," And I sat down on a pile of folded blankets before the fire, not yet sure that I was not dreaming and that the strange chests and stranger figures of turbaned men and barbarically dressed barefooted women would not vanish when I awoke.

"I did not think," said Lulash, "that any of our houses would be as fine as an American house." He was so pleased that his hand quivered a little on the long handle of the tiny brass pot in which he was making the coffee. So I told them that only our finest houses are of stone, that my house was of wood, and much smaller than his. But all our houses had windows, I said.

"Yes," said Lulash, wistfully. "Windows are very good; I always wish that all our houses had windows. But first we must have a *besa* of peace among all the tribes; it is not safe now to have windows, a man never knows when his tribe will be 'in blood' and enemies will shoot him through windows. You see that mine are so placed that it would be difficult to shoot through them, and I have heavy shutters for closing them at night, when the firelight makes it easier to see us from outside."

But he was pleased that I praised his windows; he had gone through many other tribes and down into Scutari to bring up the glass of which he had heard, and made them with his own hands. They were on leather hinges so that they would open and let in the air; he said he had observed that sunshine and air were good things, and, if good outdoors, why not good in houses? "But it will be a long time before my people can have windows," he said, sadly.

He did not think it was good to keep the sheep and goats with the family, either; all his flocks were driven at night into their own quarters, on the lower floor of the house.

Houses are the most endless subject in the world; all of humanity and its history is expressed in houses, and while the coffee cup was passed back and forth I told about American houses; about the log cabins of the pioneers, such a little time ago as crude as those of the Albanians; about the loophole glassless windows, and the pegs on which rifles were hung; and about farmers' houses in New England, where the cattle live under the same roof, at the end of long sheds; and suburban houses with gardens, and apartment houses where whole tribes of people live, going up and down in movable rooms. And then I spoke about water power and said that it became electricity – Lulash asked me eagerly how it was done, but I did not know – and that brought us to the whole subject of machinery. I drew a picture of a spinning wheel for them and explained it, but they said it would not be practicable on the trails, where the women did most of the spinning; a woman could not carry her baby in its cradle and a spinning wheel, too; the spindle was better; and I agreed with them. But if men and women did not work so hard carrying water from the springs, they would have time to sit in the house and work a spinning wheel, and I said that water could come into houses in pipes, and Lulash and I discussed for some time how a hollowed-out log could bring part of the waterfall into his house.[13]

A Visit to the Home of Sadri Luka

"I'm going to upper Thethis myself," said Perolli, at length. "Like to come along? We've been invited to visit Sadri Luka, the richest man in the Five Tribes."

We roused ourselves with some little effort, for the grayness of the day, the chill, and the ceaseless sound of pouring water were like an actual weight on muscles. We swept the floor painstakingly and long, with the pine bough. We went down the draughty stairs and out into the downpour to bring back a wooden bucket of water; we tried to stir the sullen embers into a blaze to warm it; we gave up in despair and washed the coffee cups in water cold and sooty. We made the beds; we went up and down the stairs, bringing water, emptying wash basins, carrying ashes and wet wood. Our admiration and reverence for Padre Marjan grew like Jonah's gourd while we did these things, which he does every day before beginning his work. At last we set out, opangi laced and staffs in hand, to go to upper Thethis.

A day of comparative dryness had broken our fish-like habits, and water seemed again an unkind element in which to be moving. Crossing the flat valley in single file, accompanied by the sucking, slushy sound of water-filled stockings, we said little. The sheets of rain blurred our sight, and the sound of it dulled our hearing. But when we began cautiously to climb the slippery trail that edged up the mountain side, exercise had begun to warm us, and we escaped from the silence which is to human beings a more unfamiliar element than water.

"How can he be the richest man in the Five Tribes? I thought these people were communistic," said Alex.

"The tribes own only lands and houses and most of the forests," said Perolli." A man or a family can own flocks, or buy and sell when they go down to the cities. Sadri Luka's the richest man because he went down to Ipek. He was a merchant there, and everyone is rich in Ipek. How I wish I might show you that valley, my own valley – it is more beautiful than you can imagine. There are such rich fields – the cows stand knee deep there in greenness like a carpet – and the best fruits of all the Balkans grow there. And butter, and honey, and fine flour, and quantities of the finest wool that makes the beautiful rugs of my people – there is everything in Ipek that you could wish to have, and both hands running over.[14]

The house of Sadri Luka was notable for its stone-walled courtyard and its broad balcony. The heavy arch of the gateway was medieval in its grim solidity; we escaped from the rain to the peace of its shelter, and there were welcomed by Sadiri Luka. He was middle-aged, sturdy, even a little stodgy of figure, among the lithe mountaineers, and this appearance suggested the successful business man – a suggestion incongruous with his picturesque clothes. His trousers were the purest white that new wool can be, his fringed jacket the densest black, the colors of his sash were clear and gay, and his

---

13 ibid., pp. 159-163.
14 ibid., pp. 165-166.

silver chains were massive. There was even a heavy silver ring on his finger. And there was no rifle on his back.

The courtyard was a litter of cornstalks, almost entirely covered with a roof of woven branches; evidently it was the home of flocks now out in the rain attended by a shepherd cutting leaves for them. An arched doorway opened into the first floor of the house, where we saw a pensive donkey gazing profoundly upon the liquid gray weather.

Obviously this was a rich house, and we followed Sadri Luka expectantly, up the stone stairs and down a long hall mysterious with closed doors, to a large room full of color. There were rugs on the stone floor, rugs on the stone walls, floor cushions covered with rugs in front of the fireplace. There was no other furniture save a row of old rifles on a wall. Their slender four-foot-long barrels were inlaid with silver, their curved thin butts were of silver chased and enameled, their triggers were intricate flint-lock affairs, and we tore our eyes from them with a wrench, to reply with proper courteousness to the welcome of our host.

While he made the coffee a woman came quietly through the door beside the fireplace and greeted us with poised and gracious dignity – one of those many beautiful Albanian women who, because they were so poised and so silent, remain a background for all our memories of the mountains, more mysterious behind their level eyes and courteous phrases than Turkish women behind their veils.

Sitting on the cushions, we drank the coffee and the rakejia, from time to time responding to the greeting of other guests come to meet us. Perolli was quiet, fallen into one of the moods which we had learned not to interrupt with requests for interpreting. There was constraint in the atmosphere, and when, presently, he fell into low-voiced talk with Sadiri Luka, we tactfully engaged the others in such conversation as occurred to us.[15]

Sadri Luka Ponders at Dinner about a Balkan Federation

It was midafternoon, and since early morning the women had been preparing the feast they offered us. A special dispensation had been asked, and granted by Padre Marjan, for that feast, for though this was Lent, we were not Catholics, and never before had Americans been guests in upper Thethis. Far and wide the rumor had gone that in our own tribe we were daughters of chiefs, and it was with apologies that the village offered us its best.

When we had washed our hands in water poured from a silver pitcher, and dried them on a towel of white silk, a large brass tray was set on four midget legs in the midst of our cushions, and the other guests withdrew to places near the walls. Much urging persuaded Sadri Luka to sit with us and share such parts of the feast as did not break the Lenten fast. Newly made wooden spoons were given us, and a silver bowl of hot chicken broth was set in the center of the tray.

Sadri Luka spoke little, but his remarks were sound and well considered. While our

[15] ibid., pp. 168-170.

spoons rhythmically dipped the delicious broth, he said that the whole question of good government in Albania depended upon the fixing of the frontiers, and that the League of Nations talks too much and does too little. He suggested, as explanation of this fact, that the League is made of human beings.

While we gorged upon pieces of miraculously tender roasted lamb, fished from a heaping platter, he said that any definite frontier, however unjust, would be better than the prolonged uncertainty which daily encouraged further Serbian invasions.

While we chose morsels of stewed chicken, he said that the greater danger was not from Serbia, which fought with artillery, but from Italy, now driven to intrigue. Italy, having been promised southern Albania and much of the eastern Adriatic coast in return for joining the Allies in the Great War, had now been cheated of payment, driven from Albania by the Albanians, and refused Fiume. However, Italy had authority from the League of Nations to occupy Albania again if the Albanians could not maintain a stable government. Italy would, therefore, do two things; first she would spend money and munitions in trying to stir rebellion within Albania and in encouraging the already savage discontent of Montenegro, Bosnia, and Croatia; then she would develop an aggressive foreign policy, drop all pretense of accord with France or England, and fight it out with Jugo-Slavia. When this occurred, of course both Serbia and Italy would fall on Albania; any trouble in the Balkans was a signal for that.

The chicken being taken away, we were given a bowl of little cakes, light as whipped cream, cooked in brown butter and served with honey. Sadri Luka said that the only hope of peace in the Balkans was a Balkan federation; nothing less, he said, would persuade the European Powers and Turkey to leave the Balkans alone. It was true that for fifteen centuries the Slavs had been attacking Albania and tearing territory from her; it was true that more than a million Albanians were suffering under Serbian and Greek rule to-day; it was true that Albanians had won the Greek war of independence, and the Young Turk revolution, and their own revolution, only to see their country mutilated by their neighbors and by European diplomacy. But if it were possible for free Albania to live, he believed she would be the leader in a movement for a Balkan federation, and he pointed out that, with frontiers free and military expenses pooled, all the Balkan peoples could develop lands and mines, water power and industries, and in time readjust their boundaries by purchase, which would be cheaper than war.

This solution was so logical that I suspected it to be in the realm of pure fantasy, for I have long observed that human affairs and logic have little in common. But we listened with great interest to these opinions of Sadri Luka, which came strangely from an Albanian mountaineer whose trousers proclaimed in black braiding his descent from a tribe older than history.

The feast continued for a long time; there were bowls of kos, which is sweet milk made solid in texture, but not sour, a joy on the tongue, and there were platters of fluffy rice with gravy and giblets, and many kinds of cheese, and little individual spits of broiled lamb, onions and potatoes, and a cream made of powdered rice, milk, and honey, and breast of chicken baked in sour cream, and crisp cakes of whipped white of egg browned in butter and smothered in beaten raw eggs and sugar – which is strange in words, but unexpectedly good to eat – and many other things which we tasted absent-mindedly. For the setting sun had briefly conquered the clouds, the rain had stopped, and we thought of the trail to Thethis.

It was good to be out in the rain-sweet air, and the waterfalls were music in the evening quiet. Sunshine gleamed on the peaks of snow, blue and purple shadows filled the valleys, and bells of flocks came tinkling down the trails. When we had said farewell to Sadri Luka and the chiefs of upper Thethis, by the arching glass-clear torrent to which they had accompanied us, we went on light-heartedly, humming to ourselves. And Perolli sang a song of the mountaineers which is more sound than words, being a song of evening with rippling water in it, and sleepy birds, and the bells of the flocks answering one another across ravines and from far mountain slopes.

"Yes," he said, "I am happy. I am happy, for Sadri Luka is a true Albanian, and when I go back to the plains I shall see that he is released from the price on his head which has been offered in Scutari."

"What!" we cried. "Yes," he said, in a matter-of-fact tone, "ten thousand kronen were officially offered for the head of Sadiri Luka."

"And he doesn't even carry a gun?"

"Why should he? He is among his own people. It is no shame to go unarmed among his own people. He would carry a rifle, certainly, if he had to go to Scutari."

"But you are from Scutari – we are all from Scutari – Cheremi, Rexh – and he asked us to his house?"

Perolli looked at us with scorn. We had been guests in the house of Sadri Luka, he explained, with weary patience. If he had been twenty times a traitor to Albania, could a guest have killed him? And on the trail he had not carried a gun; no one could kill him, unarmed. He could go to Scutari in safety, if he went unarmed. But, of course, he would not do that, for that would be shameful. For two years he had been living in upper Thethis, unable to go to Scutari without risking his life, though he was a merchant, and poor, and could have made a business for himself in Scutari. But it had all been a mistake, said Perolli, which he would clear up.

Sadri Luka had lost all he owned in Ipek when the Serbs came in. He escaped with only his rugs and the few pieces of silver we had seen. But his flocks, which were in summer pasture on the high mountains, had not been taken. Sadiri Luka had come back to his people in upper Thethis, and in the winter he had brought his flocks there. And in the spring he had sent them back to their summer pasture, now on the other side of the 1913 frontier. For this the price had been put on his head, as a traitor. How could his shepherds come and go with his flocks across the new frontier, guarded by Serbian troops, unless he were a traitor to Albania, unless he had secret dealings with the Serbs? For two years his sheep had got safely to their summer pastures and back again, while all the other flocks of Thethis had been taken by the Serbs or killed at home because there was no longer pasture for them.

The explanation, however, was quite simple. Sadri Luka was a successful smuggler of his sheep. He explained to Perolli how he did it, for both of them knew by heart these mountains, which were strange to the Serbs. Once safely across the frontier,

Qamile and Sadri Keqi and family, 1900-1919 (Photo: Kel Marubi)

the flocks were comparatively safe, for the high plateaus where they grazed were uninhabited and hard to reach; so far, none but Albanian shepherds of Ipek had seen them there. Sheep, when they had no bells or lambs, were silent things, and the flocks were moved by night. Sadri Luka said that, if he had reached Thethis in time, he could have saved all the flocks by smuggling them through the ways he knew; already his shepherds were taking with them the few lambs born in Thethis in the last two years.

There was no question that Sadri Luka was a true Albanian. For the Serbs had relied on their possession of the pasture lands to starve the tribes on the border into treason to Albania, so that the frontier could again be moved forward. Sadiri Luka, with his flocks, could have been a powerful weapon in Serbian hands, an object-lesson to the people of the advantages of friendship with Serbia which would have been well worth paying for. But he preferred to risk his sheep by smuggling them. The price on his head had been a mistake. The chiefs of Thethis had already said this to Perolli, and talk with Sadri Luka had convinced him that it was true. Therefore he was very happy, and sang along the trail.

Kol Marku and Vendetta

But joy is not a lasting thing on Albanian trails. We had gone but a little way, perhaps half an hour, when the skies opened again. The water fell with such force that we feared we would be washed from our foothold, and, gasping and drenched, clutching bowlders and deformed trees, we struggled into the shelter of a leaning cliff. We had hardly reached it when around its corner came two woman under loads of wood. One was old and withered, with a strange, sharp expression; the other, as she put down her burden and straightened her back, showed us a most beautiful face. The pose of her head was regal, her forehead and eyes and mouth struck the heart with their perfection of beauty and sorrow.

"You are a happy girl," she said to Frances, after our greetings. "I have never before seen anyone so happy. Why do you come to our sad country?"

Frances said we came because we loved the Albanian people and wanted to know them better.

"We would bless the trails that led you to our house," they said, and added, "but ours is a sad house."

"Why?" we asked, and the old woman answered, while the younger stared into the sheets of rain that veiled Thethis from us.

The son of the house, Kol Marku, husband of the younger woman, was an exile from his home. His wife had been brought to his house only a week before the night when he killed his cousin, Pjeter Gjon. He had not meant to do it. With a number of other men they had been sitting by his fire, their rifles on their knees, as usual. They were cold and tired and had been talking of crops, when suddenly Kol's rifle spoke and Pjeter fell back and died. Kol swore that he had not touched the trigger, but when the body was carried to the house of Pjeter, Pjeter's family said that Kol had killed him

"*Once a week she comes walking over fifteen miles of mountain trails ready for business bright and early on Bazaar Day. This week she has brought jars of kos (the thickened but not soured milk that she makes by putting three sprigs of grape vine into the boiled milk) and plums and baskets, and on the way she has been knitting. When she finishes the gay sock pinned to her jacket she will sell that too.*" Shkodra, 1922. (Photo: Annette Marquis)

in order to become the head of the family and move with his bride into Pjeter's rich house. They claimed blood vengeance, by the Law of Lec.

It was a killing within the tribe, a matter for the chiefs to settle. They had conferred, and decided that Kol's family should pay to the family of Pjeter twelve thousand kronen, or that value in goods. The family of Pjeter had refused to accept this. Again the chiefs met. Twelve hundred kronen had been blood payment within a tribe before the Balkan war, but everything was higher now, and the chiefs offered fifteen hundred kronen. But the old mother of Pjeter was bitter, and the family said that no money would pay for the blood of her only son. They demanded blood for blood, life for life; only the death of Kol or one of his brothers would pay the debt. Kol fled from the mountains and his brothers walked in fear.

Without their men the family could not live. The land was poor, was too hard for the women to work. The irrigation ditches were down, and they could not lift the rocks to rebuild them. And the lives of the men, hunted without rest, became no longer good to them, so that they became morose and sat always by the fire talking of death. Then the women went to Padre Marjan, to ask of him the last ultimate effort.

The good padre granted their plea. Wearing his holy robes and attended by twenty-four chiefs walking in silence, he took the crucifix itself from the church, and went to the house of Pjeter in upper Thethis. For twelve hours he stood, holding the crucifix before the eyes of that family and telling them as God's messenger that they must forgive Kol. For twelve hours the twenty-four chiefs stood beside him, waiting. But the old mother was bitter, and upheld the spirits of her nephews, so that they refused.

Never before in all the mountains had anyone refused forgiveness asked by the crucifix itself. It had been carried back to the church above twenty-five bowed heads, and the people of Thethis knelt before it in shame. And Kol could not come home, the men could not work in the fields. The family was always hungry, and the young wife had wept till her eyes were dry of tears.

"We could not again ask Padre Marjan to take the crucifix," said the old woman, looking at us with eyes that begged that we would do so. But the young woman's eyes were somber and hopeless. The violence of the rain had lessened; below us we saw the green valley, the many little houses linked by tiny fields and a network of overflowing irrigation ditches, and the wounded church which had no steeple. But a column of smoke from the chimney showed that Padre Marjan was there. The women lifted their packs, bent forward under them, and slowly went out of sight down the trail.[16]

A Few Days Later
We came back to the fireplace where Padre Marjan was stirring the tantalizing contents of the cooking pots, and were clutched by a radiant Frances. She had ventured to speak to Padre Marjan about the family of Kol Marku. And this was the news he had told her. The bitter old mother of Pjeter was relenting. Because the holy Easter-

16 ibid., pp. 190-199.

time was near – so Padre Marjan said, but we guessed that Padre Marjan himself had caused her change of heart – the family of Pjeter had told him the day before in upper Thethis that Kol Marku might come home, and the men of his family work in peace, for two weeks.

This was the law of the blood-feud truce; that the injured party might grant, when it desired to do so, on holy days or at a time of common danger from without, a reprieve of a stated length of time. During that time the families or tribes involved would meet and greet each other courteously, although on the day that the truce ended the law of the blood debt applied again, and they must kill each other at sight. The family of Pjeter had granted two weeks – fourteen days of burden lifted from the spirit of the family of Kol Marku. A great deal could be done in fourteen days, Padre Marjan said – fields cleared, ditches repaired, seed sown, family councils held. And he was hopeful that this was the beginning of complete forgiveness.[17]

A Mountain Chief Looks for a Wife: A Marriage Proposal from Lulash Keq
Perolli, taking me aside, said to me: "You say you love the Albanians and the Albanian mountains. Do you want to stay here?"

"I'd love to stay here for years," I said. "It's the most beautiful country I've ever seen, and the most interesting people. But I can't, of course. Why?"

"Because you can, if you really do want to," said he. "I have a proposal of marriage for you."

"What!" said I. "You're joking!"

"Not at all," said Perolli, indignantly. "Do you think marriage is a thing to joke about?"

"But I never know what you mean," I complained. "And why should anyone want to marry me, here?"

"You needn't take it as a compliment to your personal charm, if that's what you mean," said Perolli, coldly. "It's really your short hair. But I can get twenty thousand kronen for you, if you want to marry and stay here."

"Twenty thousand kronen!" said I. "Two thousand dollars? For me? Here? But for Heaven's sake, why? You don't mean anyone thinks me beautiful, among all these Albanian women?" said I, indignantly.

"Of course not," said Perolli.

"And I can't even talk their language. What do you mean, twenty thousand kronen? And what has short hair to do with it? Don't be so annoying, Perolli. What *do* you mean?"

"Well," said Perolli, "Lulash would like to have an American wife. I don't mean he put it to me so crudely as that. He didn't actually put it to me at all, in fact. But I know that he will give twenty thousand kronen for you, and you can stay here and make over the whole life of Shala, if you like."

"But why me? Why not Frances, or Alex?"

17 ibid., pp. 210-211.

"Because you are all a long way past marrying age, in Albania, and their hair is long, so naturally these people think they are already married. But your hair is short, so they think you are a sworn virgin. In these mountains, when a girl is old enough to marry and absolutely refuses to marry the man to whom she has been promised, she may escape the marriage by swearing before the chiefs of the two tribes an oath of life-long virginity, and she cuts her hair and takes a man's place in the tribe. Naturally, when they see you, at your age, with short hair, they think that is what you did. If you were an Albanian no one would dream of marrying you, for the man to whom your parents gave you would have to kill your husband to clear his honor, and all the chiefs before whom you had sworn would be bound in honor to see that your husband was killed. But America is a long way off; that man and the chiefs would hardly come so far after you, especially as your customs are so different. Besides, I think Lulash would take the chance, anyhow. He really very much wants a woman to help him with the people, and he will not marry a mountain woman."

"You mean he would listen to my ideas and take my advice – you mean he wants a wife who will be his equal, a sort of partner?"

"Of course. What else is a wife? He would like nothing better than to have you give him American ideas."

"But I thought a woman had no rights at all, here."

"How absurd! She has all the rights that a man has."

"But women aren't in the tribal councils?"

"They are when it's a council of the whole tribe. They aren't chiefs, no. But chiefs always talk things over with their wives."

"But women are bought and sold. You just said so. Didn't you say you were offered twenty thousand kronen for me?"

"It's an unusual situation. Here you are, without a family; I'm the only man in the party; naturally he thinks of me as in the position of a brother or a father. The man's family always pays money to the girl's family before a marriage, but the girl isn't sold; she's been betrothed in her childhood, for any number of reasons. The money the man pays is spent for the girl's clothes and household things."

"Then you'd be supposed to give me the twenty thousand kronen? And then it would be his again, after all."

"Of course not. It's yours, isn't it? No one has any right to a woman's personal belongings, except her."

"You mean I could do anything I liked with it? I wouldn't have to have his consent?"

"Of course you could do anything you liked with it," Perolli said, wearily. "This isn't Europe."

"Obviously," said I. "Nor America."

"Well, what do you say? Do you want to do it?"

Men ask women to marry them for many reasons and from many motives, even though they are all lumped under the word "love." Sometimes the asking is an honor that should make any woman, either happily or regretfully, proud. And sometimes it isn't. For myself, I shall always remember as one of my finest experiences this offer of

Shala guide, 1922 (Photo: Annette Marquis)

a scalplocked Shala chief to pay twenty thousand kronen for me. There was no eager clutching in it, no selfish, grasping, personal asking for personal happiness; he could have had no idea whether or not this strange woman would bring happiness into his house; his motives in asking her to marry him had their roots quite outside himself. He believed that she would help him in his work for the tribe.

And I thought that a woman might have a much worse life than in this remote, stranded fragment of primitive times still left among the Albanian mountains, where respect for women is not taught like courteous manners, but is as natural as breathing, so natural that it is never discussed nor even thought about, and where marriage is not centered in small egotisms, but in the larger idea of the family and the future.

But I must admit that to live that life requires other training than any daughter of the twentieth century has received, for one's ideas have little to do with one's actions; my mind might admire this alien concept of life, but I fear that nothing will ever lead a Western woman to marry for the good of anyone but herself.

"Why, Perolli," I said, "of course I can't marry a Shala chief!"[18]

18 ibid., pp. 206-210.

Two English Minstrels in the Mountains

Jan and Cora Gordon in Theth (1925)

Who were Jan and Cora Gordon?
The British couple Jan and Cora Gordon performed, acted and lectured across Europe and America. They are still remembered for their travel books, including one on Albania.

Cora Josephine Gordon, née Turner (1879-1950), who was born in Buxton in Derbyshire, was an accomplished pianist and violinist, and graduated from the Royal Academy of Music in London, but she was first and foremost a painter. In Paris around 1907, she met Godfrey Jervis 'Jan' Gordon (1882-1944), born in Finchampsted in Berkshire, a parson's son who had studied at the Kensington School of Art in London. They got married in 1909 and were determined to live as artistes.

Their first contact with the Balkans was in February 1915 when they volunteered for hospital service with the Red Cross in Serbia. At the end of that year, their adventures took them on to Montenegro, Shkodra and Shëngjin where, amidst the confusion of war in the Balkans, they managed to catch a steamer and get away to Italy.

This curious "pair of vagabonds" was then based in Montparnasse in Paris until 1932 and thereafter in Notting Hill in London, and over the years, they produced no less than twelve volumes of unconventional travel writing. Their ashes were scattered on the lawn of Golders Green crematorium in London, mixed with those of Edith Durham.

Among the books of Jan and Cora Gordon is the 300-page volume *Two Vagabonds in Albania* (London 1927), the delightful record of their return to Albania over a decade after their first short visit during the Great War.

Why Theth?
Jan and Cora Gordon found themselves in Shkodra in 1925, set for an adventure in the northern mountains to follow in the footsteps of Edith Durham. As they noted: "We were now preparing to make a fortnight's ride through the northern mountains, to trespass upon the almost unpoached preserves of Miss Edith Durham, whose memory still lingers here. In the towns they have made her godmother to some back street, but in the country, even in the none too retentive memories of the everyday people, they still call her 'Kralitza' or 'The Queen.'"

The Gordons had initially planned to begin their journey in Mirdita, and visit the "Christian clan sombre and taciturn by reputation," and then to continue northwards to the Drin River and the Shala Valley and from there, to carry on back to Shkodra. The Prefect of Shkodra, however, suggested that they would find the voyage much more instructive in the inverse direction. Behind this polite suggestion lay the fact that there

Jan and Cora Gordon as performers (Photographer unknown)

was political unrest in Mirdita at the time, and the government forces of King Zog were gathering to quell it.

Having been given a "nebulously ignorant" German speaking dragoman called Nikola, an 18 year old hairdresser, the British vagabonds thus set off for Shkreli, and thence, with a guard of two policemen from Boga, Corporal (Tetar) Si Ali Ahmed and Corporal (Teatar) Djok's Nok, over the mountains to Boga and distant Theth.

Travelling to Theth
Half-way between Ducaj and Boga, where we hoped to spend the night, we encoun-

Nikola the hairy hairdresser, 1925.
(Drawing: Cora Gordon)

Woman from Boga that wanted to be photographed, 1925. (Drawing: Cora Gordon)

tered a man and a woman sitting on the hill-side. Both were dressed in the height of mountaineer fashion: the woman had on all her best clothes and jewellery; over her black, clipped, and probably dyed hair, was an expensive silk handkerchief; her broad silver marriage belt dangled with coins and chains; in front of her wide, bell-shaped black skirt was an elaborately embroidered apron; her canoe-shaped shoes were new and of red and yellow leather. The two stopped the hairdresser and talked for some while with him. The hairdresser argued with them, but at last condescended to translate. "This woman heard you were coming and asks you to take her photograph."

"Where has she come from?"

"From Boga."

"But we are still an hour and a half from Boga. Why has she come thus far to meet us?"

"She doesn't want her family to know that she has been photographed. I have told her that she will get beaten if her husband hears about it. But she says that she won't mind being beaten if you will promise to send the photograph."

I took the photo and wrote down her address, in order to ensure the beating. Presently we saw coming towards us along the road a small cavalcade, which She Ahmet recognized.

"That is Sadri Luka," he said. "In his splendid house you must lodge when you arrive at Thethis. He is the most important person in all these higher mountains."

Sadri Luka, warned by our guards, gave us a courteous welcome and placed his own apartments at our disposal. But rain had begun to fall; he was pressed for time and the interview was of the shortest. Each took his route again.

"Ha," exclaimed Ali the muleteer, who had been once already in Thethis, "you will be in clover at Sadri Luka's. He has a wonderful mansion, and his own apartments are..."

Words could not express it – he kissed his hand instead.

Just before we opened up the settlement of Boga we passed a grave recently made by the roadside. It was a pretentious grave, a tall wooden cross stood over it, and palings painted crimson and blue fenced it round.

"What grave is this?" we exclaimed.

"It is the grave of a police officer," answered the hairdresser." He was killed recently on Shtegut-Dhenvet by the brigands, who ambushed him there. His orderly too was shot; both his arms were broken and a bullet went through his chest. The brigands did not finish him off because they were sure he would die, but he walked down along from Shtegut-Dhenvet to Boga, four hours' climb, and he has recovered and is well again now."

Stay in Boga

Boga lay in a turn of the valley; the mountains had piled up higher and higher as we had proceeded, but the clouds had fallen lower and lower. The drizzle had become persistent, and we were glad enough to reach the little presbytery. A limping hunchback man welcomed us and ushered us up to a whitewashed room containing a bed and a table, in which his brother, the priest himself – small, vivacious, beady-eyed, a complete contrast from our aridly Christian hosts of last night – gave us a wholehearted greeting.

The little priest and his invalid brother lodged in a style not much better than did the mountaineers – the latter harboured, as it were, in the barn over their cowshed, the former in the harness-room; theirs was a plain, unvarnished poverty, his was tinged with a tentative refinement only rendered the more harsh from knowledge of better things. Yet no doubt he painted over the rawness of his exile with illusions and so existed philosophically enough. Formerly he had been secretary to one of the higher dignitaries of Scutari, and was musical. He had once composed a little oratorio which had been performed by the school-children before the bishop, and for which he said he had received a money present from the President himself. The writing of music was no mystery to him. Indeed, he dreamed of installing in his presbytery a wireless telephone, and said that he had ordered a quite expensive apparatus to be sent from Germany, but we have reason to believe that this latter statement was only another example of Albanian illusion. He wished that it were so, but he was barebones poor... "If wishes were horses," he was already astride.

His home of three rooms, his stables, barns, storehouses, and the church were all under the one roof. Early in the morning he jangled the bell, the rope of which hung outside, to call himself to church, where he performed the service to a congregation of himself and one small acolyte; had he only possessed a harmonium he would have played himself out with a voluntary. The chapel was tiny and damp; the ceiling of it had been made and decorated by a Moslem, who had played on it an emblem of triumphant tolerance composed of the crescent and the cross in a fraternal embrace. The little priest pointed this out to us with a humorous twist of the eyebrow.

Outside, a narrow cemetery was deep in grass, from which stood up tall crosses, many beautifully chip-carved. Poised, as if in contemplation, on the crosses were primitively shaped wooden birds with wire nails for legs. They are probably meant

Child in traditional dress on the cemetery of Boga, 1940 (Photo: Giuseppe Massani)

to be cuckoos, the Serbian bird of grief, for the Serbian word for "woe" is *kuku*. But the Albanians have lost both derivation and meaning of the birds, and we saw them nowhere else.)

As we had come along the road from Scutari on the first day we had passed groups of peasants going to market, and others who were accompanied by troops of sheep or goats, women carrying armfuls of babies, others with babies in cradles strapped to their backs.

These latter the hairdresser had said were the migratory peasants from Boga who moved seasonally between their own hill-pastures and the woodcutting trade at Marmoras between Scutari and Kruja. Now the lad was very persuasive that we should go up into the hills above the church and visit families of these folk who had not yet moved away to their winter quarters. In the morning the rain had been falling with such persistence that any hope of continuing our journey was impossible, but the rain lightened during the afternoon, and since the cheery little padre was hurriedly called off to an extreme unction, thus depriving us of his company, we decided to make the walk.

Had we known that even for so simple a stroll as this an escort would be considered necessary we might have hesitated. We reached the wretched two-roomed hovel where the Tetar Ahmet lived, and here the yelling and shouting of messages and the inevitable delay warned us that even an hour's stroll up the mountain-side was of consequence when we were in question. We were forced to accept the guardianship of Tetar Djok's Nok, of a gendarme with a blistered heel, and of two armed village bravoes before we were permitted to proceed on our visit.

Half-way up the hill we heard a distant voice crying from the far mountain-side. Every such cry must be attended to, and after a moment Tetar Djok's Nok announced that the message was for him. Setting his thumbs in his ears to preserve the drums from danger of bursting, he bellowed an answer. Back came the voice again, thin and clear.

"That is a message from my post," said Djok's Nok "it has been sent across the mountains. I must return at once."

"And how far away is your post?" we asked.

"Six hours' walk towards the Serbian frontier."

"And which road must you take?"

He pointed straight up the opposing cliff. Over our heads the mountains rose steeply into a crest nearly four thousand feet above, but in one spot the peaks lowered to about two thousand feet, and this notch Nok indicated.

"But is there a road?" we asked.

"There is a man's road," replied Nok; "animals cannot pass across it."

We said good-bye to the amiable and good-natured post-commander and resumed our own way uphill.

An hour's climb through dripping woods, up the beds of waterless torrents, and across boggy grazing brought us to a green gate woven of boughs, through which we stooped into a glade of beech trees which overshadowed a long plank hut and a series of wattle shelters, where lank, rough men lay sprawlingly asleep. At the foot of the trees was a clutter of wooden churns. A tall Albanian with handsome moustaches greeted us, his hand on his bosom.

"How have you come?"

"Slowly, slowly!" we answered. (Ngadal, ngadal). He greeted the others.

"Are you a man?" he exclaimed, touching his rough cheek to theirs in turn. He had to a high degree that easy dignity which is one of the mountaineers' most pleasant assets, a savage Beau Nash who had slept for three months in his clothes. After him came slouching out an old greybeard whom our guides at once began to chaff. The

Woman with cradle, 1936 (Photo Erich von Luckwald)

hairdresser stooped to explain.

"The old man has just married a very young wife. They are joking with him."

There was evidently a spice of acid in the jests, for the old Romeo seemed to hang half-way between annoyance and boasting, between pique and perk.

And, lo, his young bride, who stooped to our shoelaces at the doorway of the hut, was no other than the girl who had waylaid us on the road from Ducaj. She paled at our entry; no doubt she expected us to divulge her crime in order to watch her suffer the merited drubbing, and before she had received the vain consolation of the photograph. But we held our tongues. She went timorously about her bridal duties, manipulating with her silver tongs pieces of glowing charcoal for our cigarettes. Jo attempted more than once to signal to her by means of facial expressions that "Mum was the word"; but the poor bride, girt with her wide silver belt, jingling with her silver chains, evidently mistook this for mere feminine malice; she seemed more and more distressed the more Jo subtly grimaced. At last, reassured by our unaccountable and continued silence, she dexterously caught up a red-hot cinder in her bare fingers and pressed it upon the tobacco in my pipe.

The interior of the long wooden hut was divided by low wattle partitions, which stretched perhaps half-way across. At this end was the fire on the floor. The smoke drifted out through a corner space where two or three planks were missing. A few threadbare carpets on the earth made the ceremonial divan. The wattle partitions were in lieu of dormitories, for here a whole brotherhood lived all together, and the wattle partitions, semitransparent though they were, represented the first notions of a connubial decency superior to that even yet found amongst the peasants of Bosnia, where the married members of a family all couch down together upon the same divan and often under communal rugs.

Grouping themselves around the fire, the dark-faced, dramatic herdsmen sat waiting until the women had made the coffee. They discussed with the hairdresser news from Marmoras, whither they were shortly to migrate for the winter, and where they had known him during his days as a cafe waiter. This explained his eagerness for the visit. In one of the partitions a man lay tossing with fever, and the account of our miracle at Shkreli at once called down on us a clamour for medicine.

The news spread of our presence here. From time to time other men or women sauntered in until the back of the shed was tiered with heads watching Jo as she drew portraits of the more characteristic men. A couple of youths came in, boys apparently on the point of reaching manhood; one was dressed in the tight white and black clothes of the mountaineer, the other had loose cotton trousers such as are more worn by the townsmen of Scutari.

The conversation turned on to family affairs, and our host with a laugh pointed to the first lad.

"Manners are degenerating," he said. "See, there is my son. He is seventeen, his wife is seventeen also, and, will you believe me, he doesn't beat her? He's getting soft. Aha! The good old times are going."

The other lad had occupied a stool near the fire and at once fell into conversation with the women. This surprised us, for hitherto in Albania we had seen no man who considered it worth his while to exchange any unnecessary words with the womenfolk. However, looking closer, we began to doubt the sex of this person, and the hairdresser confirmed our suspicion.

"That girl," he said, "has vowed never to marry, so she dresses like a man and does man's work."

"But if she breaks her vow," we said, "does her family pursue her to kill her?"

"She doesn't ever break her vow," said the hairdresser; "she would be ashamed to. And, anyway, no man would want her any more than he would want his sister."

"But," we persisted, "if she did fall in love with somebody, and if the man did fall in love with her?"

This was a little puzzling for the hairdresser. Stendahl says that three-quarters of humanity would not fall in love if it had not read romances; the Albanian might almost prove this statement. Here is a passionate, excitable race, but it doesn't fall in love. Desire it knows, affection it knows, parental or filial love it undoubtedly knows also, but that mating love, that juxtaposition of inevitables that we make so much fuss about, has on the whole escaped them. A young man does not desire a sworn virgin any more than he desires his sister; she is out of reach, wholly undesirable.

Yet we repeated our questions, "If? If? If?" we insisted.

"She would have to leave the clan then," said the hairdresser; "she would be disgraced for ever."

"But they would not kill her?" we asked.

"Oh, no. She can marry if she likes, but she would not want to. You understand, mein lieber, she has sworn she won't."

The normal Albanian woman's condition is still Eastern: a little more than my dog, a little less than my horse. Yet she must find contentment in her lot since the virginal vow still seems to be a comparative rarity. May we be permitted to wonder whether the first clamour for emancipation might not produce a plethora of sworn virgins, and thus we would see in the family politics of the Malcija the ruse of Lysistrata triumphant.

Higher yet we came to places where the peasants camped in houses of basketwork, and where for a living they chopped out massive segments of wood for cartwheels, which they strapped to their wives' backs for transport to Scutari, one and a half day's laborious journey. A horse can carry six or eight segments, a woman must carry three. The total earnings after some three days' work for the man and three days' walk for the woman amounts to less than five shillings: little wonder that they eyed with delight the silver twopences that Jo distributed amongst the children.

Back to Boga for the evening we went. There the priest's cat had discovered and eaten one of our precious roast fowls, but in revenge our horses had broken into the priest's private corn supply. All now seemed really good-humoured for the first time since our setting out. Once more the hospitable little priest insisted upon giving up his bed to Jo, while he himself camped out on the floor of the kitchen, in company with the hairdresser, Ali, and the invalid brother.

The new day dawned loweringly. We sat over the hearth in the priest's kitchen and discussed the possibility of departure. Autumn was fast approaching and we might soon expect torrential rains, so that it was very necessary to get on, if any getting on were possible. With unusually little delay we packed for the road. Ali was in the best of spirits. Thethis, our next stop, had pleased his fancy; he had passed through the place once before on his flight from Serbia and the beauty of it had clung in his memory.

On the whole, however, Ali had been quite happy here. The little priest had found an old woman of the village who had been willing to sell hay, and each evening Ali had staggered up the stony paths under massive bales of fodder, which he and the priest had scrupulously weighed with an old steelyard. Further, his horses had feasted on the poor priest's corn supply, so that they were well fed for the moment. Ali was, as we have said, primarily a barometer of his horses' stomachs.

We started off without the usual exasperating wait and took the upward road along the river-bed towards the Tetar She Ahmet's hovel. As we proceeded an acid and angry voice was raised in our rear. The old woman, owner of the hay, was following Ali and cursing him in adept measures. Ali trudged along ignoring her vituperation with a look of passive glumness. We glanced back at him and he sent us a shrug of expressive resignation and a twisted smile. Suddenly the little priest who came with us intervened. But the old woman showed no respect for her pastor; she diverted the biting flow of her wrath from Ali to him.

"She is cursing us," the father said, "because she says the muleteer has robbed her over the payment for the hay. She guessed the weight optimistically and will not believe that we checked it honestly. She is now accusing me of conspiring with the muleteer. I sent the Mohammedan to her to help her because she is very poor, but the people of these mountains are completely lacking in any sense of gratitude."

Little awe as she had for the priest, she showed more for the gendarme. As we came nearer to the post-commander's house her voice dwindled and she stamped resentfully off. Then we understood why we had got so easily away from the priest's: the delay had been transposed to here. During a full hour we loitered, sitting on damp stone walls, first for the post-commandant himself, who had to be shouted up from the valley, then for village guards whom the post-commandant in turn had to shout up from the valley. More than once we protested against this loitering, but the hairdresser exclaimed:

"You can't go till the village guards come. It is much too dangerous. Shtegut-Dhenvet is full of bad men."

The Sheep Trail Pass (Shtegut-Dhenvet)

However, at the end of an hour, after continual shouting and screaming on the part of She Ahmet into unresponsive space, we grimly got on our horses, said a final goodbye to the little priest, and, heedless of the dismay of the hairdresser and of the policeman, we started off. With a volley of new and more urgent curses into the valley the policeman dashed into his hut, hastily armed himself with cartridge belt, revolver, and rifle and plodded in our wake. At once the rain began to fall, gradually increasing in weight as we went upwards, until after an hour we were forced to take refuge under some trees, where two lank woodsawyers in sheepskin coats were ripping lengthwise wheel segments which their comrades had carried laboriously down upon their shoulders from the mountain above. One of the shepherd's houses was near, and thither we went to shelter and to drink coffee as long as the downpour continued.

Here one by one, dripping, sombre, but apparently resigned, the lank village guards, all fully armed, slouched in until a full escort of seven had assembled. They squatted round the fire smoking with gusto the Scutari tobacco which Jo passed round them, and discussing the possibility of crossing over Shtegut-Dhenvet that day. If the rain continued, they said, the pass would be insurmountable: there were many places which the horses would be unable to climb as long as the stones were wet.

But after an hour and a half the rain diminished. The clouds gradually rolled up the

Okol and the accursed mountains, 1925.
(Drawing: Cora Gordon)

pass and only the mountain tops remained cloaked. An attempt was judged practicable.

An hour and a half later we understood quite conclusively that Shtegut-Dhenvet would indeed have been impassable in wet weather. Sometimes the rocky track seemed to stand up on end, and from boulder to boulder the horses scrambled like goats, and the high packsaddles rocked and strained under the convulsive efforts of our steeds. We, clinging to the mane to minimize the strain, were often keenly aware that our necks depended solely on the quality of a narrow girth of plaited goats' hair.

The pass itself lies some five thousand five hundred feet above the sea, and we were glad enough at last to reach a grey amphitheatre of bare stone which lies just beneath the final ridge to be surmounted. Here it was that the police captain, whose gay grave lay at the entrance to Boga, had been ambushed and killed by the wild men. From hence downwards over the treacherous track that we had climbed the wounded orderly had made his way for help. We had wondered at the feat even when we had heard it told of in Boga, but now that we had ridden the road ourselves we saw it as something almost impossible.

Here She Ahmet was to turn back with three of the guards. He was indeed in more danger than were we ourselves; he was meat for any outlaw's rifle. In fact, we believed that the guards were sent with us more for the protection of the gendarme who was theoretically protecting us. His life might be sometimes in positive danger, while we ourselves risked no more than the looting of our baggage, or, even more remotely, abduction for ransom, though actually these risks were, I believe, small enough.

We had, though, during our first day's ride changed our plans and were now taking a much wider swing into the hills than the Scutari authorities had given us permission to do; for into these very hills only three weeks earlier the police had dispersed a band of two hundred outlaws under a chief named Pjeter, of Kiri.

So She Ahmet, with his three protectors, stood below in the glacial amphitheatre watching us as we slowly mounted the steep zigzags of the last ascent. Before us our three guards had slung their rifles horizontally across their shoulders, and, hanging their arms over the guns' butts and nozzles, they seemed to lean forwards on the air. Pad, pad, pad went their india-rubber shoes, taking the rocks and boulders on tiptoe with such unconscious precision that, no matter how accidental the nature of the ground might be, the rhythmic fall of their feet never faltered. They made no false steps nor indeed seemed to employ much exertion.

"In a moment," said Ali the muleteer, "we shall reach a narrow gap and you will see Thethis."

We passed into a narrow chasm. Far below us She Ahmet and his guards fired a farewell volley, waved their hands, and shouted, and, though we could no longer distinguish their words, we knew that they were wishing us "a white road."

We emerged from the chasm into a bank of mist. Our guides halted in dismay. The hairdresser was almost panic-struck with fear.

"This is very dangerous," he said; "the brigands might attack us at any moment."

"If there are any," we answered.

We stood on the edge of nothing. The cliffs rose perpendicular above our heads and seemed to fall straight down beneath our feet. The mist was a flat wall before us. Down the face of the precipice a narrow, rough causeway sloped at a steep angle. Ten yards below the road had already faded away into the mist.

Suddenly a gust of wind came into the dank fog. The clouds suddenly drifted apart and we were looking straight below us down into Thethis. A mile away, but three thousand five hundred feet beneath us, a white riverbed was scored across the deep, dark gulf of the valley. From this bed the tall, purplish-blue cliffs of the opposing mountains rose up as steeply as these which we stood upon fell below our feet. We drew our breaths and gazed enchanted. It was like the moment of climax of some wild romance by Haggard. Suddenly the mist was swept back again and the vision of Thethis was blotted from our sight.

Arrival in Theth

They decided that Ali should go down first with the horses. One of our guards declared that as the mists had cleared he had espied a man lurking amongst the pines upon the mountain-side – a suspicious being of whom the hairdresser told us at least six times before we could quieten him. With Ali below us we would hold a superior position in case anyone might attempt to cut off the baggage. We gave the muleteer a reasonable start and followed him down the cliff stair. Now and then when the mist thinned, below us, we could perceive the awkward forms of the horses as they care-

Path to the house of Sadri Luka in Okol, 1940 (Photo: Giuseppe Massani)

fully and grotesquely lowered themselves from step to step, and upon Ali's turban, beneath which his legs worked valiantly. Striding with seven-leagued stretches down the precipice-edged causeway, we soon came through the mist, reached the first of the pine trees, and guessed that Pjeter of Kiri had moved his hunting ground for the moment; or maybe, under the laws of hospitality, he had disdained to touch mere tourists.

The rain, which had held off long enough to see us over the crest of Shtegut-Dhenvet, now began again. As fast as we could we made our way down to the post-commandant's house, and from thence, after some delay, through a now pelting storm, afoot, sploshing over marshy hill-sides, scrambling down into river-beds, wading over swollen streams, clambering up clay-faced banks by means of roots and pieces of notched tree-trunk, visiting and prescribing for a sick man, pushing a way through drenched coppices and so on, we came up to the settlement of Okoli and to the so-called splendid mansion of the Captain Sadri Luka.

The four-square mansion of Sadri Luka stood in mud; a puddle six feet in diameter

At Sadri Luka's, 1925. (Drawing: Cora Gordon)

was immediately before the door and made access splashing and difficult. The roof was of wood slats and sloped steeply to throw off the winter snow; from the almost windowless walls projected square, loop-holed stone bays on corbels. The inside of the house was in pitch darkness because there were no windows, and we felt our way up two flights of broad, wooden ladders to the uppermost floor, where a gaunt, roughened woman in rags of black and grey ushered us into a large room lit greyly by two tiny windows and a small skylight. Near one end of the room a fire smouldered on the floor; the acrid pine smoke drifted in the slight draughts and in the course of time had tarred the walls to an almost even blackness. The smoke at last found its way into the open through interstices between the wooden slats of the roof. We could hardly help comparing this rough, uncleaned, undecorated barn with the white, pleasant rooms and the gay rugs of the south. While apologizing for the absence of the men, the gaunt woman threw wood upon the fire until the flames leapt up with a friendly warmth. We turned ourselves round and round and began to steam to dryness the drenched clothes upon our bodies.

"This is a strong house," said the hairdresser; "it counts fourteen fully grown gunmen, and it dominates the country round about. The Captain Sadri Luka is a powerful chief; he is a partisan of the President, Ahmet Zogu, while all the other clans are secretly opposed to him."

One by one the members of this powerful family assembled – dominating, dark-faced men all. Their heads were wrapped up in clouts of various colours, their bodies were clad in rough, often embroidered, homespun of different degrees of dirt and raggedness. But rags here implied no disgrace. The habit of apparent poverty has so long been a protection not only from tax-gatherers but from marauders that it implies none of the shame that it has in our Western life. As each man came in he hung his rifle on the wall. Two little girls crept in also and crouched on the other side of the fire staring at us with eyes of wide curiosity. Their clothes were at the limit of patches, tatters, and ingrained earthiness; their legs, hands, and arms must have been awaiting a yearly bath in the autumnal downpours. A dishevelled man in a sheepskin coat, the front

The living room of the Sadri Luka family in Okol, 1940.
(Photo: Giuseppe Massani)

part of his head shaved, his hinder hair falling in tangled and clotted ringlets behind his ears, arranged for us on the floor a rough couch with carpets that would hardly have been rescued from the dustbin by a Parisian rag-picker.

Those splendid rooms of Sadri Luka we were destined never to see. They were locked up, we were told, and Sadri's wife had carried the key with her up to the high pasturages. But later, Sadri's wife, a plump and pompous woman in the full panoply of a Shala heiress, came down to inspect us; she said no word of the splendid suite, and so we stayed quite contentedly where we were, lounging round the hot, leaping fire, Jo drawing one vivid Albanian head after another, handing her tobacco box about, and insisting so much on the prerogative of the Western woman that she awoke memories of Miss Edith Durham, the *Kralitza*, or "Queen."

"Aha, that was indeed a woman!" cried Nëij Miraka, the man in the goatskin. "She went about in man's clothes, and I tell you that she was here with us, and over the mountains too, for fourteen days before I as much as suspected her sex."

It was from this village of Okoli that Miss Durham set off on her attempt to photograph Gusijne, in defiance of the Turkish interdiction.

And yet, in suite of the self-sacrificing work that she has done for the Albanians, Miss Durham is being rapidly forgotten. All the priests that we met insisted upon one thing, that the Albanian peasant does not feel gratitude, and such ingratitude is nowhere more exemplified than in this instance. We often had great difficulty in extracting memories of her from the very places that must have known her best.

The darkness came on quickly. Soon there was no more light in the room than that given by the fire, which, however, was damped under the circle of a ponderous clay baking-pan roasting in the flames. At the back the gaunt woman, upright before a large, carved chest, was sifting and damping the maize meal that was to make a new loaf for us. Picking from the corner a broad board of pitch-pine and an adze Nëij Miraka began to hew long splinters of resinous wood, which were placed upon a hanging grille of wrought-iron and fired. This was the sole lamp that they possessed, the most primitive means of illumination we had yet encountered. During the whole evening one or other of the big, dark brothers or cousins was wielding the adze to provide sufficient of the bright burning pine chips.

The loaf was moulded, the big earthen pan, with a holy cross inscribed in its base, was turned, almost red hot, off the flames, the bread was slapped in and embers were piled over it. Nëij Miraka now took his turn as cook. Sitting almost in the overpowering fire he stirred persistently a copper bowl full of a meal dish for supper.

We had fully expected to wait till midnight for our supper, but they were wasting little ceremony here over us. The war has brought too many strangers through the mountains – Serbs, Austrians, Germans, and so on. The fatted kid is slain no longer; the voyager takes pot-luck more or less. Hospitality has lost most of its pleasures and has not yet gained the right to earn profits. Mountain honour has not fallen so low that the farmer may charge strangers for their food or lodging, but he must speculate on the probable *quid pro quo* of a parting gift to the women, sordid creatures who can accept cash.

The children of the Sadri Luka family, 1940. (Photo: Giuseppe Massani)

We supped as usual squatting on the floor. Jo and I, Nëij Miraka and the hairdresser alone were deemed worthy of the first table. The meal was simple but quite pleasant to the taste. Here we were above the line of grape-growing, and so outside of the frontier of homemade intoxicants. We quaffed pure spring water from a wooden jug, dipped our wooden spoons into the communal dish, and chewed the tasty maize bread, which was warm and crisp under the fingers. The rain still fell persistently in the valley, and from time to time water dripped upon us. The drops had gathered some tarriness from the smoked roof-slats and made long stains down my coat.

"You must not think that our roof is in bad repair," said Nëij Miraka; "this water is coming through the bullet holes that our enemies made last time that they attacked the house. All Shoshi came up against us, but they never even dared to set foot upon our lands."

After supper the table was picked up and removed to the other side of the fire,

In the Sadri Luka house (Sadri Luka sitting in the middle), 1940. (Photo: Giuseppe Massani)

where the rest of the men and Ali the muleteer dined. When they in turn were satisfied the poor women ate up the scraps; and after all had been cleared away the family hen walked about between our feet, admirable and productive substitute for the dustpan and crumb brush, a feathered housemaid which in other lands might have become a feathered broom.

Singing songs

We, of course, asked if they had music here, and a handsome, almost clean peasant with a great rope of silver necklace as a watch-chain borrowed Jo's umbrella and went off into the rain to the next house, from which he brought a one-stringed vellum-faced *lahuta*. The singing of the southern Albanian is complex; that of the northern proved to be well-nigh as simple as music can be conceived. A tune of six notes was almost all that the vocalist could achieve, a chant which he accompanied by a peculiar rhythmic sawing on the one-stringed *lahuta*, with its limit of four hoarse notes. These were produced by the fingers widely spaced, touching the string at the second phalange. The vocalist intoned a long, dramatic poem, the repetitive musical theme of which was but four bars or so in length. It told the heroic history of a band of Shala men who went down to Scutari to kill an unjust Turkish *bej*. They penetrated into the palace, achieved their purpose, and were all slaughtered there except two who escaped by jumping from the palace windows. Covered with blood and wounds these two made their way back to Shala, but their own mothers reproached them. "Why have you returned while your comrades lie dead?" At once the two turned back, marched down again to Scutari and fought till they were killed by the guards.

The song finished, Nëij Miraka said:

"There were some American Red Cross women here once. They sang queer songs to us. Can you sing these things?"

So to try the Albanian musical taste we sang to them various Western songs. We found that beyond the childish rounds of France and England, such as "Three Blind Mice," "Frère Jaques," or "Sweetly Sings the Donkey" their comprehension could not go. The lastnamed roused them to the wildest joy, and completely sealed Ali's devotion to us. For him henceforth we were the folks who knew that wonderful donkey song, and, wherever we stayed, after supper he would creep into the room and murmur respectfully:

"These people sing a marvellous song about a donkey."

And after having had his donkey song he would creep off to whatever corner had been assigned to him, smiling broadly with satisfied contentment. The hairdresser also proved to be the possessor of a good voice. He sang Scutari love songs with almost exaggerated passion. Then we knew why he was proving so unsatisfactory. We had thought to hire a dragoman but had instead engaged a tonsorial and vocal artist, and he had the second-rate artistic temperament fully developed. He would have been quite in his element at the Café Royal or at the Rotonde in Paris.

Bed-time came and we were led off to a separate room. The gaunt woman seemed reluctant to leave us. We had brought some strong carbolic soap, and its pungency had convinced her that it must be very efficacious for the complexion. We had brought it as a parasite deterrent, but we did not like to deceive her and chopped off a small quarter at her request. Poor woman, she would have needed skin peeling for at least three layers down to undercut the infiltration of long years of neglect. She still loitered coyly in the room, and at last offered another request: Would we let her see us go to bed together? But this we declined to do. We manoeuvred her tactfully from the room and shut the door.

Our bed was formed of a goat-skin spread an the floor and two very grimy cushions; the room was pungent with a mixed smell of cheese and half-cured hides, but we managed to extract a wooden stopper from a six-inch loophole in the wall and so preserved ourselves from being quite asphyxiated. However, there were no bugs, or the night was too cold for their sallies, and thus we fared better than we had hoped or indeed had expected.

* * *

Our couch was neither soft enough nor cosy enough to give us lie-a-bed longings. We rose in time to catch Nëij Miraka at his toilet in the big room. This was performed by pushing his long, lean arms through various rents in his shirt and scratching himself luxuriantly with his finger-nails, walking to and fro in the meanwhile and uttering tones of ecstatic satisfaction:

"*Krukje Krishti kjoft*" ("If the cross of Christ should be").

The assonances of the phrase were so excellently suited to the action that they tickled my sense of the apposite and I at once memorized them in case the exigencies of this mountain travel should make me also use my own nails as toilet luxuries. If anything could render scratching respectable surely such an incantation should do so.

Nëij Miraka was the earliest riser. On the floor the others lay shrouded in various ways – in sacking, in old sheepskins, or in the rags of once vivid rugs. There was plenty of room here to sleep. The room was, as I measured it, forty-two feet long by twenty wide, and contained no more furniture than a clumsy loom, a carved bread chest, and a pile of farming utensils. The low table was rolled out of sight, and the only seats were low, three-legged stools and one stumpy but noble chair.

This chair had at once excited Jo's possessive sense. The seat was but a foot from the ground, cut from a segment of pine tree, but the back and arms were astonishing examples of use developed simply and beautifully from nature with the easiest grace. Jo's possessive instincts thirsted to carry that chair off by some means or other. Later in the day we compelled the hairdresser to make inquiries; he did nothing voluntarily. The peasant with the watch-chain said that a man near had a chair and that he might be persuaded to part with it.

The rest of this Albanian mansion-fortress was formed of dark rooms lit only by loopholes, dark rooms filled with tall churns, or with produce or ill-cured hides, all tinged with the earth as though the troglodytic habit had not yet worn out. What sense of decoration there was had been expended all upon the clothes or on pieces of carving, such as that upon the corn chest or on the arms of the chair; one man had carved the stock of his gun into a veritable masterpiece of intricate pattern; but the idea of house decoration so freely employed in southern Albania has not yet developed in these severe mountains. The house is here shelter, barn, and fortress – nothing more. Yet the folk had a keen appreciation of Jo's drawings, provided only that she assisted Nature in her art by adding a little to the length of their moustaches.

To one man who showed some reluctance to pose they cried:

"Why, your moustaches will be exhibited in all the English newspapers. What more could you desire?"

During the morning we went to visit our patient of the afternoon before, and found him apparently in a dying state. We had given him a linseed, liquorice, and chlorodyne lozenge dissolved in a little hot water, for we had learned that we must never

The mountaineer chief, 1925 (Drawing: Cora Gordon)

leave such people without some magic draught. A simple Couéism[19] may achieve what medicine cannot. But here Jo's magic had evidently failed. Sympathy and distress, the only things we could offer him, except a good glass of Greek brandy from my flask, which undoubtedly cheered him up. But our Albanian guides showed little signs of sympathy with their dying companion; they laughed and joked and at last clamorously insisted that Jo should sketch a later visitor in sheep-skins, "because he hasn't got a shirt to his back."

19 Émile Coué (1857 – 1926) was a French psychologist and pharmacist who introduced a popular method of psychotherapy and self-improvement based on optimistic autosuggestion.

In contradiction to the Boga families who migrate downwards for the winter, we found here families from the plains about Scutari who had migrated upwards for the summer. We also visited the post-commandant, a young man nicknamed "The Frog," because of his prominent eyes. He said that he would not guarantee our journey on the morrow from Thethis to Lower Shala unless the Sadri Luka family would place a *besa* upon us and send a representative to ensure it. After an argument Nëij Miraka promised to do so. The *besa* is a family vow of protection, and should any attack be made upon the *besa*d person the family's honour is blackened until the injury has been avenged.

During the afternoon we bought the chair. The peasant with the watch-chain said that we would hardly buy such a chair for less than thirty crowns, or about ten shillings. The man who had a chair for sale was a sly-looking fellow with a sharpened nose. Knowing nothing of the probable value of such a chair we flung ourselves upon this boasted Albanian sense of honour; we told him that we did not know the value, we told him that we trusted him not to overcharge us, and we added that under no circumstances would we bargain. He should name his price, we would say yes or no; he at once said forty crowns, which was obvious robbery.

The Albanian honesty had shown thin in his hands. So, ignoring him, we had to calculate whether the chair would be really worth that amount to us. Once back in Paris sixteen shillings would be a tiny price to have paid for so remarkable a piece of furniture. Moreover, we have learned by experience to seize anything desirable where and when we first see it. Often, it never appears again. There had been none of these chairs in Boga; how could we expect to find others in Lower Shala? Of course these chairs were not made for sale, and it was mere chance that this man was willing to sell. So we decided to smile, pay our forty crowns, and to take the chair. In Spain we would have lowered ourselves in popular estimation, but here in the East a soul above bargaining may be esteemed as an indication of nobility. When we had returned to Sadri Luka's the hairdresser announced in almost awestruck tones that we had paid a napoleon, without bargaining. Nëij Miraka was crouching over the fire; he looked up at me quizzically.

"That man has sweet blood," he proclaimed. "If I had known him longer I would have asked him to be a blood-brother with me."

It may have been a compliment – the noblest compliment, indeed, that Nëij Miraka could have paid me. My vanity would persuade me that it was, and yet I suspected him. He had more than a touch of malicious humour, which we had hitherto enjoyed. I would not bet a halfpenny more on the flattery of an Albanian than I would on that of an Irishman.

The two little girls of the family were winsome creatures, shy as wild woodland things and incessantly at work. During the morning they had sat half within queer wicker-work frames plaiting with a tremendous click of tossed bobbins an interminable string of goats' hair, with which to make the black embroidery for the mountaineer's trousers. At other moments they plied their knitting, inseparable accompaniment to the mountain woman wherever she goes, and which she plants as an ornament

Girls of the Sadri Luka family constructing wicker work frames, 1925 (Drawing: Cora Gordon)

in her hair whenever her hands are busy. Their names we learned were "Sky" and "Flower." The hairdresser now suggested that we should give them some slices of our stale loaves. So stale indeed was the bread, already five days a-journeying, that we demurred; but he replied that such staleness would be nothing to them. Nor was it indeed. They grasped the already rocky stuff as though it were the most delicious cake, they giggled over it, tasted it with precious gluttony, and submitted that a half of the treat should be subtracted by their mother to prolong delight till the morrow.

"They don't eat bread more than once a year," said the hairdresser; "all they get is *pogac*."[20]

Veritably wealth and power as they deem it in these mountains does not include luxury.

In the evening the sharp-nosed chair-seller came in and paid us a hundred compli-

---

20 Stale maize cake, exceedingly unpalatable and indigestible.

ments. We sat on talking and smoking in the flickering light of the pine-chip lamps. I remembered that somebody once had remarked of a friend, "She makes a god of comfort," and it struck me how inaccurate that phrase was; "She makes a demon of comfort" would have been truer. Jo and I are the people who make a god of comfort, because just as the true Christian finds God everywhere, so we can find some comfort everywhere. To multiply the conditions that can render you uncomfortable is not to worship comfort.

Presently the sharp-nosed man whispered to the hairdresser and the hairdresser spoke in turn to us. The fame of our donkey song had reached him. Would we be so good as to sing it once more? Ali at once brightened. "Yes, yes, the donkey song," he urged. And so we tuned up our childish rondeau:

"Sweetly sings the donkey
As he goes to grass,
If you don't sing better
You will be the ass.
He-haw, he-haw,
He-haw, he-haw, he-haw!"

I rather pride myself upon the verisimilitude of my "he-haw" effect.

The usual delay at setting off was if anything exaggerated here. We judged that Sadri Luka's family had in reality become bored with visitors; at the rate of one set per annum. Ali had been moderately distressed about the fodder supply, which was a fairly sure indication of the different people's attitude towards ourselves, much more accurate than all their pleasantries or blarneyings.

The truth is that for the traveller the Albanian mountaineer's sense of honour is already an unmitigated nuisance. If the tourist could pay properly and make his decent previous bargain all would be clear. Although the hospitality of the north Albanian has been vaunted above that of the southerner, we personally have found the real southern peasant apparently more spontaneously and more really hospitable than the northerner.

The duty of having to escort voyagers from one village to another undoubtedly weighs heavily on the peasants. It belongs to the unpaid offices which can be claimed from the man who owns a licence to carry the rifle, a kind of vigilante committee work. In spite of whatever risk there might have been we ourselves would far rather have travelled alone with a guide, but mountain traditions shuddered at the proposal. The Government had insisted on an accompanying policeman, and the policeman insisted on the guard. He would never have dared to come home alone; so that wherever we voyaged we had to drag this comet's tail of half-reluctant bravoes, who often complained of the wear and tear on their shoes.

The gigantic man of the Sadri Luka house, who represented our *besa*, strode along on huge bare feet, and at one place asked me in an undertone to sell him half a dozen

*Gigantic man of the Sadri Luka house, 1925.
(Drawing: Cora Gordon)*

packets of cigarette papers. Mr. Suma of Scutari had advised us to carry tobacco and papers in plenty with us, and we had procured what seemed on starting out to be a very large supply. But we could have bought friendliness everywhere had we carried five hundred packets of papers with us. As it was, I could only give him one packet, since we had to ration our generosity or we would leave ourselves without any provision for the latter parts of the trip. Cigarette papers and salt are the two things most lacking in these regions. On their ride the English police officers had encountered a woman who was making a two-and-a-half days' journey down to Scutari solely in order to sell a dozen eggs with which to purchase sixpennyworth of salt.

Leaving Theth
Before we had passed the church of Thethis we had gradually, by shouting, amassed four policemen and seven armed villagers. Our escort down the valley of the Shala River numbered eleven armed men. Even so, our little command took no risks. Twice the sergeant made us halt for twenty minutes while the men scouted ahead and searched the hill-sides to be sure that the road was clear. Evidently the men themselves were quite nervous. The road lay down the cleft of the river – sometimes it mounted high above, sometimes it scrambled almost to the water-line – and though the riding was rough enough, nowhere did it approach the difficulty of the ascent and descent of the Shtegut-Dhenvet pass.

After some seven stony miles the valley opened a little, and on the opposite side of the water we saw three stone houses in the fields of yellow-green maize such as spread out wherever there was any hint of flatness. This was the village of Nerlymza. We splashed across the river, turned our horses loose in a little graveyard, and sent a messenger to say that we would honour Nerlymza by lunching there. Soon we were being conducted along a mud causeway, between deep fields of maize, to the usual rectangular house with an exterior upper balcony and narrow, defensible staircase.

Already the women had begun to sift the maize for our bread; the fire was heaped high, and the earthen bread pan with a cross moulded into its base had been placed over the flames. Here, too, were evidences of the communal life of these families. There were three or four women to the house. Several babies in cradles were wholly hidden under thick cloths, though some of the babies had grown much too big already, and the ends of the cradles having been removed, their little feet projected, dangling in the air, beyond the coverings. Our guards had distributed themselves amongst the three houses of Nerlymza, and so we had but one man with us, the police sergeant, who could introduce Jo's sketching idiosyncrasy and persuade the men of the house to submit to portraiture.

In this, however, he was assisted by a keen-eyed, large-headed peasant, who understood almost at once what was necessary and who conveyed it to the others by a set of excited signs, more expressive than words. He was deaf and dumb. But this handicap had developed a keen wit and quick intelligence, which more than balanced his defects. Indeed, after a quite satisfactory little meal of new bread, cheese, and omelet, as soon as the sick were spread before Jo, the deaf and dumb man rather than the hairdresser became her most useful interpreter.

We were appalled at the amount of illness we had encountered. You would expect that these mountaineers would exhibit robust health, though at Boga most of the migrationary folk had caught malaria or sand-fly fever in the swampy forests of Marmoras. But at Thethis every house we entered has its quota of sick and fevered, not counting the old women, who, like all old women everywhere, would swallow medicine as a luxury, even if they were not ill. At this house the illness reached its climax. Scrofula, inherited syphilis, fever, and itch afflicted somehow or other almost every person in the house. Such simple hygienic advice that Jo could give she had to repeat to the women over and over again, for the men showed no interest as long as they were not themselves ill. One baby was in a dangerous condition. Jo said that it should see a doctor without delay.

"And how can I get it to a doctor?" replied the poor mother. "The nearest real doctor at Scutari is three days away, and over these roads the baby would be shaken to pieces before I could get him there, carrying him in the cradle strapped to my back. I could not even get him as far as *Pater Kiri*."

The little store of medicines that we habitually carry was already much depleted. Jo measured out quinine to those cases where it might be really useful, gave a linseed, liquorice, and

A deaf and dumb peasant became Cora's most useful interpreter, 1925.
(Drawing: Cora Gordon)

chlorodyne lozenge dissolved in hot water, which made a warm sensation in the stomach, to others, and malted milk tablets for the quite hopeless. Luckily we had ointment for the itch, and did not neglect to smear our hands with a little as soon as we had escaped into the open once more.

In the deaf and dumb man we had encountered a remarkable character. "Other people have ears and tongue," he said to us clearly by signs; "I have only eyes, but because of that I think the more and understand more than they do."

When we said adieu in the little graveyard by the river, he insisted upon giving Jo a man's salute, so he laid his hands upon her shoulders and rubbed alternately first one and then the other scrubby cheek against hers.

Luckily he was not one of the diseased.

From Nerlymza (now Nderlysa) to Shala Church, where we hoped to spend the night, was a long, slow climb of some thousand feet. We had now passed out of Thethis and had apparently traversed the riskier section of the journey. Our policeman shouted up a couple of villagers from the fields, put us into their charge, and turned homewards with the men of Thethis. But while we were waiting to make the change of guards, a lean and ragged fellow came sauntering down the path. The men at once arrested him and brought him to Jo.

"Make a drawing of him. Isn't he ragged?" they cried. "Why, see, even his *Celshe*[21] is full of holes."

The church of Abat, 1925 (Drawing: Cora Gordon)

The man gazed at the drawing. He made a face, his vanity was touched, though Jo had indeed flattered him, giving him more moustache than was his due. "Surely," he said, "I do not look as old as this?"

Slowly during the afternoon we rode higher and higher. Wherever the land was at all suitable, terraces had been cut and the maize planted. The farms were always the same – two- or three-storied windowless oblongs with steep wood roofs an which rickety crosses were standing at the corners; the farm out-buildings were queer erections of plaited wicker-work, and the stacks of maize stalks were perched half-way up the trunks of lopped trees to lift them above the snow during the hard winter.

The first object that struck our eyes in the welcoming little presbytery of Abata was a native chair even more desirable than the one we had purchased, which I had been carrying lashed in sections to the side of my packsaddle, where it had galled me horribly during the ups and down of the road.

The fine-moustached Franciscan of Abata told us that all through the mountains between Thethis and Pulti we would discover such chairs, whereas the fellows of Thethis, and the hairdresser in conspiracy with them, had said that nowhere else in the Malcija would we find the like. The honest price should have been some twenty crowns, so we had been finely swizzled. We don't repine now that we have it lodged in our Paris studio, the marvel of all our visitors, the envy of our friends, the only chair of its kind in Europe, except one other in the museum at Vienna. Nor perhaps did the transaction do us actual disservice. The hairdresser had been, I think, almost ashamed of us; we were so hail-fellow-well-met with everybody, for ever jumping down from our saddles to seize a likeness from the chance passer-by – not lordly by any means. But he tried to redress our lack of poise by a counterweight of plutocracy, insidious modernism creeping in. He said, more or less, "These people don't look much, and they behave just like you or me, but they paid a napoleon for an old chair, just like nothing, and that leather satchel of theirs is full of medicines and of gold" – which latter statement, considering his own terror of brigands, was hardly the best way to safeguard us over the passes where he believed that outlaws might lurk.

The Horseshoe Inn

A. den Doolaard in Theth (1932)

Who was A. den Doolaard?
A. den Doolaard is the literary pseudonym of the Dutch writer Cornelius Johannes George Spoelstra, who was born in Zwolle in the Netherlands in 1901 and died in 1994. His father was a minister of the Dutch Reformed Church who was long active in South Africa. He attended school in The Hague and held a job there as an accountant with an oil company for several years (1920-1928), but he was restless by nature. In 1928, after he had begun writing, he quit his job to travel in France and through the Balkans, financing his journeys with various odd work, including photography and travelogues for Dutch newspapers.

Den Doolaard was the author of over fifty books, published between 1926 and 1983. His Balkan travels took him initially to Yugoslavia and Greece. In early 1932, he decided to return from Salonika to Sarajevo via Albania. After spending two weeks journeying from Struga, in good part on foot, he reached Shkodra and from there visited Theth up in the mountains. Den Doolaard was fascinated by blood feuding, of which he had heard from a German traveller. His trip to northern Albania gave rise to his best known novel *De herberg met het hoefijzer* (The Horseshoe Inn), Amsterdam 1933, that centred on murder and vendetta in that region. He wrote the book in early 1933, mostly in Skopje and Mavrovi Hanovi in western Macedonia where he was staying with his French wife, Daisy Roulôt.

A recent Dutch-language biography of the writer by Hans Olink entitled *Dronken van het leven: A. den Doolaard, Zwerver, schrijver, journalist* (Drunk with Life: A. den Doolaard, Wanderer, Writer and Journalist) has uncovered that on 1 March 1933, while absorbed in the Albanian novel of blood and vendetta, Den Doolaard murdered his wife's lover, a Serbian infantry lieutenant. The murder is recounted candidly in his later novel, *Samen is twee keer alleen* (Together is Being Alone Twice Over), Amsterdam 1976, but no one recognized at the time that it was based on fact.

Among Den Doolaard's other works of Balkan inspiration are: *Quatre mois chez les comitadjis* (Four Months with the Komitadjis) Paris 1932; *Oriënt Express* (Orient Express), Amsterdam 1934, *Van vrijheid en dood* (Of Freedom and Death), Amsterdam 1935; *De bruiloft der zeven zigeuners* (The Marriage of the Seven Gypsies), Amsterdam 1939; *Het land achter Gods rug* (The Country Behind God's Back), Amsterdam 1956, and *Joegoslavië: kaleidoscopisch reisland* (Yugoslavia: Kaleidoscopic Travel Country), Amsterdam 1956.

Den Doolaard was early to warn of the rise of fascism in Europe and fled to England during the Second World War. In later years, he returned to Yugoslavia, which he came to regard as his second home, particularly Macedonia. A monument was raised in his

A. Den Doolaard on horseback in Macedonia, 1931. (Photographer unknown)

honour in the town of Ohrid in May 2006. He is buried in Hoenderloo near Arnhem.

Why Theth?

It was a mere coincidence that Den Doolaard ended up in Theth. He described the events that led to this visit in his autobiography *Het leven van een landloper: Autobiografie* (A Vagrant's Life: Autobiography), published in 1958. In the spring of 1932, Den Doolaard was working as a journalist for the Dutch newspaper *Algemeen Handelsblad* and was on his way to Athens to report on the "revolution in Greece." He got stuck at Budapest airport because the revolution had already broken out and Athens airport was closed. Seeking an alternative, he took the train to Belgrade, hoping to catch a connection to Salonika. In Belgrade, however, Janko, the night porter at Hotel Albanija, forgot to wake him up in time. Nonetheless, Den Doolaard managed to jump on board the Orient Express as it was moving slowly out of the station, while the taxi driver threw the clothes at him that had fallen out of his suitcase and were strewn along the platform. He found himself in a first-class carriage so decided to stay put and travel and dine in luxury. The revolution was already over by the time he got to Salonika. He had arrived too late and – to make things worse – he had used up all of his money. He thus decided to return through Albania – a country he had earlier wanted to visit – and get to Sarajevo where he had a friend who could lend him some cash. He stuffed a few clothes into a rucksack, sent his suitcase back to Belgrade, and got a lift with a truck driver. The final twenty-five kilometres to the Albanian border he walked on foot.

Shkodra bazaar with Rozafa fortress in the background, 1932 (Photo: Shan Pici).

Travelling to Theth

'The barrier went up and I walked into the Kingdom of the Albanians. Before I got to the first town, Leskovik, I met a German *Wandervogel* hiking with a guitar on his way to Yugoslavia. We went over and sat under the bushes at the side of the road for an improvised picnic, exchanging bits of sausage and cheese, and then some linguistic tidbits. In exchange for one hundred words of Serbian (anymore than that he regarded as superfluous), I got his list of one hundred words of Albanian. At the top of it was "*Tn-gat jeta!*" meaning "Long life to you!" This greeting had its origin in a rarely explored area where vendetta had been practised for generations – the mountainous region of

Woman from Dukagjini at the market of Shkodra, 1936. (Photo: Erich von Luckwald)

*Highland woman in the bazaar of Shkodra, 1932.
(Photo: A. Den Doolaard)*

the Albanian Highlanders. The German fellow told me that he had not succeeded in getting into the northern Albanian mountains. He had hiked for several hours from the port nearest to Scutari [Shkodra], but had been caught by some gendarmes who sent him back. I decided to give it a try and got to Scutari two weeks later. This was the capital of the region known for its blood feuding and it was here that I first saw Albanian men walking around armed. Many of the peasants selling onions and peppers in the market had revolvers stuck in their red and yellow striped sashes. Others held a rifle in close proximity. At the press office in Tirana, I had received solemn assurance that blood feuding was a thing of the past. Any violations of the prohibition on feuding were subject to capital punishment. This may be the case, but the difference between theory and reality was more than evident at the market in the long cartridge belts that the peasants, in loosely fitting white woollen trousers, had slung around their hips.

Scutari was certainly the most flee-infested town in the Balkans. Late in the evening, I fled from the Turkish *han* (inn) where I had found a place for the night for one Albanian *lek* (about a dime). The weather was warm and I climbed up the slope of the devastated citadel where I had seen sheep grazing during the day. In the short, fragrant grass I soon fell asleep. When I woke up, I noticed someone at a stone's throw away from me. From his shoes, jacket and blond hair I was certain he was German. He turned out to be a student of anthropology from Munich, who was on an extended Easter vacation. Like me, Helmut D. was hoping to explore the arid mountain region of the Highlanders. I asked him a couple of trick questions and it seemed to me that

Lemonade vendors in Shkodra, 1932.
(Photo: A. den Doolaard).

The young highland bride who inspired the figure of Katharina in the novel, The Horseshoe Inn, 1932. (Photo: A. den Doolaard)

he was anything but a Nazi. Good prospects for two like-minded people to travel together. We deliberately 'forgot', as the *Wandervogel* fellow had done, to go the Prefecture and ask for permission to travel in the highlands.

The Highland Bride

The next morning before sunrise we set off eastwards over the sombre plain. The lead-grey mountains loomed under a stormy yellow sky. There was nothing growing in the fields but corn and onions. Together with a few eggs, these were the only things we got to eat over the following two weeks. The Highlanders were a hardy bunch – they looked like they were cut out of stained leather. Three hours later we came across two women near the first village where the mule track passed along a roaring brook. They were walking pensively, hand in hand. When we got closer to them, we could see why. One of them was a bride and the other was her chaperon.

The bride's face was covered in a white linen cloth that she had draped sideways over her shoulders with her fingers, adorned with sparkling rings. Behind the veil, her thoughts were no doubt as turbulent as the water in the torrent tumbling down the mountainside. A hundred paces away from her were the house and the bridegroom whom she did not know. What would her new life hold in store for her? Onward they strolled, the two of them – the old lady in black with a face wrinkled deep like the furrows of a field ploughed a lifetime long, and the young bride in a white veil, a silver-embroidered flared skirt, a wide silver belt and several tinkling necklaces of gold. The bridegroom stood alone in the distance waiting for her. Lying next to him at the farmhouse were a scythe and pickaxe in the dirt. He would not do any work today. His hands would be too busy caressing the bride. In his red and yellow striped sash were the obligatory revolvers, and leaning against the wall was his rifle. The eyes in his skinny head were fixed on the veil, as he shuffled in the dust like a jittery stallion. He tugged nervously at his moustache and then made a patient fist. For the first time, he would now see the bride that his mother and father had chosen for him. With a sudden jerk he pulled off the veil. The short curls of her black hair adorned a curved childlike brow. Her eyes were fixed firmly to the ground as she fingered her necklace, with nails painted red with henna, but her sensuous lips betrayed an unchaste smile.

Adultery and the Blood Feud

We were in the first chapter of the novel about marriage and it was only the next day that we heard of the dramatic sequel that followed. Old laws on water rights and disputes about inherited property easily led to feuds in this land, but they were also caused by marital infidelity. At the least challenge, the Highlanders are wont to draw their arms to defend their property, and thus their women. Later in the day, a young Highlander standing in front of his house invited us in. He had heard that there were two foreigners in the village, one tall and lanky and the other one shorter and stocky, and both of them completely unarmed. The Highland telegraph had spread the news of the strange newcomers. A goatherd we had seen at the first turn of the mountain path had let out a series of strange cries when he passed us, with his hands around

Highland bride and her mother in the Northern Albanian Alps, 1932. (Photo: A. den Doolaard)

Living room of a peasant family in North Albania, 1938. (Photo: Shan Pici)

his mouth like a trumpet. We then heard a second and third man convey the news that resounded over the mountain pass and down into the neighbouring valley.

We greeted him with a "tngat jeta" and he responded with a friendly grin, gesturing at us to visit him. His timber-framed cottage was made of clay and covered in a thatched roof that overshadowed the entrance. The windows were small. We were not above the tree line, but we were certainly above the windowpane line, that ran somewhere along the foot of the mountain range. Over the stove, right under a hole in the roof hung a pot of milk simmering. Around the smouldering fire there were a few footstools. I sat down on the nearest one. Nailed to the wooden seat was a cream-coloured wolf skin. Almost immediately, however, our host emitted a scream as if the ghost of the dead wolf had taken possession of his body, and I sprang to my feet. He was fingering the Luger in his sash. I must have looked petrified and he gave a stiff laugh. At that moment, his elderly father came into the room. He had worked in Yugoslavia for a long time. In faltering Serbian he explained to me what a grave error of Highland etiquette I had made. I had sat down on the footstool reserved for the wife of the house. We then had some mastika liquor which we drank out of little wooden cups. His wife, an attractive young woman, entered the room and brought us coffee. That her husband was jealous was more than evident as she moved graciously through the room with almost unbridled coquetry. In her make-up and fine dress, this Highland beauty would have awakened longing and envy in any fashionable salon. I turned the conversation to the subject of vendetta which was said to have been eradicated. The old man told us a story as he sat and stirred the milk. His low voice and slow gestures only served to magnify the horror of what he revealed to us, better than any lecture could have.

"My niece was a beautiful woman and very industrious, too. Everything went well with her marriage until the day her husband took the fatal decision to go to Macedonia to work as a lemonade seller. You know how it is. Poverty forces our people to go abroad in search of work. While he was away, one of his friends seduced his young wife. However, the husband's fifteen-year-old brother discovered what was going on and forbade the lover from entering the house. The fellow laughed at the boy and made fun of him so he decided to avenge the shame done to his family by taking revenge, as our customs demand. He stole two cows belonging to the lover and drove them up to a distant mountain pasture. When the fellow went off in search of his animals, the boy was laying in ambush behind a rock, and shot him dead. The lad then fled into the mountains, but was betrayed and caught by the gendarmes. Nonetheless, after a brief skirmish, his tribesmen managed to free him. The boy later found out who had betrayed him and killed the man right in the middle of the market in Scutari. Now there are three families involved in the feud, and four men have died over the past three years. Six men and one boy are up in the mountains, fleeing from one another and from the gendarmes."

How "The Horseshoe Inn" Came About

I slowly absorbed the words, like raindrops falling onto barren field singed by the heat of the sun. I now knew why my subconscious had sent me to this land. It was in unwitting expectation of the tale I was to tell. If Janko had woken me up on time in Belgrade, I would never have arrived penniless in Salonika. As a result, I would never have been in Albania at all. But there is no use brooding over coincidences. A coincidence is just a term used for the sake of convenience to describe what is inexorably written.

Two Shoshi men in the Northern Albanian Alps, 1932. (Photo: A. den Doolaard)

A whole year passed before I began writing The Horseshoe Inn. The tale of vendetta that it contains is only one level of the narrative and is interlaced with another adventure – the discovery of one's conscience. I certainly had sufficient material when I met the Highlanders and heard about their blood feuds. Our host gave us enough proof of suspicious behaviour. A glass of water was always served with the sweet Turkish coffee, but the jug was empty. He felt for his pistols, hung the vessel over his shoulder and took his rifle. The fountain was less than a hundred metres from the farmhouse, but a sniper could be lurking anywhere in the scrub. We roamed through the mountains for several days, over the high passes and along grey, stony promontories that loomed over dark green groves of oak trees. In every village there was a police station with lazy servants of the new law who spent their time playing cards and spitting sunflower seeds. Each of them insisted on accompanying us to the next post to ensure our safety. However, we usually managed to escape their attention and to get away before dawn. It was on such days of unhindered travel that we twice came across men escaping from a blood feud, accompanied by shepherds who had brought them food.

We used gestures to communicate with them. While one of them remained on the look out, we exchanged snuff boxes as a sign of mutual esteem. Much later in life, when I had had contact with many other foreign peoples, I came to realise what drove the Highlanders to engage in eternal feuds. In appearance, they were poor mountain farmers, who often suffered from skin diseases and hereditary syphilis, but their finely sculptured faces showed traits of inherited nobility – they were men of a realm that

Men in the Northern Albanian Alps, fleeing from a blood feud, 1932. (Photo: A. den Doolaard)

Shepherd playing a flute in the Northern Albanian Mountains, 1932. (Photo: A. den Doolaard)

no longer existed, and every heartbeat reminded them of it. They lived like banished kings on their small and solitary farms and demanded more of heaven and earth than the dull monotony of their highland community.

For this reason they were willing to play jeopardy with their lives. A matador enters the arena but once a week during the season, but the Highlanders do it every day as soon as they set foot outside their homes. Man is a creator and a destroyer, and this is what distinguishes him from animals. In the West (in peacetime at least) we pay tribute to Abel who cultivated the fruits of the fields. Nowadays, these fruits are called railways, factories, aeroplanes and chemical products. But the Highlanders pay tribute to Cain. As individualists, they allow their lives to be ruled by a perverse interpretation of "honour," whereas elsewhere on earth, the collective masses have equally perversely devoted themselves to wars. But above all, aside from this mythical interpretation, there was a practical explanation, that is the only one valid for historians and materialists. In the institution of blood feuding lies an ancient and cruel piece of wisdom that has been handed down from generation to generation among the "savage" peoples of the pre-industrialised world. Their land can only hold a limited number of people or they will starve. Eskimos in Greenland let a surplus of babies freeze to death. Tuareg women in the Sahara manage birth control with the help of an ingenious device that the men make from hollow bird bones. Elsewhere, wars ensure that the population is kept under control, and primitive peoples have always been victim to epidemics. Then came the white man with his need to "pacify" and the result was overpopulation which often, as I later noticed in Morocco, resulted in mass starvation. Among the Montenegrin neighbours of the Albanian Highlanders, feeding methods and child care(lessness) mean that weak children under the age of two usually die. In mountain regions, this is equivalent to at least half of the newborn children. The rest die of old age. Nowhere on earth did I see so many old people as in the land of the Black Mountains, which was to be my next destination.[22]

Dinner at the Vicarage of Theth

Two days later, we set off to the northeast for Theth, the most charming village of them all in the mountains. Theth reminded me very much of Lauterbrunnen in the Swiss Alps. It was small and very attractively set, yet although there are many roads that can take you to Lauterbrunnen, there is but one through a rugged landscape and over a 2,000 metre pass that leads to Theth. Whereas swarms of tourists spend their time in Lauterbrunnen, the people of Theth, at least for the time being, will continue to be all alone with the sparkling waterfalls that cascade down the slopes of their dark mountains. Theth does have the one advantage over Switzerland, in that you can buy old silver pistols and embroidered costumes for virtually nothing, and it offers hospitality that would cost a fortune in Lauterbrunnen. The commander of the guard post lounged on a veranda in front of his whitewashed cottage, and we joined him, sitting down on a chest that had once contained tinned vegetables. He was playing with a couple of chicks, but they were not destined for dinner, so we swallowed everything we had with us for our frugal evening meal, a hard crust of corn bread and an onion.

We then noticed that one of the grey houses was larger than the rest, and it had a cross on the roof. Was this where the pastor lived? Yes it was, and he was said to speak three languages. We hastened across the fields and were invited into a large room full of footstools and sheepskins. The ceiling was black with smoke, but what mostly caught our attention were the strips of shiny bacon and racks of lamb hanging on strings from the beams. Our mouths watered as we spent the next five minutes staring upwards. Then the pastor came into the room and, to our great joy, addressed us in German. Coffee was soon brought in and a glass of mastika or Balkan absinthe that only increased our hunger. Our eyes were constantly fixed towards heaven above us. The pastor was a very busy man because, in this region, he is not only a minister, but also the doctor, the pharmacist, the veterinarian and the school teacher. An old woman came by to pick up a bottle of cough syrup. Then he had to write a letter for a farmer who knew how to use a rifle but not a pen. All the time, we kept nudging at one another. "Do you think we could ask for something to eat?" Had we been dogs, we could have leapt towards the ceiling and made off with the bacon, but as "civilised" Europeans we remained at our seats. Finally, the good Franciscan must have heard the rumbling of our stomachs because he swiftly rose and pulled a beautifully woven tablecloth from out of a carved chest. And then a meal was served, from which we took sustenance all the way until we got back to Skutari.[23]

22 A. den Doolaard (1979). *Het leven van een landloper: Autobiografie.* Amsterdam: Querido.
23 A. den Doolaard (1935). *Van vrijheid en dood*, Chapter 18 "In the Wild Mountains of Albania,

View of the Shala Valley from the Sheep Pass, 1936. (Photo: Erich von Luckwald)

Theth and Beyond

A day's journey beyond the village of Theth, more sparkling than even Lauterbrunnen, in a deep valley and surrounded by roaring cascades, I took leave of my travelling companion. Helmut D. wanted to go further southwards and return to Skutari. I crossed the pass leading to the north, in the direction of the Yugoslav border which, for lack of a visa, I crawled over in the dark through the bushes. I later solved the visa issue in Belgrade because, in view of my many lectures about Yugoslavia, I had good connections with the press office. I only needed my passport to register at hotels and the state of my finances did not allow me such luxury. The whole trip through Albania had not cost me more than five Guilders and I still have one and a half rix-dollars left.'[24]

Theth, the Most Charming Village of Them All." Amsterdam: Querido.
24 A. den Doolaard (1979). *Het leven van een landloper: Autobiografie.* Amsterdam: Querido.

The church of Theth on the plain, 1933 (Photo: Shan Pici).

The church of Theth and the vicarage, 1933. (Photo: Shan Pici).

Franciscan priests in Theth, 1936. (Photo: Erich von Luckwald).

Father Anton Kiri, Theth, 1940. (Photo: Giuseppe Massani)

A young girl spinning wool in riverbed, Theth, 1936. (Photo: Erich von Luckwald)

Two young girls wearing the traditional xhubleta, 1940. (Photo: Giuseppe Massani)

The Burial of Ujk Vuksani

Reimer Schulz in Theth (1937)

Who was Reimer Schulz?
Dr Reimer Schulz (d. 1941) was a German anthropologist. Like his American counterpart Carleton Coon (1904-1981) in 1929-1930, he carried out research in physical anthropology in the mountains of northern Albania. In 1937, Schulz took part in a German-Italian expedition to the northern Albanian mountains on behalf of a so-

Two shepards from Theth 1940. (Photo: Giuseppe Massani)

Two Albanians smoking, 1940. (Photo: Giuseppe Massani)

called Thuringia Institute for Racial Studies (*Thüringisches Landesamt für Rassewesen*) in Weimar. During a longer stay in Theth, he measured body shapes and sizes and noted the physiognomic particularities of the natives for an academic discipline called anthropometry that – then strongly infiltrated by fascist ideology – was soon to fall out of fashion. In the course of his research in the Shala Valley, Schulz also took over two hundred photographs of school children and other pictures. These photos are said to have ended up in an archive in Halle, but may have been destroyed during the Second World War. Schulz himself died as a soldier on the eastern front on 14 July 1941.

Why Theth?

By 1937, Albania was well within the sphere of influence of fascist Italy, with which Nazi Germany was allied. Two years later, the little Balkan country would be absorbed by Mussolini and would become part of his new Roman Empire. It was within the

Funeral in Dukagjin, 1929 (Photo: Shan Pici)

framework of this alliance that a joint anthropological expedition was sent to Albania, specifically to the isolated region of Theth in the Shala valley. Theth was also chosen in particular because it had the only school, and a teacher, K. Liadja, who knew some German. It was also a Catholic region, which gave the scholars greater access to the female population. Reimer Schulz intended to complete his anthropological research on a second trip to Theth and had begun learning Albanian, but the Second World War intervened. What he did leave us at any rate is the following fascinating account of his participation at a local funeral as well as several spectacular photos taken in Theth.

"Nik Ndou, our dragoman, arrived at our camp earlier than foreseen. It was about 6 A.M. A call had echoed long through the valley early that morning. It began in the north and spread from cliff to cliff. The "Albanian telephone" then fell silent when it reached the end of the valley. This is the name the Austrians gave to the masterful way that the highlanders, the mostly Catholic inhabitants of the Northern Albanian Alps, spread news, by calling and taking advantage of the echo. Nik had heard the news and transmitted it, as a matter of course, to the next house. Now he wanted to inform us of what had happened, so he arrived at our camp earlier than usual. But he did not hustle. Albanians never hustle.

From Nik we learned that Ujk Vuksani, a wealthy farmer from the northern end of the valley, had died the night before and was to be buried that day. Nik wanted to attend the funeral, and we joined him.

A burial in the highlands that includes all the funeral customs lasts a whole day, often late into the night. The tribesmen related to the deceased gather to pay their respects to him and to take part in the wake.

Funeral Customs in Theth, 1937 (Photo: Reimer Schulz).

We got to the house of the deceased in the late morning hours. Nik accompanied us first to the home of the dead man's brother. In the courtyard, large vats of food had been put out for the guests.

The dead man's brother was waiting for us at the doorway. We greeted him and his son with "Paçi baftin" which means more or less "May the deceased leave you good luck." They replied, "May the deceased leave you good luck, too," and accompanied us from the stable on the ground floor to the living room upstairs. Visitors were standing and squatting everywhere - in the stable, on the stairs and in the upstairs

room. Five low, round tables had been set up in the living room. At each of them ten men sat on the floor, with their legs crossed. To make room for everyone, they sat sideways, with their right flanks towards the table. Cornbread and sheep cheese were brought in for the guests. One man at each table broke the large round loaf of bread and the cheese into bits. A jug of water was also handed around. Corn mush was then served that the guests dipped into liquefied butter. On every table there was a large wooden bowl that everyone ate out of. The guests had all brought their own spoons with them. After this came *kos*, a type of sour milk. When the meal was over, they all

The family of Mirash Vuksanaj, 1930 (Photographer unknown)

took to smoking. Albanians hardly ever let their cigarettes go out - only when they are eating or sleeping.

After we had eaten, we proceeded to the house of the deceased man. His body was already laid out. From outside we could hear the wailing of the women, and the noise continued when we were inside. The women were sitting around the body, with one of them at his head waving a fan made of fern branches to keep the flies away. The deceased was dressed in his finest clothes. He was wearing a richly embroidered red waist jacket, typical for elderly men. His head was wrapped in a pure-white scarf that covered his new woollen fez. On the jacket were his medals, a Turkish one and an Austrian one, and a skilfully fashioned filigree chain. Around his waste was a loaded cartridge belt, with a pistol in it. His rifle was leaning at his side.

He was also wearing white woollen trousers with black strips and a pattern on them, as well as beautifully embroidered socks and pointed Albanian shoes on his feet. A cigarette butt had been placed in his fingers. In his arms there were three apples, a bundle of tobacco leaves, a tobacco box and a bottle of *raki*. These were symbols of the generosity and hospitality of the deceased. In the afternoon, the body was taken to the graveyard on a narrow bier. Two boards were placed flat under a tree and the deceased was laid out there with all the gifts. The women carefully ordered his clothing, tightened his scarf and fanned the flies from him with the fern branches. Some men then began digging the grave.

Twelve men, however, remained to one side, about two hundred metres away from the rest. They were standing in two lines, brow to brow. Their leader was in the middle. He bent his knees slightly, took a deep breath and began the tribal lamentation, emitting loud sighs. of "*Mjeri, o, o, vëllathi i êm -, mjeri – o, o eh, eh!*" ("Woe, my wretched brother!"). The words were repeated over and over, each time louder and with greater vehemence, and was accompanied by gestures. The men beat their breasts and rubbed at their temples. Then they held their noses and moaned, "*eh, eh, eh.*"

The group took several steps towards the body and repeated the lament and gestures in the same sequence. Step by step they approached the deceased until they stood in a semicircle around him. Once again they began lamenting and fell to their knees, leaning forwards. They held themselves up with one hand on the ground and placed the other at their sides. "*Mjeri, o, o, o!*" The cries were repeated, louder and louder. The brother of the dead man then came forth and placed his hand on the backs of the moaning men, to tell them that it was enough. The men fell silent and rose to their feet, withdrawing to one side to smoke a cigarette.

The women then approach the corpse and sat closely around it. One young woman covered her face in her scarf and began the wailing of the women. Every phrase she uttered was echoed by the other women with groans of "*eh, eh, eh*". The young woman mourned her beloved father who had left them forever. She told of his life, his family, his children, his virtues and his hospitality, but also of his suffering and death. The wailing of the women lasted for about half an hour and ended in groaning and sobbing.

We returned to our camp. We could hear the wild cries and lamentations of the men until midnight, echoing eerie in the night. The corpse was later placed in the grave filled with leaves. Two long boards were placed over it and were covered with earth.

The lamentation of the highlanders, the primarily Dinaric inhabitants of the Northern Albanian Alps, is a moving ceremony evincing tribal solidarity among simple peasants and shepherds. All the relatives bring forth their lament and do so as part of a cult tradition. Solemn and earnest, they reveal devotion and fervour, yet show no sign of ecstasy or demonic frenzy. The lamentation is the way the tribe honours its dead. It is not a fraternity of men or a secret society that is acting here, it is the entire tribe that is openly paying farewell to one of its members.[25]

---

25 Reimer Schulz, "Leichenbegräbnis und Totenkult bei den Malisoren." in: *Atlantis, Länder, Völker, Reisen*, Leipzig, vol. 10 (1938), pp. 257-259.

The First Agricultural Co-operative

Kurt Seliger in Theth (1957)

Who was Kurt Seliger?
The Austrian journalist Kurt Seliger had always wanted to go to Albania. He was particularly interested in history and was fascinated by the exotic country, having read much about the scandals and corruption at the court of King Zog in the 1930s and of the Italian invasion just before the start of the Second World War. As a boy, he had devoured the adventure tales of Karl May, like so many writers of his age had done. Kurt Seliger was especially fascinated by the dramatic political break-up of the one-time socialist allies, Yugoslavia and Albania, in 1946. As such, he got on his motorcycle and set off for Albania after having, with some difficulty, persuaded his wife Fritzi to go with him. The couple left Vienna in July 1956 and made their way through Yugoslavia, via Banja Luka, Jajce, Sarajevo, Mostar, Dubrovnik, Kotor and Titograd, until they got to the Albanian border post of Han i Hotit. There, they made quite a stir with their bike. Albania did not have any tourists at the time, and certainly none on a motorcycle.

In Tirana, the German-Albanian Friendship Committee provided the couple with an interpreter named Kambo, who was a young teacher of chemistry at the Agricultural University there. Kurt and his wife spent two weeks in Albania, far too short a stay, as he later noted.

In April 1957, they returned to the country for a second time. On this occasion, they rode took them from Vienna to Rijeka in northern Yugoslavia, where they caught a ship sailing to the Albanian port of Durrës. In Tirana, they parked their motorcycle at the famous Hotel Dajti and stored it there until it was time to leave the country. The state tourist agency Albtourist provided them with an automobile and a driver. On this trip, Seliger and his wife spent three months touring the country, with the same interpreter, Kambo, and got up into the mountains of the north.

Why Theth?
Kurt Seliger wanted to visit the northern region of Dukagjin and he finally got his way. He spent a couple of days in the Shala Valley and paid a special visit to Theth where he met the village priest and took part in the ceremonies for the opening of the first agricultural co-operative there. Seliger was one of the few journalists allowed to visit Communist Albania in the 1950s, before the practice of religion was banned in 1967.

His German-language travel book, *Albanien, Land der Adlersöhne* (Albania: Land of the Sons of the Eagles) was published in Austria in 1958 and in East Germany in 1960. It was also translated

Right: *Cover of Kurt Selinger 's travel book Land Der Adlersöhne, 1958.*
Left: *Kurt Seliger on the Yugoslav coast, while traveling to Albania, 1956. (Photo: Fritzi Seliger)*

Woman on horseback with two men, 1936. (Photo: Erich von Luckwald)

into Hungarian (1959) and Polish (1961).

On their second tour of Albania in 1957, the Seligers thus journeyed by car from Tirana up to the Shala Valley. The car and driver had great difficulty getting over the mountain pass to Theth and it was night when the group arrived. Their interpreter and driver were lodged in different quarters. Kurt and Fritzi were given a house for the night but they were terrified of the idea of lice and other bugs, and used their tent instead. They set it right up on a field and inflated their air mattresses – without the help of a pump – to the great interest and amusement of the locals. The next day, they went hiking through the Shala valley, taking two hired mules with them for the baggage.

In the evening, they arrived exhausted in the village of Breglumi. The Seligers met many of the inhabitants who told them willingly of the blood feuding that had ravaged the region before the advent of communism. Kurt wrote all of their tales down and used many of them in his book. A few days later, when they were on their way back, they got to Theth again and met the local priest. There they had the opportunity of taking part in the inauguration of the first agricultural co-operative in Dukagjin.

The Priest of Theth

" Our excursion took us back to Theth. The little parish there, as we were told, was run by the seventy-three-year-old Franciscan priest, Sebastean Deda. He had studied in Salzburg and Klagenfurt in 1913, had visited Vienna at that time on several occasions, and spoke fluent German. We made up our minds to go and pay His Grace a visit.

As soon as we got to the little vicarage at the foot of the imposing mountains, the elderly gentleman came out to greet us. He was delighted to have an opportunity to talk about the past and to speak German a bit once again. He asked us about the "Steffel", as he called our St Stephan's Cathedral in Vienna, and inquired as to whether the beer in Salzburg was still as good as he remembered it to have been. We then sat down outside in front of the padre's house and he made us a cup of Turkish coffee. We were interested in hearing what a Catholic priest might think of the changes that had taken place in the country since 1944.

"You in Austria," began the Franciscan, "have a culture that has been advancing for centuries. Your country is civilised. We are just beginning to construct what you have had for centuries. For the first time in our history, we have a real government and a semblance of public order, and blood feuding has been eradicated. But there has been progress in other fields, too. In the past, in the whole Dukagjin region, there was only one little health clinic, no hospital and no schools. Now we have six health clinics, a hospital in Breglumi and enough schools."

"And what is your opinion about the agricultural co-operatives?" I asked.

The old man chuckled. "I understand why it is me you are asking. Well, I will tell you what I preached last Sunday, a week ago, here in my church. When the farmers heard that an agricultural co-operative was to be set up here, too – the first one in the whole Dukagjin region – people started coming to me from Okol, from Gjecaj and from Markdedaj to find out what I thought about it and what they should do. In my sermon, I said the following, more or less: "A co-operative is like a beehive. If all the bees are industrious and work together, there will be honey. If each bee were to work on its own and were not industrious, there would be very little honey. We all know what the situation has been like here in the past."

"This is my view on the co-operative."

Nonetheless, there were certain aspects of the co-operative that the Franciscan considered problematic. He was particularly sceptical as to whether an agricultural co-operative would be economically viable here in the mountains. "You know," he told us, "life is very difficult here in the winter. Almost every year we are snowed in and isolated from the rest of the world for months. The situation was so bad once that airplanes had to fly food in. And the soil is not particularly fertile. I wonder whether a co-operative can survive here."

Priest Sebastean Deda in front of the church and vicarage of Theth, 1957. (Photo: Kurt Seliger).

Kambo told the padre that the co-operatives in the lowlands were almost all economically viable. In the mountains, the government would probably have to provide subsidies, but things in the valley would certainly improve if modern methods were applied and if better farming equipment were used. In addition to this, the government was trying to persuade the farmers in the barren mountain regions to resettle in the fertile lowlands. Some 170 families had already settled near Milot, along the road between Tirana and Shkodra. The new settlement was called New Dukagjin. However, many of the families in the mountains were so attached to their land that they would not leave it.

"I am sure that the mountain people in Tyrol would never agree to resettle in the flatter regions of eastern Austria," noted my wife.

To this the padre replied: "That is the way things are. People never like to leave their homes, even if conditions are difficult where they live."

The Franciscan permitted us to inspect his vicarage and the little garden he tended to himself. While he was showing us to the door and we were saying good-bye, several shots rang out, disturbing the tranquillity of that Sunday afternoon. We were petrified. The padre could read our minds. "Don't worry," he grinned, "it is not a feud as in the old days. The co-operative we talked about is being inaugurated today. The shooting is simply part of the celebration."

There will be honey...
Fortunately, the celebrations for the founding of the co-operative had only just begun. We got there in time to see it come into being, the first agricultural co-operative in the Dukagjin region. Men and women, boys and girls were scurrying about in all directions for the final preparations. Others were standing at the entrance to welcome the visitors. As soon as they saw us, they formed two rows leading through the festively decorated garden. We shook everyone's hands and took our seats as guests of honour, right beside those of the secretary of the Party of Labour for the district of Shkodra, the head of the co-operative and his wife, the only woman who had the courage to show herself among all the men. As we later discovered, she was not from the mountains. The future co-operative farmers had strung a canopy of foliage between the trees so that we were all protected from the glare of the sun.

It was only we, the guests of honour, who were given chairs to sit on. All of the farmers sat cross-legged on the grass. Then the official ceremonies started up and the party secretary rose to speak. He stressed the great importance that the founding of a co-operative would have on a region such as Dukagjin. When he was finished, he raised his glass, and we, too, downed much raki after numerous toasts to the success of the new co-operative.

The secretary, who was also a member of parliament, emptied his glass and was just about to sit down when the head of the co-operative came up to him and gave him something that I could not see at first. I soon found out what it was because the party secretary lost no time in pointing the object into the air and shooting with it. The party secretary fired the pistol off until it was empty and thus declared the co-operative open. The weapon was then reloaded and given to a foreign guest of honour to express his joy at the foundation of the co-operative. Alas, this guest (me) had never had a pistol in his hand before and was thus unable to express his delight in the form they desired.

My inability to use a gun caused not only disappointment but also amazement, and, I believe, a certain disdain that I thought I could make out among some of them. The farmers were probably thinking to themselves, "What kind of man is this who doesn't know how to shoot a gun? What good could he possibly be?"

The party secretary then turned to me and explained – he knew a bit of Italian, about as much as I did – that shooting guns was an old Albanian custom and something they greatly enjoyed. In earlier day, when the priest held a moving sermon, they even shot their guns off in the church. The tradition of firing guns had remained up to the present day, and while a foreign guest might be excused, an Albanian party secretary was obliged to conform.

With these shots, the co-operative was declared open and we now turned to the informal part of the festivities. We were asked to leave our seats and to sit down with everyone else on the carpets laid out in the grass. We would actually have preferred to stay put. Sitting on the ground cross-legged for hours is not everyone's cup of tea. But there was no way around it so we did our best.

Round tables, about 20 cm. high, were placed out on the carpets and set in a jiffy. While everyone around us was looking forward to the meal, we were aghast at what we saw coming at us. We were more than familiar with Oriental cuisine and had learned how to avoid all the greasy food swimming in fat. Here in the mountains we had restricted our intake as far as possible to tinned food and natural products, such as eggs, bread and fruit, and had more or less survived. But what was going to happen to us now?

Stories abound in Albanian literature about traditional food and table manners. Here in the mountains it was usual, and perhaps still is – who knows? – to add salt to sheep milk and use it to make coffee.

While the meal was being served, I turned to my wife to explain in a whisper an eating custom I had read about. Whenever a man from the Shala region, to which Theth belonged, had guests over, it was custom that his most important guest receive the greatest attention. It was considered a special honour for the guest to be given the eye from the skull of a roasted sheep. Sheep eyes were considered particularly delicious. Custom had it that the most important guest was not to keep the whole skull to himself, but was to hand it to the person beside him. The next fellow was not to keep it either – hospitality knows no bounds – but to pass it on. The sheep skull was thus passed all around the table until it got back to the head of the household who set it aside. The other tribes looked down upon this tradition of the "uncouth" Shalas whom they regarded as "backward". In their regions there was no passing around of a skull. The guest of honour was to keep for himself and savour it.

The very thought of the coming meal made our stomachs turn. We could not excuse ourselves by pleading a lack of appetite. Hospitality involved obligations not only

Women from Theth, 1938 (Photo: Shan Pici)

for the host but also for his guests, in particular when they had not yet tried such delicacies. One is obliged to eat one's fill because the host can otherwise be insulted.

The festivities were approaching their climax. Bowls of tomatoes and cucumbers were brought to the tables, with sheep cheese and liver swimming in grease. Mutton, bread and eggs also appeared, accompanied by gallons of *raki*, a strong Albanian *schnaps* distilled from grapes. We were surrounded by the other guests. There was no escape. However, to our great fortune, the custom of picking meat and eyes out of a sheep skull being handed around, turned out to be a thing of the past. Indeed there were no skulls in sight, although we certainly had enough food on our hands without them. We initially stuck to the bread, tomatoes, cucumbers and eggs, and the really excellent sheep cheese. But our driver, who was otherwise a very nice fellow, had it out for us. He watched us closely with the intent of ensuring that we try everything. Not for a second did his eyes turn away. He soon realised what we were up to and asked in Italian: "Il carne non è buono?" ("Is the meat not alright?")

"It's fine, very good, but you remember, we have been having problems with out stomachs," I strove to explain.

He shook his head disapprovingly and continued to study us. The rest of them caught what we had said and began watching us, too. They all seemed to be staring at us now. "Eat up, eat up! There's plenty more to come!"

There was no way out. I grabbed the food waiting on the plate in front of me and began stuffing myself. I had to eat for my wife Fritzi, too, because she steadfastly refused to touch a thing, being prepared to infringe upon sacred custom rather than take one bite of the tasty mutton floating in the grease. I had no choice and swallowed each chunk of the meat with a good swig of *raki* to get it all past my taste buds and down the hatch as quickly as possible. The result was inevitable. To put it in brief

Woman from Theth, Dukagjin, 1938 (Photo: Shan Pici)

Woman from Dukagjin (Photographer unknown)

Two women from Dukagjin (Photographer unknown)

terms, I kept a fine young physician in my employ in Tirana for a whole week until he got my stomach back into order.

But let us return to the festivities. While everyone was busy eating and drinking, an old farmer suddenly rose and made it know that he wished to speak. When the noise had died down somewhat, the old man, looking solemnly around him, went over to a tree. We could not see what he was doing until he returned with a little package. In his hands was something wrapped in newspaper that he began rather clumsily to unpack. It was a piece of rusty iron. Holding it up triumphantly, he declared: "This is the symbol of our shame and misery! It was with such tools that we used to work. I intend to keep this piece of iron with me in memory of the shame and suffering we went through."

Yes, the old man was holding a piece from a primitive old farming tool. He then came over to us: "I remember the Austrians from the time of the First World War and know that they have a highly developed culture. We will soon begin a new life. There will be honey here, too…"

The farmer was given a stirring round of applause. Among the people sitting a bit farther away from us, however, I noticed that his solemn words were somewhat out of place amidst the general merriment. We had noticed earlier in Albania that men, women and children sat at separate tables. Nowhere was there a woman to be seen at the men's table, and vice versa. The young people were tired to listening to speeches and just wanted to have some fun. Would there not be a dance?

Those attending the festivities were all clad in the fascinating costumes of northern Albania. The men were wearing a fez, white trousers made of sheep wool that only reached to their thighs, a sash around their waists, and a lambskin jacket. Particularly fascinating were the costumes of the women.

We had already caught sight of some wonderful native costumes in the better neighbourhoods around Shkodra where they were colourful and richly embroidered. On feast days the women also donned abundant amounts of gold and silver. I was told that an expert would immediately know whether a woman or girl was Catholic, Orthodox or Muslim by the patterns of her costume. Here up in the mountains there were only Catholics and the costumes are not nearly as colourful and richly embroidered as on the coast. A good costume costs a lot of money. It is a sign of prosperity and in some cases a depository of great wealth. Both of these had been lacking in the mountain valleys for generations. However, the costumes were no less artistic and original. Some of the girls were wearing old highland dress with a stiff black skirt made of goat hair that was bell-shaped at the bottom. I remember reading that scholars believe this type of skirt has been around for a thousand years. Several years ago, Illyrian vases were found in Yugoslavia with this very same bell-shaped dress on them and it is assumed that the northern Albanian skirts date from that period.

There was some agitation among the guests who were dressed up in their finest costumes. The youth people eventually won the day. Hardly had the round of applause given to the old man died down when we heard the sound of a harmonica a few tables away from us, and the young men and women hastened out onto the grassy meadow. It was beautiful to watch the exotic costumes of the young people with the rocky cliffs in the background. Rising behind them was the oblique peak of the Mali i Pejës. They all formed a circle and began to dance, initially taking slow, hesitant steps. Soon their legs were twirling over the grass at great speed. One of the boys then entered the ring with a full roast of mutton in his arms. All the attention was now on him. Different dances followed, and with them other dancers joined in. The girls teased the boys with fluttering kerchiefs that the lads tried to catch, but the girls kept them deftly out of their reach. Finally one of the boys caught a kerchief, or did she let him get it?

The echo of the harmonica subsided. In the middle of the circle that was gradually breaking up stood two men. Everyone else sat down in the meadow to watch. The two men began to dance, though without any music. One of them moved around while the other imitated him with gestures. Then they changed roles. The first dancer slowly approached his partner who took over the rhythm of the dance, but still all without music. One of the many unusual features of this country.

The two men then returned to the other dancers. On the spot where they had been dancing appeared a man in traditional costume. In his hand was a curious instrument. It looked something like a mandolin but had a longer neck and only one string spanned tightly of goat hair. The music he played was unfamiliar to us and seemed rather monotonous at first. But we got used to it and even started enjoying it. The text which the singer had composed himself was translated for us. He was one of the great bards of the north, a well-known singer of highland ballads, and the song was about the harsh life of the Albanians under the Turks, under the reign of King Zog, and during the Italian and German occupation. He sang of the great days of the liberation and the profound changes that had taken place since then. His recital went right to the present day and he closed it with: "Long live the Party and the Albanian people!"[26]

---

26 Kurt Seliger (1960). *Albanien: Land der Adlersöhne*, pp. 78-87. Leipzig: Brockhaus.

Adventures on a Motorcycle

Nina Rasmussen in Theth (1994)

Who is Nina Rasmussen?
Nina Rasmussen is an experienced motorcyclist from Denmark who has been on the road since 1981 with her partner Hjalte Tin and their children Emil and Ida, on a wide range of motorcycle trips to some of the most exotic places in the world: South Africa, New Guinea, Indonesia, Australia and Africa.

Nina did her trip to Albania alone on a motorcycle in the summer of 1994. She was extremely curious to know more about the country that had been cut off from the rest of the world for such a long time under communism. She was prepared for an adventure, but she didn't know anyone in Albania. Before she left Denmark, a Danish priest gave her the address of Vjollca Dervishi, who worked for a Christian development organisation for children in Tirana. There were many foreign-run Christian organisations active in Albania at the time that supported a wide range of social endeavours.

Nina Rasmussen began her journey in Durrës where she had arrived by ship from Trieste. From there, she set off on her motorcycle (a 50 cc Honda that she brought from Denmark with her) for Tirana and managed to find Vjollca. Vjollca's husband

Nina Rasmussen on a motorcycle on her way to Theth, 1994 (Photo: Nina Rasmussen).

Eddie had an elderly aunt called Roza, with whom Nina was able to stay. Aunt Roza's apartment was thus to serve as base camp for all of her Albanian expeditions. She returned there each time to recuperate before setting off again. Nina's first excursion took her into the interior. In all, she spent two months in Albania and covered 4,000 km of territory there. She did the south of the country first and then the north, and endeavoured as much as possible to stay with people she met on the road, or with friends and relatives of these acquaintances. Nina took a copy of the *Blue Guide of Albania* with her, and the rest of the information she needed she acquired from the Albanians themselves. She hardly knew anything of the Albanian language, but most of the people with whom she had contact spoke some English or knew someone who did. Towards the end of her book, she notes that she was the first woman to have explored Albania alone after the fall of communism. This was not exactly what the *Blue Guide* recommended for women, but in view of her extensive travel experience, the fact that she was 51 years old and dressed modestly, she did not have any major problems. One exception was an encounter with a man carrying a pistol who tried to steal her motorcycle and other possessions. This happened at the end of her stay when she had learned how to avoid or at least keep her distance from Albanian men. The fellow held his pistol at her, but her furious reaction unnerved him. His attention slipped and she managed to get away from him. Otherwise the book is full of pleasant encounters and of many delightful stories told to her by people she met by chance. Nina Rasmussen combined these stories with much background information on Albania and, as such, readers not only get to know the Albanians as friendly, hospitable and good-humoured people, but also learn much about Albanian history as seen from her perspective.

Nina Rasmussen spent two months in Albania, from July to early September 1994. She first biked through southern Albania: Durrës, Tirana (at Aunt Roza's), Elbasan, Lake Ohrid, Tirana (at Aunt Roza's again), Divjaka, Fier, Berat, Këlcyra, Përmet, Korça, Pogradec, Tirana (at Aunt Roza's once more), Fier, Vlora, Dhërmi, Himara, Saranda, Gjirokastra, Lushnja, Divjaka, and finally Tirana and Aunt Roza's.

Why Theth?

In the second part of her stay in Albania, Nina Rasmussen travelled to northern Albania. Her first stop was Shkodra. She devotes a few passages in her book to earlier descriptions of northern Albania that she had read: *High Albania* (1909) by Edith Durham, and *Peaks of Shala* (1923) by Rose Wilder Lane. She also refers to Joseph Swire's book *King Zog's Albania* (1937). She was unable to find any more modern texts about the country. Nina also devotes part of her book to blood feuding.

From Shkodra she first explored Lake Shkodra. While travelling along the banks of the lake, she observed oil smugglers on their way to Montenegro (then part of Yugoslavia under embargo). The journey took her on to Tamara, a village in the Catholic Kelmendi region, where she stayed with Marika and Dod. She was able to communicate with Marika and Dod with the help of their nineteen-year-old daughter Luljeta, who knew Italian. Her next stop was Vermosh, the northernmost settlement in Albania. There she got to know Alexander and his family. Alexander spoke German since he had worked for some time in Switzerland. He held the view that Albania's borders were wrong because half of the surrounding territory outside the country was populated by Albanians. Vermosh was Catholic, too, and one of the inhabitants told her the story of a Muslim family that had wanted to settle there but was made unwelcome. She also made an outing to a farm up in the mountain pastures, at 2,195 metres in altitude, and then returned to Shkodra via Tamara and Koplik. There she met Alexander again, whose family was on the point of going home. With Alexander's help as an interpreter, she conversed with many of the inhabitants of Koplik. No one had anything nice to say about the Muslim population. "But the Muslims must be killed anyway." When she mentioned that she wanted to go to Theth, there was visible consternation among the men. One of them protested, "They will kill you up there, they are all Muslims, bad people." When questioned, he admitted that he had never visited Theth, although he had been to America. The other men in Koplik also advised her not to go to Theth. It was too dangerous for a woman travelling alone. When they realised that she was going no matter what they said, another fellow called Tom declared that he would not allow it if she were his wife (and Nina was quite relieved that she wasn't). However, if she insisted, he would be willing to drive her there in his car. Nina declined the offer.

Then begins the central chapter of her Danish-language book *Som en albansk jomfru: en rejse gennem et ukendt land i Europa* (Like an Albanian Sworn Virgin: Travels Through an Unknown Land in Europe), and Nina Rasmussen's encounter with the Valley of Theth.

Travelling to Theth
"Having left Koplik, I took an old cobblestone road with the stones set sideways in it. The road had not been repaired for over a decade and it was often easier to drive beside it than on it. My motorcycle rattled furiously every time I attempted to drive over the cobblestones themselves.

In Dedaj I stopped to ask for information about the road before continuing my journey through the mountains of Kastrati. All I had to do was to decide which direction I wanted to take. They rest would be determined by the people I met on the way.

When I went into the café, there was complete confusion. I found myself surrounded by about thirty men, all wanting to tell me where to go. It was as if I had taken a poke at a hornets' nest. They were waiting there for a lift on the truck that passed by daily on its way to Dedaj, Theth, and Ura e Mesit, and they all did all they could to convince me to leave my motorcycle at the café and take the truck with them. I did not like this idea.

The truck driver offered to take me and my motorcycle with them. I did not like that idea either. He was insulted when I refused, and told me I was a fool and that I would never find my way on a motorcycle. I would most certainly drive off a cliff or bandits would attack me, etc. Why were all these old men trying to stop me?

Fatmir, a serious-looking young man of eighteen, spoke good French, a language that I alas did not know very well. But he understood that I intended to take my bike

Top: *Family traditions in the mountains, 1994.* (Photo: Nina Rasmussen).
Below: *Traditional family in the Shala valley, 1925.* (Drawing: Cora Gordon)

whatever they said. From what he was saying, I understood that he was offering me accommodation at his place.

"Oui," I replied, not really knowing what I had said yes to, but he seemed like a reliable fellow. I was to follow the truck until he got off. But the truck driver insisted that I ride in front of them and that the truck would catch up to me later. He was determined? I still had no idea where the road led. At any rate, the passengers climbed into the back of the truck and I turned on my bike. In *Peaks of Shala*, Rose Wilder Lane described the region as rough and difficult to reach, but she and her girlfriend managed to get to their destination on foot and on horseback. That was before the road was built.

Initially the road wound its way up through a few villages. I suspected that the truck driver was driving faster than usual to scare me. The road was extremely bumpy. With its big wheels, the heavy truck had no difficulty, but the motorcycle was constantly jumping up and down. I rode for my life and prayed to the god of bikes and tires that I would not get a flat. After a while, the terrain became more difficult. The road was suddenly steep and strewn with fallen rocks and boulders. Now it was the men's turn to pay acute attention to where they were going, because this was the sort of terrain I could whiz through. My jewel of a bike glided around the rocks and boulders like a top-class slalom skier, with me standing on the gas pedal all the time. The truck, on the other hand, had difficulty advancing. It groaned all the way up the mountain road, swerving left and right, and I could imagine the poor passengers in the back who must have been clinging to the rails all the time. It was a long climb with many a narrow bend in the road. In addition to my pride, I had another reason to accelerate and get ahead of the truck. A call of nature forced me to try and reach some place where I could get off the bike, pull the toilet paper out of my back pocket and get my trousers down and back up in time, so as to be standing serenely at the roadside with a smile on my face by the time the truck came by to greet the men who would all be waiving at me. I managed this before we made a stop halfway to Theth.

After the rest, the driver turned the engine back on and set off again, higher and higher up the mountain road until we reached a grove of beech trees. I don't know how beech trees could possible grow here. After the village of Boga, the road flattened out. Suddenly, I found myself picking up speed. The truck was going faster, too. There were no curbs at the roadside and the descent was precipitous.

Through the large beech trees I caught a glimpse of the long sunlit valley between the mountain ranges. On the other side rose the majestic peaks of the Jezerca range to an elevation of about 3,000 metres. The road wound its way back and forth down the mountain, with many steep hairpin turns. There were a few houses around now.

Arrival in Theth

When we reached the floor of the valley, Fatmir hopped out of the truck. "Bravo, bravo," cried the men from the back of the vehicle. This was quite a compliment coming from Albanian men, who are not wont to praise women, but of course they could not know that the woman they were complimenting was an experienced biker who had been over worse roads than this one. The truck driver still looked a bit sullen. He helped the other passengers unload their flour sacks and gave me an angry look that made the other men laugh.

The seven children of the Rupa family in Theth (left to right): Fatmir, Alfred, Diana, Mirela, Sokol, Valbona and Roza, 1994. (Photo: Nina Rasmussen).

"Where are we?" I asked Fatmir.

"In Theth," he replied. I gave the truck driver a signal that he could carry on without me.

How could I be so lucky as to have arrived here without any problems. It was one of the most beautiful places I had ever seen. My two cameras were of no use. They were too small to take in the majesty of it all. Before us was a primitive bridge of tree trunks that spanned the sparkling creek. Fatmir looked worried, but I had no problem getting the bike over it. The only signs of inhabitation that I could make out in the valley were two tall slender houses and a church.

The atmosphere was surreal. As we approached a beautiful little cottage, the sunlight streaming into the valley seemed to unite heaven and earth. However, when I stepped into the house, my fantasies suddenly turned into bitter reality, the reality of wretched living conditions and gnawing poverty. Fatmir lived within the uninsulated walls of this dark stone house with his parents and six brothers and sisters. I suddenly found myself surrounded by horde of children. To my good fortune, his sixteen-year-old sister Valbona spoke good English. She translated for me and introduced all the rest of the family.

This was the house of Pal Nik Rupa. He was a tall, gaunt-looking fellow, fifty-eight-years-old, who seemed sharp and intelligent. His wife looked tired. She stood at the doorway turning a little copper coffee-grinder. Valbona brought me and her father two little cups and poured boiling hot black coffee into them. He told me that they were Catholics and that the seven children were a gift of God.

"No abortion here?" No, abortion is not good. This was obviously not a preferred topic of discussion for a man with seven children. We sat down on two old, threadbare sofas stained with coffee and wet diapers. This was the first house I had ever seen without a television. There was also no discussion of getting one because there were no channels available in the region.

My photo album and the lego blocks I had with me proved to be a sensation. Alfred, Diana, Sokol, Mirela, Roza and Fatmir were fascinated by the colourful little plastic bricks. Valbona and her father spent much time pouring over my photo album, analysing and commenting on every single photo.

"Who is that? Is that Emil? How old is Ida? Fifteen and a half?"

When we finished our coffee, I went out for a walk with Pal and Valbona. The family owned a field with a crop of maize growing on it. They ate the maize and also used it to make bread. Up in the cliffs behind the house there was a small cave. In earlier times when things were less peaceful, it had been used as a place of refuge. Looking up at the cliffs, I spotted a cloud of smoke.

"The Italian mountain climbers," said Valbona.

"You should open a campsite for hikers and nature fans here," I suggested as I looked around the valley. "All you need to do is build a toilet and get some garbage bins."

Valbona did not think anyone would come. The valley had nothing to offer.

We walked down to the church. It was the same one I had seen in old photos. The church had been destroyed by the Serbs but it was now standing again, although without any windows or furnishings. Everything had been plundered by the locals.

In the cemetery there were ancient gravestones dating from various ages. On some of them, animals and round suns had been engraved. No one knew exactly how old they were.

On the way back, we paid a visit to the neighbours who lived in a house Pal's father had built. The current owner was a carpenter. He had got himself some tools and had now started carrying out some small repairs for the neighbours. His wife and sister came home while we were there, each of them carrying a heavy load of branches and twigs on their backs used for feeding the cows.

The man asked us to have a seat on the veranda and brought out a bottle of *raki*. He poured drinks into three glasses, one for me, one for Pal and one for himself. It was obvious that I was being treated like a man. They could not treat me like a woman because this would have been insulting for a foreign guest.

"Gëzuar," said the carpenter as he raised his glass. I took a sip. It was dreadful and tasted like some pesticides used for farming.

"Don't drink it," whispered Valbona in my ear. I put the glass down, realising that imbibing their home-made moonshine was probably not a good idea. Pal and the carpenters had a few glasses each. They were used to it. Fortunately no one took excep-

The church of Theth in ruins between 1991 and 2005 (Photographer unknown)

tion to the fact that I did not drink with them. It was custom for the women to remain sober so that they could take care of the children and drag their drunken husbands home.

When we were finished, we got up and returned to Pal's house.

"Where is the village?" I asked innocently because I had not seen the centre.

"Theth has seven hundred houses in all," explained Pal, "but they are spread out over the whole valley. More than seven thousand people live here in this area. I am the mayor and am responsible for eight regions." The municipal building where Pal had his office was in Pedaj, twenty kilometres away.

"How does your father get to work?" I asked Valbona.

"He walks."

"On foot?"

"Yes, he leaves early in the morning at six and gets to the office at nine. When he finishes work in the afternoon at four or five, he has another three-hour walk to get home. Sometimes he is lucky and gets a lift on the back of a truck, but it is too expensive to do that every day."

Pal told me that his administrative activities for the municipality were rather complicated. The old system had broken down and there was no more funding. "Could you ask a Danish municipality how they would manage a situation like this? I would be interested in knowing."

We got back to Pal's house. He understood how important it was for his children to get an education. For this reason they spent all their money on schooling. The two eldest, Valbona and Fatmir, attended a boarding school in Shkodra. Pal had paid extra so that they could study English and French, too. Fatmir and Valbona took their studies seriously. They were a poor, but talented family struggling to get along.

All of the children in the family did the best they could. It was moving to see how they constantly helped and supported one another. The youngest of them, a lad who was one and a half years old, had brown ringlets and looked like a little troll. He rummaged around in the dirt around the house, with wet pants and a crust of bread in his fist. Whenever he fell down, there was always a helping hand around to get him back on his feet, and there was never a sound of crying or fighting in the house.

The mother of the family was called Pashkë. She was a forty-five-year old, a tiny, withered woman. She was the mother of seven children and was completely ignored by her family. I met her in the kitchen where she was sitting on a footstool peeling potatoes. From time to time, she stirred a ladle in a blackened pan on the open fire. The room was dark. From the ceiling hung a fifteen-watt light bulb that looked as if it would give up the ghost at any time.

"Pak korrent" – not much electricity – she laughed innocently. Here, up in the mountains, the voltage was not high enough to keep all the lights on. She got up, dried her hands and shook my hand in a rather bashful manner. I was a whole head taller than she was.

Pashkë Rupa squatting in the kitchen of her home in Theth, on the right is her son Alfred, 1994. (Photo: Nina Rasmussen)

Pashkë was a doctor. She visited all of her patients in the village and up to a distance of twenty kilometres on foot. Whenever anyone fell sick, they would send a couple of men around to get her. She would walk with them to see the patient. Whenever a truck passed by, she would try and get a lift for free, but most of the time she had to walk. On her way back, the relatives of the patient would walk her home.

"When I turn fifty, I get my pension," she said wearily as she continued peeling the potatoes. A doctor's work is never done here.

"What do the people in Theth lack most?" I asked.

The little grey woman in her creased dress looked up at me. Her expression now took on the authority of a physician. "The people here in the valley are actually in good shape due to the healthy climate."

"What diseases are most prevalent?"

"The children often get bronchitis and we have several cases of contagious hepatitis."

The kitchen walls were black with soot, and behind a half-height wall was the toilet, which also had the water tap. The running water from a natural source, gushed in through a pipe, splattered onto the floor and disappeared into the hole in the ground. It served at the same time to flush the toilet. Right above the water pipe there was a large hole in the wall that led to the pigsty. It was built as part of the house so that the leftovers could easily be thrown to the pigs. In one corner of the toilet was a cupboard with some food and various junk in it.

The family was extremely poor. They were honest people who worked hard and got very little income for the effort. The people of the valley had to pay for the doctor themselves, but because few of them had any money, the doctor was not getting rich by any means. Pal made a thoroughly honest impression, although many Albanians told me that they had to bribe officials to get any assistance. Otherwise they were told to come back next week. Pal's family was not the only one that was poor. The villages in the region had been starved out for years because they were Catholics and extremely anti-communist.

Valbona was now exhausted from speaking English and interpreting. Ten days earlier, she had had an appendix operation.

"Doesn't it take too much time to get a patient with a swollen appendix to hospital in Shkodra?"

"Yes, it does, so we do it ourselves here."

"You mean, your mother knows how to operate on an appendix?"

"Yes, she does them quite often."

"But you don't have any equipment here for the anaesthesia."

"No, we have to do it with ether."

A meal was served and I was given my food on a low table in the living room. Baked potatoes with a plate of sweet but watery milk rice. Valbona's younger brothers and sisters came in from time to time with hunks of bread or plates of milk rice in their hands. Some of them ate on the sofa and, of course, much of the food was spattered on the ground. No one seemed to mind. It was normal because there was not enough room at the table for everyone to eat together.

"Is this a new house or an old one?" I asked Valbona.

"It's new. My father built it four years ago. We still don't have enough money to finish it." She points to the unplastered walls of rough stonework.

"We used to live in the house built by my grandfather, but it was too small."

There was not much furniture in the living room. Seven children slept in the adjacent room. Only a couple of them had a bed. The rest slept on the floor. They had no mattresses, only thin blankets that they used as coverings. A wide wooden staircase led to the attic where the parents slept on the floor, right under the shingles.

"Why is the roof so high and steep?"

"It's so that the snow can slide off it in the winter."

"Why don't you leave the snow on the roof in winter to isolate the house?"

"If it stayed on the roof, the house would collapse."

This was probably true. Traditional Albanian house construction is nothing to write home about. These stone houses lacking insulation must have been freezing cold in the winter. The only heating they had was the wooden stove in the kitchen.

Night fell and I prepared for bed. The children brought me a jug of water so that I could brush my teeth. I poured some water into a glass and out plopped a little figure made of legos. Seven observant children giggled at my surprise. Valbona took them all back to bed and then returned.

"There may be a few little creatures around if you turn the light out, so it would be better to leave it on." She pointed to the light bulb on the ceiling that was still struggling to get enough electricity out of the wires.

"Little creatures?" I had a closer look at the sofa and saw them emerging from all the cracks. It was swarming with flees and lice! Fortunately it was a cool evening, cool enough for me to sleep in my sleeping bag. I unfolded my mosquito net and, turning the light off, crept in and pulled the cover well up around me. What were these things crawling around my pillow? It was like having my own private zoo. There was not much I could do about the situation, so I decided to get to sleep and ignore what was going on around me.

Pal got up at five in the morning to go to work. The children were still on vacation and got up later. Valbona helped her mother in the sooty kitchen and brought me my breakfast: white homemade cheese, delicious home-baked maize bread and onions. It looked healthy and tasted healthy, too. I inspected my clothes to see if there were any creatures I could do without.

Valbona wanted to look her best for school, as all girls do, and this was not easy. The family had only one comb, so I gave Valbona my hairbrush that she could take to Shkodra with her. In my bag I also had an orange blouse that I did not wear very often, and two bras. Valbona's mother didn't have a single one. Indeed, she only owned one dress. I wondered if my nicely embroidered culottes would be something for her? Valbona inspected the clothes with great interest.

"Mother would never wear this because of this stuff." The problem was the piping along the skirt. Loosely fitting culottes were all the rage that year.

I did not have much luggage with me and, as such, not much to give to family. Valbona was pleased most of all by the lipstick and a little compact of eye shadow I gave her, and swiftly stuffed the sinful objects into her bag. Most useful of all, I was able to give her a new toothbrush and a tube of toothpaste. No one in the house owned a toothbrush!

We took a long walk in the vicinity of the house. Valbona had so many things she wanted to ask me. What could they be? When we were out of sight, she began:

"Do you mind that your daughter Ida has a boyfriend?"

"No, if that is what she wants. I do not check up on her. I trust her to know what is best for her." To break the ice, I asked Valbona:

"Do girls use contraception here?" Valbona did not know what I was talking about.

"I mean, family planning, condoms, the pill?" She knew nothing about these things. I was not able to explain everything in detail, but she understood that they were things to avoid getting pregnant or getting Aids. She probably did not understand why her father had forbidden her from having a boyfriend. It was of course to her advantage to wait as long as possible before tying herself to a man, but ignorance was a dangerous strategy that often led to the wrong result. Everything to do with sexuality was covered in a mantel of silence, as it was in Denmark a hundred years ago. Obscene words were never uttered, and not even written on walls. The first expressions we teach foreigners in Denmark are *rødgrød* (currant pudding) and *jeg elser dig* (I love you), but there are admittedly places where the first words you learn are 'shit' and 'fuck.' In Albania, the first words I learned were 'man' and 'children.' I never heard any swearwords and only once did I see an obscene drawing on a wall. It was a naked woman with breasts folded over her shoulders, and with no genitals.

It was cold that morning so I had my jacket on. I also put a pair of loosely fitting jeans over my embroidered culottes. It was still chilly at 9:30 when I was preparing for my departure. Fatmir walked me down to the road. He eyed my jacket and blue jeans and nodded in approval.

"It is a good thing that you have all those clothes on." When I said good-bye and put my helmet on, he pulled the visor over my eyes, saying earnestly: "Keep the visor down. That way, nobody can see that you are a woman."

"You look like a sworn virgin!" he called out. Marriages in Albania used to be arranged by the parents, and engagements were made when the fiancés were still children. Brides were cheaper than horses. The men always accepted the brides that had been purchased for them, but there were some rare cases when a bride refused to marry the man she had been promised to. There was only one way of getting out of such a marriage, and this was for her to swear, in the presence of twelve witnesses, that she would remain a virgin. She then had to cut her hair short and dress in men's clothes for the rest of her life. She would also do men's chores and bear weapons like the rest of them. Women were bought and sold up until the Second World War and it was nothing unusual here in the north of the country to come across these Albanian sworn virgins. I was given to understand that there were still some old ones alive.

When Rose Wilder Lane got to Theth, an Albanian tribal chief offered her a lot of money to become his wife. Because she kept her hair short and was wearing long trousers, he thought that she had refused to marry the man her father had promised her to. Because America was so far away, the rejected bridegroom would not be able to take revenge easily. His offer of marriage was thus practical and generous. Nowadays, women who dressed in men's clothes and did men's jobs were nothing unusual, but for other reasons. They were a vestige of the communist period. If sworn virgins still existed, I would not recognise them.

Fatmir was very worried at the thought of me travelling alone through the mountains. He thought it better that I wait and go back with him on the truck. But I had other plans. I wanted to continue on through the mountains to Ura e Mesit in order to avoid taking the same road back to Shkodra.

Leaving Theth

On my journey southwards through Dukagjin I did not encounter a single vehicle, only horses, donkeys, cows and pigs... and a frog that jumped out of the bushes at me with a loud croak. The sun was out and it began to warm up. Taking my jacket and extra pair of trousers off, I once again became a woman. In Pedaj I stopped to buy a watermelon, my only food for the day. A couple of young men were galloping up and down the road on bay horses. All the people I met were friendly and full of curiosity. One man surprised me by telling me my name. I realised that news of my arrival in the valley with the truck had spread faster than I could travel.

At one lonesome spot on the road, when I had not seen any human beings or animals for over an hour, I stopped and sat down for a while to listen to the world around me. There are few places on earth where you can sit and not hear some the sound of some motor in the distance. Here, there was absolute silence. After a quarter of an hour, however, I realised I could hear the mountains. At first they were almost inaudible, like sand running through an hourglass, but then I caught the vague sound of gravel and then the noise of rocks tumbling down the mountainside.

Suddenly, I was shaken out of my reverie by a nearby thud. A boulder had broken off a cliff and come crashing down onto the road right beside me. I sat there with the impression that the mountains were moaning and groaning, and very slowly collapsing around me. I could hear them. The rustling of sand and gravel, then the echo of a falling boulder, then another.

When I finally got up to continue my journey, I was in bliss at that moment of peace and tranquillity. I hoped that the solitary peaks around me would stay with me forever. For a long while down the canyon I had the impression that my wish was becoming a reality, but eventually the road emerged from the valley, and the mountains turned to hills. The dusty road now wound its way along a river where men and boys were swimming and fishing for trout. I thought of taking off my clothes and jumping in for a swim, too, but the men would all have stared at me. There were lots of children around so this would not have led to any great problems. My only worry was about leaving the motorcycle alone at the side of the road. Later on, when the countryside was flatter, I drove along a lengthy irrigation canal out of which horses were drinking. At one end of it there were some little watermills with old tins attached to them, squeaking as they turned."²⁷

This is the conclusion of Nina Rasmussen's chapter on Theth. She continued her journey to Ura e Mesit near Shkodra (where everyone recognised her because of the white helmet she was wearing - no one wore a helmet in Albania) and, from the dam at Vau i Dejës she caught a ferry to Fierza. On the way, she met Tom Prekelezaj of Koplik who insisted on going with her. To avoid him, she made a detour to Puka, thus taking the same route that Edith Durham took in 1908. Edith Durham had to travel with packhorses. The road was now somewhat better than it had been in 1908. Nina got to Fierza and continued on to Bajram Curri. There she came across a gang of rowdy men. She was afraid that they would follow her to her next destination of Valbona and therefore changed directions and carried on to Kukës. On the road from Kukës to Shkodra, she was stopped by a fellow with a pistol in his hand, someone she had met earlier, but reacted swiftly and managed to get away from him. She had now been in the country for quite some time and had met a lot of people. These acquaintances told other people about her and, as such, she was recognised wherever she went. In Shkodra she visited the citadel and then continued her journey via Lezha and Shëngjin back to Tirana, back to Aunt Roza. From there, she made one final trip to Kruja and Burrel, where she saw the burgu i vjetër (old prison) from the outside, and then rode on to Peshkopia and Qafë-Murra, before returning to Tirana. By now, it was September and, after a few days at the beach in Durrës, she left the country.

---

27 Nina Rasmussen (1995). *Som en albansk jomfru: en rejse gennem et ukendt land i Europa*, pp. 139-150. Copenhagen: Gyldendal.

Part III Present-Day Theth

Gerda Mulder

The Road to Theth

Hiking over Mountain Passes

The Shala Valley in northern Albania is one of the most isolated regions of Europe, one could almost say that it is cut off from the rest of the world. It takes determination to get there. None of the travellers who visited the village of Theth in the early decades of the twentieth century fail to mention the arduous journey and the suffering they went through to reach the fabled valley. To get there from Shkodra, they had to cross one of two mountain passes: the more northerly Sheep Trail Pass (Qafa e Shtegut të Dhenjvet) or the more southerly Bishkas Pass (Qafa e Bishkasit), both journeys requiring two or three days of travel and spending a night or two somewhere in the wilds.

Karl Steinmetz, Franz Nopcsa and Edith Durham clambered over the Sheep Trail Pass (some with the aid of mules and guides, others without) when Albania was still part of the Ottoman Empire. Their reports all tell of their attempts to outwit Turkish gendarmes and guards who tried to prevent them from getting into the interior without official escorts.

After the First World War, Rose Wilder Lane, Jan and Cora Gordon, and A. den Doolaard found themselves in an independent but volatile country over which the government in Tirana had little control. The Shala Valley was situated in a disputed border region between Albania and the recently created Kingdom of Yugoslavia (Montenegro and Serbia) and was, to boot, the scene of warfare, rivalry and much blood feuding between the various Albanian tribes.

The Gordons and Den Doolaard took the northern route over the Sheep Trail Pass and describe in enthralling detail their struggle to get over the narrow trail without falling into deep ravines or without being swept away by raging torrents.

Rose Wilder Lane and her companions took the southerly route over the Bishkas Pass, no less exhausting. Passing through the isolated settlements of Pult, Xhan, Pog and Plan, they reached Ndërlysa, ten kilometres south of Theth, after a grueling journey.

The return journey was even worse. Rose had fallen ill during her stay in the Shala Valley. She caught pneumonia and had to get back to Shkodra for medical attention. For twenty-four hours, without stopping for the night, she and the 12-year-old Rexh – a less than reliable guide – trudged through the mountains and over the snow-covered Bishkas Pass once again to reach the coast. Jan and Cora Gordon, who travelled over this pass three years later on their way back from Theth, read her account of the journey and thought that she had exaggerated ("our horses were now growing so consistently fatigued from undernourishment that we looked upon the final ascent of the Qafa e Bishkasit with some anxiety, espeecialy as it has been honoured with a particulary dramatic and stirring account by an emotional American woman traveler. However, the pass was much easier than we had imaged...") [28]

[28] Jan and Cora Gordon (1927). *Two Vagabonds in Albania*, p. 295. London: John Lane.

The Northerly Route

In the years preceding the Second World War, the Albanian government gradually came to exert its control over the northern mountains and the region became somewhat more stable. In 1936, on the initiative of King Zog, the narrow track to Theth was widened and made suitable for motor vehicles. Now it was finally possible, via Buni i Thorës, to reach Theth by car or by motorcycle.

Reimer Schulz was the first traveller included in this book to have reached Theth over the new road by motor vehicle. Kurt Seliger and Nina Rasmussen were to follow in later years on their motorcycles.

We chose to take the car.

The northerly route to Theth is about sixty kilometres long. From the town of Koplik, north of Shkodra, the road sets out eastwards through the settlements of Dedaj, Xhaj, Dukaj and Boga and then snakes up over the Buni i Thorës Pass (where travellers can stop and see the memorial to Edith Durham) until it suddenly plunges down the mountainside to Theth on the valley floor. The journey over the mountains, with its breathtaking views, takes four or five hours if the weather is good. In the spring and summer it can be quite an adventure when storm clouds gather. The road is in fact not bad up to Boga, but thereafter a four-wheel vehicle and an experienced driver are recommended. It is all the more adventuresome in the dark.

Herman and I have taken the northerly route to Theth on numerous occasions - in good weather, in a rainstorm, through deep snow and even at night. Each time, it was an experience we had not counted on.

The Buni i Thorës route is closed due to snowfall for about six months of the year (from November to May) and, when it reopens in the spring, it is always uncertain as to how much of the road has remained intact. Whole sections are often washed away and need to be repaired before it can be used by vehicle traffic.

The Southerly Route

On our most recent trip to Theth in mid-May 2013, together with Robert Elsie, we learned that the shorter, northerly route over the Buni i Thorës was still snowed in, despite with warm spring weather. We were thus forced to take the much longer southerly route that sets out from Shkodra on the road past the famed Mes Bridge (Ura e Mesit). This journey required a bit more organisation and persistence. Robert and his companions had already rented their own four-wheel drive, but Herman and I still had no transport.

The car rental company we approached in Tirana categorically refused to give us a four-wheel drive for Theth unless we accepted 100% liability in case of accident. The risk was simply too great.

To our good fortune, while we were in Tirana, we met Pavlin Polia, the proprietor of a guesthouse in Theth, and he arranged a four-wheel drive for us in Shkodra.

The car came with an experienced driver, Sadik from Abat, who knew the road well. He travelled back and forth on it virtually every day.

The southerly road from Shkodra to Theth starts out well. It is paved up to Drisht and Ura e Shenjtë but then winds its way up the Kir River valley as a dirt road and finally as a dusty trail. The seven-hour journey over the mountains of Shosh is exhausting but spectacular and well worth the effort. There is no food to be had on the way, only a couple of very basic cafes that serve cold drinks and black Albanian coffee.

We were surprised to see that highway maintenance crews were actually at work to keep the road open. Dump trucks had, however, left piles of gravel on the road and, on one occasion, we were brought to a complete stop. Roza Rupa, the daughter of the proprietor of another guesthouse in Theth, was with us and had made the trip many times. Without giving a shrug, she got out of the car, grabbed a shovel and got to work. We all pitched in and, in a quarter of an hour, we were able to continue our journey. Finally over the mountains, we reached the Gates of Shala and the small administrative centre of Breglumi. From there on, we made our way along the dusty gravel road up the Shala River to Ndërlysa and Theth. Jolted, shaken and coated in dust, we reached the Rupa guesthouse just before sunset. We were exhausted, but exhilarated to have reached our goal - the elusive and breathtaking village of Theth.

The Village of Theth Today

Theth is a peculiar village because there is no real centre to it. This was the reason why I was so disappointed when I finally got there in 1995, thirty years after having read the novel The Horseshoe Inn. What I encountered there was not a village in the classical sense of the word but a collection of little hamlets scattered far from one another throughout the valley. All of the houses were situated along the valley of the Shala River.

Each of the hamlets, such as Okol, Nik Gjonaj, Nderja, Qendër, Nën Rreth, Gjeçaj, Ndreaj, Kolaj, Grunasi, Ulaj and Ndërlysa, was but a couple of houses surrounded by enclosed yards and fields. Fences and hedges that divide property are very important in the northern Albanian mountains. The kanun has very detailed provisions as to property rights and borders.

I was not the only person to have been fascinated by the village of Theth. A major international research team from Millsaps College in Mississippi visited the Shala Valley for four years, from 2005 to 2009, to carry out the Shala Valley Project under the enthusiastic direction of Dr Michael Galaty. This project was inspired by a book, too. Galaty had followed Rose Wilder Lane's 1921 journey, with a copy of Peaks of Shala in his rucksack. The scholars and photographers involved in the project spent four summers with their laptops and measuring equipment at the little inn of Fran and Kristina Frashnishta in Theth Gjeçaj. They systematically mapped the whole region and collected material on archaeology, history, geography, anthropology and linguistics and published the results in the book Light and shadow, Isolation and Interaction in the Shala Valley of Northern Albania.

The Houses

In the first year of the Shala Valley project, the scholars investigated the history of all the houses and other buildings in Theth with the help of travel reports, official documents and photos. The team came to the conclusion that five different construction phases were to be distinguished in the valley.

The village of Theth is first recorded in a mediaeval chronicle dating from the year 1465. At that time, it had seven houses and accordingly few inhabitants. In the seventeenth century, the population grew substantially, caused by campaigns carried out by the Turks to force the people to convert to Islam. Many families and tribes from the southern part of the Shala Valley moved to the more isolated northern region of the valley, but none of the houses of this period remain.

The oldest surviving houses in Theth were built in the period between the second half of the nineteenth century and the 1920s, when blood feuding raged. These characteristic grey stone houses were small and did not originally have upper floors. What they did have for windows were narrow slits (*frëngji*) framed in stonework that served as loopholes for shooting in blood feuds. They also had grey wooden shingles.

King Zog, who reigned in Albania in the 1930's, did much to combat blood feuding in the north. He wanted to put an end to the isolation of the region and to the *kullas*, the traditional fortified houses. Most of the homes built in the 1930s and 1940s were accordingly constructed with larger windows, no slit for shooting anymore, as if feuding had become a thing of the past. People continued to live in large extended families, with two or three generations under one roof.

There was much construction in Theth after the Second World War because the communist regime that had taken power in 1944 made property available for small families. This caused many of the large family units to break up into smaller nuclear families and there was a modest boom in new housing construction. Many of the inhabitants of Theth also began adding a second floor to their originally one-storey homes. They made the windows larger and used other material than wooden shingles for covering the roofs.

The buildings of the communist period, such as the Party headquarters, the health clinic, the school and government shops, were all constructed of new material such as bricks and cement. In 1966, Theth received its own little hydroelectric power plant and all the homes were attached to the grid. At this time, there were two hundred houses in Theth, and the village now had almost a thousand inhabitants.

In the early 1990s, the inhabitants began to emigrate to the Albanian coast and abroad and Theth was rapidly robbed of its inhabitants.

Theth currently counts sixty-seven houses, however few homes are inhabited all year round. The families that do spend the winter months in Theth suffer from great isolation because the road from Shkodra over the high mountain pass, the Buni i Thorës, in snowbound from October to May. Most families live and work in Shkodra in the winter and now only spend the summer months in Theth. The rise in tourism means that many of them have put on additions to their homes to make room for guests or transformed them entirely into guesthouses.

The proprietors of the vacant homes live mostly in Shkodra or elsewhere in Albania. Some have settled abroad and have abandoned the properties entirely. This process has accelerated since the fall of communism, and twenty-four houses are now in such a state of disrepair that they can be considered ruins – a tragic situation even though they are a delight for photographers.

Fortunately, many of the traditional pre-war constructions in the village, such as the church, the vendetta tower, the ethnographic museum and some of the watermills, have been preserved. Most of them were in a desolate state and several of them had collapsed entirely, but with the help of emigrants and international aid organizations, they have been renovated.

The Church
In the middle of the plain is the small, white Catholic Church of Theth that was built

in 1892. This old-fashion church and the Franciscan priests who ran it played an important role in village life until 1967. It is mentioned in virtually all travel narratives up until the Second World War because foreign guests were always received there. At that time, only the priests knew foreign languages and were able to appropriate provide shelter to visitors. There were no inns or hotels in the valley.

Thanks to the spectacular reports left by Karl Steinmetz, Franz Nopcsa, Edith Durham, Rose Wilder Lane, A. den Doolaard and Kurt Seliger, we have much insight into the daily life of these hard-working priests, who spent most of their lives in this isolated valley. All of the travellers who reached the valley before the Second World War stayed with the various priests in the vicarage. Kurt Seliger camped out in 1957, but did have extensive contacts with the pastor while he was there.

Albania declared its independence in 1912 but was soon caught up in the Balkan Wars and the First World War that were fought in this region, too. It took some time before the new borders were definitively recognised. The church was regularly pillaged by Serbian troops passing through the area.

In 1916 and 1917, Theth was the home of Shtjefën Gjeçovi (1874-1929), one of the best-known priests in the country and a figure of great significance for Albanian culture. With the help of local tribal elders, he put to writing the ancient code of Lekë Dukagjini (1410-1481) that had been transmitted orally from generation to generation.

It was in the church of Theth that Gjeçovi also opened a school in which the children of the valley first learned to read and write Albanian. This tradition was carried on by all the priests who arrived after him. Such was the success of the school that the church was soon too small to hold it. In the early 1920s the village therefore applied to the government for the construction of a proper school building. This was the reason why representatives of the American Red Cross, including Rose Wilder Lane, visited Theth in 1921.

In 1957, the Austrian journalist Kurt Seliger visited the parish and got to know the old Franciscan priest Sebastean Deda. They exchanged views on tension between the Church and communism, and on the recent establishment of an agricultural co-operative.

The last priest of Theth was Daniel Gjeçaj. In 1966 the communist regime launched a fierce campaign against religion. As a result of the campaign, the church of Theth was closed down. The vicarage and the bell tower were razed and the church was transformed and transformed into a cultural centre on 10 June 1966. Church services were banned and all the priests were taken prisoner or interned. Gjeçaj had no choice but to leave Albania and fled to Italy, where he maintained contacts with other Albanian emigrants from the region.

In the 1990s, after the fall of the communist regime, all the buildings built under communism were plundered and destroyed. The old church with the health clinic in it was abandoned and began to decay. During her visit in 1994, Nina Rasmussen noticed that the church was in a bad state. ("We walked down to the church. It was the same one I had seen in old photos. The church had been destroyed by the Serbs but it was now standing again, although without any windows or furnishings.")

In 2005, an Albanian from Theth who had emigrated to America provided funds for a new roof and the church was renovated. The bell tower that had been torn down was rebuilt on the site where it had originally stood, but not the vicarage. The church is used from time to time by the few remaining inhabitants. There is no resident clergy anymore, and mass is held by a priest who visits Theth every two to four weeks only.

The Cemetery

The old cemetery of Theth, splendidly set near the church, was mentioned by Edith Durham during her visit in 1908. She was particularly impressed by the beautifully carved wooden crosses and decorations, and photographed them. Nina Rasmussen visited the cemetery in 1994 ("In the cemetery there were ancient gravestones dating from various ages. On some of them, animals and round suns had been engraved. No one knew exactly how old they were.").

The crosses are still there, but they now stand next to expensive marble tombstones. A visit to the cemetery is a veritable lesson in history. All the families in the village have relatives buried here.

The Vendetta Tower

The most important tourist attraction in the village is the Vendetta Tower (*kulla e ngujimit*). This is one of the few such towers still preserved in the northern Albanian mountains. A vendetta tower is a fortified stone building where a family caught up in a blood feud can take refuge for a few months. Men who committed murder in accordance with the provisions of traditional law were considered outlaws until they were tried in court, but could take shelter here with their families.

At the request of the inhabitants of the valley, the Dutch Embassy in Albania financed the restoration of this 150-year-old *kulla e ngujimit*, one of the most important historical monuments of Theth.

We were present at the opening of the building in September 2007. The day before the ceremony, we travelled with the staff of the Dutch Embassy from Tirana in a convoy of cars. There was also a group of Dutch people there who had booked a trip to the Balkans called "In the Footsteps of Den Doolaard." We met one another during the gruelling journey from Shkodra to Theth when a terrible storm broke out. They had come from the Tara Gorge in Montenegro which they had visited because of its connection with Den Doolaard's book *Het land achter Gods rug* (The Country Behind God's Back). In Theth we found ourselves in the backdrop of Den Doolaard's other great Balkan novel, The Horseshoe Inn. The verdant valley surrounded by lofty mountains and waterfalls, and dotted with picturesque houses of grey slate was there on our arrival before us, just as it had been seventy-five years earlier when the Dutch writer was inspired to write the novel.

The deputy head of the Dutch mission in Albania, Ardi Stoios-Braken, held a moving speech at the opening, in which she noted that the Vendetta Tower was fortunately no longer needed for its original purpose. Deaths caused by feuding still existed in Albania, but in Theth they had ceased many years ago. She praised the friendly ties that existed between Albania and The Netherlands and hoped that the restored tower would become a tourist attraction as a museum on blood feuding and served to remind the people of Theth and foreign visitors about the valley's turbulent history. Tourism had now become a major source of income for the local population and, in view of recent trends, she was confident that it would continue to grow. It was a good sign that this group of Dutch tourists had made the long journey to Theth, she noted, and hoped that the international press would publish more such positive stories about Albania to compensate for the often negative image the country had. Albania was often associated with mafia and corruption, with human trafficking and energy crises. A few other speeches followed, and those present were then able to inspect the restored tower.

The entrance to the tower is on a slope because of its rocky foundations. There are two upper floors that can be reached by means of a ladder. One after another, the participants vanished into the tower through the sturdy door. It was a haunting experience to climb up the ladder and see the rooms in which people once hid for months on end. Dozens of men had spent long periods in these rectangular whitewashed rooms, living in fear and no doubt in great boredom. You can still feel the atmosphere when you go in.

Because of the glaring sunlight outside, the interior of the tower was pitch-black at first. The windows were tiny, only slits big enough for taking a pot shot. The owner of the tower, Nikollë Zef Koçeku, a distinguished-looking gentleman in a black suit, grey vest, and silver hair, spoke of the history of the tower. The building was the property of his family, but had been expropriated in the communist period and used as a storehouse. Thereafter it had been empty for many years. There was no money to restore the tower and it began to decay. Koçeku was delighted at the restoration carried out by the Dutch Embassy and intended, with the rest of the inhabitants of the village, to transform it into a commemorative vendetta museum. This meant that the interior of the tower would have to be restored to its former condition. They would have to find old photographs of the tower and of the village and gather information about the history of blood feuding in the region. Fortunately, feuding was now a thing of the past in the valley, but in and particularly around Shkodra, it was still going on.

After the ceremony, Koçeku posed for the cameras and gave interviews for Albanian television and radio stations based in Shkodra and with journalists reporting for Tirana newspapers. We read the articles on the Dutch-financed restoration in Theth in the national newspapers the following evening.

When Herman and I returned to Theth a couple of years later, there was a nice sign on the tower. Sokol Koçeku, the owner's son, was now charging an entrance fee of one Euro and handing out one of Herman Zonderland's photos in postcard form as a ticket. It was a nice gesture, but Herman was appalled that they were using a low resolution copy of the photo to make the postcard and had not waited for the better-quality copy to arrive. You could count the pixels on the postcard, which was not good publicity for him as a professional photographer. Sokol promised that he would use a better photo as soon as he got more postcards printed.

The Village School
The village schools in this isolated region of northern Albanian were mostly built in the 1920s and were financed by the American Red Cross. This is the reason why the writer Rose Wilder Lane got to Theth in 1921, when she accompanied the Red Cross representatives, Margaret Alexander and Frances Hardy. Funds had been raised and they had just got enough money to build three new schools in the poorest and most isolated regions of northern Albania. Whether a school was actually built in Theth at that time, I do not know.

After the Second World War, a school was set up in the village in a home that had belonged to a large family and had been confiscated by the Communist Party to be used for this purpose.

Later, in the 1960s, a proper school building was constructed on the flat land near the river. Dozens of children graduated from this school over the coming years, but the end of communism also turned out to be the end of the elementary education here, too. Like so many other state schools in Albania, it was plundered and destroyed. The roof tiles were stolen and the building eventually caved it.

In the splendid book *Long Life to your Children: A Portrait of High Albania* in 1997, published by the writer Marjorie Senechal and the photographer Stan Scherer, the school principal, Gjokë Verrishta, gave an interview in which he stated that he had 174 pupils from the ages of six to eighteen, but that conditions in the school were miserable. "The main problem we have is the condition of the school. There is a stove for each classroom in the winter, but the classrooms cannot be heated because there is no glass in the windows, the doors are broken and it is difficult for the students to stay six hours a day at school in these conditions. The school building is badly damaged."

In 2007, the school was rebuilt with funds provided by the German government, and stands, bright red in colour, in a prominent location in the middle of the village. The only problem was that there are no more teachers or pupils anymore. Almost all the children of Theth now attend school in Shkodra.

One Monday morning in the autumn of 2007, we went to see the school with Sofia Harusha, the thirteen-year-old daughter of our host, but she seemed to be the only pupil around. The teacher did not show up that day. The school building is now only used as for assemblies and for summer courses.

The Power Plant
The Shala Valley, including the village of Theth, was long deprived of electricity. Then, in 1966, with Chinese support, a small hydropower plant was constructed in a creek that shot out of the mountains, one of the many tributaries of the Shala River.

In 1978, the Chinese withdrew their economic support for Albania, and since that time, the power supply for the village and for much of the Shala Valley has depended on this outdated, noisy, and badly maintained installation. Whenever the plant broke down (which happened most of the time), there was no electricity in the daytime, and no warm water because the water pumps did not function without power. Whenever an outage occurred at the plant, people would hook up their loud generators, but the generators often broke down, too. This caused countless problems, both for the inhabitants and for visitors to the valley. No water in the tap, and no light.

On our first evening in Theth in 2007, everything suddenly went dark. A major outage had occurred, one that could not be fixed by the local inhabitants. Mechanics arrived from Shkodra the next day, but they were not able to fix the problem entirely. They had not brought the right equipment with them and called on the Harusha family, that lived nearby, to supply what tools they had. More and more men of the village got involved in the repairs, but to no avail. The mayor, Prek Harusha, was involved in the activities too, but to his great embarrassment, he was forced to offer us a "candle-light dinner" at his farmhouse the next evening. We thought it was quite romantic, but for the women in the family, it was quite a struggle preparing meals in a dark kitchen. From time to time, the lights flickered on and went out again. Several hours later, Prek Harusha gave up and turned on the noisy generator.

The Kola Family Watermill

Near the bridge over the Shala River, not far from the Vendetta Tower, there was a watermill for milling grain that functioned until 2009. It was located at the foot of a large boulder. It is the only mill that has survived. In the old days, each of the neighbourhoods of Theth had its own mill. The locals would bring sacks of corncobs to be milled into corn flour which was used to produce firm round loaves of traditional corn bread (bukë misri). The guesthouses still serve corn bread, but unfortunately not from flour milled in Theth.

The One-Time Ethnographical Museum

It was in this building, once the home of the Lulash Keq Boshi family, that Rose Wilder Lane stayed on her visit to Theth in 1921. In her book she describes her meeting with the venerable Lulash. Through an intermediary, he asked for her hand in marriage because he wanted a modern wife, and not a highland woman. She turned him down, but mused fondly at the offer in later years.

In the communist period, the house served as a regional museum of ethnography that exhibited furniture, traditional costumes and tools made in the mountains. The museum is, unfortunately, now empty, with the exception of a device for making moonshine raki that is still sitting in the attic. Most of the exhibits vanished, as they did from most of the other museums of this kind in Albania. We thought that it had been plundered in 1991 during the fall of the communist regime, but according to the inhabitants, many of the exhibits were removed and taken to the historical museum in Shkodra. The building has been uninhabited since that time. It can still be visited, as a neighbour has the key. It is a fine fortified stone house situated nine metres high on a promontory and seems to fits in well with the rocky surroundings.

The Hotel

High about the valley in the hamlet of Theth-Gjeçaj is a modern hotel with twelve bedrooms, a dining room and a veranda. It is the property of Fran Frashnishta. This is the only place in Theth where one can enjoy a modicum of luxury (meaning that there are warm showers and electricity during the daytime). It is here that groups usually stay when they are too large for the guesthouses.

Most visitors and smaller groups in Theth prefer to spend the night in one of the guesthouses in the valley itself. Conditions are mostly basic, simple bed-and-breakfast accommodation usually including dinner. The guest family lives in the same house.

The River Café

There are no shops or restaurants in Theth. All supplies come by trucks and buses from Shkodra and are usually ordered by the families that run the guesthouses. Some of the owners of the guesthouses open little outdoor cafés in the summer, usually consisting of a self-made wooden bar with tables and chairs where they serve coffee, beer or a glass of *raki rrushi* (Albanian grappa). The *raki* always used to be homemade but, now that so many families receiving guests in the summer months live in Shkodra in the wintertime, the habit of making *raki* has died out. Most of it is imported commercially from the coastal towns.

There is a wonderful little bar next to the Vendetta Tower and another beautiful garden café belonging to the Kola family near the Shala River in Okol, right next to the watermill.

After a long winter, it is always fascinating to return to Theth and see what damage has been done by the river during the spring runoff. During the thaw it is not unknown for the café beside the river to be carried away several hundred metres downstream.

Theth and its Inhabitants

Herman and I visited Theth four times together: twice in the spring, once in high summer and once in the autumn. We have no first-hand experience about what it is like in the winter. We have long considered spending some time there over the winter, but have not yet had the courage. Our visits in the early spring were cold enough.

Because of the heavy snowfall, the valley can be cut off for months, offering only very basic living conditions for visitors and the 90 to 100 inhabitants who remain there all year round. The families who do still spend the winter in Theth have learned to come to terms with the cold, the deep snow and the isolation. They depend on one another for survival.

Other families leave the valley in early October and go back to Shkodra on the coast where the climate is much milder. They return to their homes in Theth in mid-May. The annual migration has become the norm since the fall of communism in the early 1990s.

During our many visits to Theth, we stayed with five different families – twice with the two Harusha brothers, once with the Koçekus, once with the Polia Family and the last time with the Rupas. We had occasion to visit several other families, such as the Gumnaris, the Grunas, the Pishas, the Dedas and the Nikas, and took pictures. By the time of our fourth and last visit, we had the impression that we knew everyone.

The Harusha Family (Theth Qendër)

In the autumn of 2007, we were caught up in a storm on our long car trip to Theth. It was on this occasion that we got to know the Harusha family that had only recently opened their home up to travellers.

The brothers Gjergj and Prek Harusha and their families welcomed us with an open fire one evening in the living-room of their large farmhouse. We sat on long benches and were given a hearty dinner. The daughters of the two brothers were charming and served us our meal, although with some reserve. There was more than enough to eat: rack of lamb on large platters, tomato and cucumber salad, corn bread, eggs and sheep yoghurt. Everything that they produced on the farm themselves was delicious. There was no wine with the meal, however, as a group of Czech tourist visiting in the summer had downed their whole annual supply. Nor was there any beer either because the Harusha family did not brew any. But there was certainly enough moonshine *raki* to keep us going.

Both of our hosts, the Harusha brothers, were farmers, and they were well known and well respected in the village. Prek Harusha, the younger of the two, was the mayor. Gjergj Harusha, for his part, was the regional prefect of the whole Shala Valley, including Theth. They had lived all their lives in Theth and had married women from other tribes, from the villages of Kir and Lekaj. According to the *kanun*, one is not to marry a woman from one's own village or from the Shala tribe. This is regarded as somewhat incestuous because members of tribes regard one another as brothers and sisters.

The two brothers served as role models for other farmers in the village. They were the first to invest in tourism, and seven other families soon followed suit. Most of the families in Theth now offer accommodation with simple but comfortable beds and western-style bedding, and bathrooms. In the early years, many tourists had complained. It may sound very romantic, but spending the night on a straw mattress or on a sheepskin rug laid out on the floor, as Den Doolaard did in the 1930s, is not really much fun. Prek and Gjergj Harusha assured us that an investment in tourism was the only way to stop the depopulation of the valley.

Lively discussions took place in the warm living-room of the Harusha family, in Dutch, English and Albanian. Our international group wanted to know from the Harusha brothers more about the difficulties that people in the Shala Valley faced. They asked what problems occurred when the road to the next major town of Shkodra was blocked, what ramifications the continuing depopulation of the valley would have on Theth, what tourism meant for the future of the village, and whether blood feuding had indeed been eradicated.

Warmed by the raging fire and now sleepy from the strong *raki* we had been drinking, we wended our way to the bedrooms that had been made ready for us. There were three bedrooms in all, that were normally the sleeping quarters of the family. Each bedroom had four beds so that the house could accommodate a total of twelve persons at a time. Because of the heavy downpour, a couple of Czech mountain climbers who were camping in the yard outside, fled into the house in search of a dry place to sleep. The bedrooms were thus full to maximum capacity, and there was the happy-go-lucky atmosphere of a youth hostel in the two bathrooms. All the members of the Harusha family, the two brothers, their wives and nine of their children, slept in the attic.

The storm had passed by the time we got up the next morning, and there was beautiful weather out. The rays of the sun bathed the national park around us, and there were only a couple of little clouds in the sky. The serrated peaks of the Accursed Mountains (*Bjeshkët e Namuna*) rose sharply into the blue sky. The Czech campers were already up and about, drinking their morning coffee with a glass of *raki*. After a copious breakfast, we set off to explore the surroundings. The farmhouse is situated on the Shkodra-Koplik-Boga road that comes down from the mountains and continues on to the hamlet of Theth Ndërlysa, ten kilometres to the south. It is not far from the bridge over the Shala River and is the first house you come across when you enter Theth – an ideal spot for a guesthouse.

The Harushas owned 2.5 hectares of land (2 hectares of grazing land and 0.5 hectares of farmland). They were quite self-sufficient and, in principle, could feed all of their guests from the produce of their land.

However, there were still a few products that the family had to purchase in Shkodra: coffee and wheat flour for making bread. The traditional hard round loaves of cornbread, *bukë misri*, also called *bukë miseria* (misery bread), are not longer very popular, and cornbread is actually only good when it is fresh out of the oven. The family owned livestock: eighty head of sheep, three milk cows, fifteen chickens, three pigs and twenty beehives. They also had a packhorse and four dogs to guard the flocks. The vineyard produced about 1000 kilos of grapes a year, which was enough to make 400 litres of wine and a lot of *raki*. The cauldron for distilling the *raki* was situated outside next to the farmhouse. In the garden, they grew pumpkins and squashes that they fed to the animals, beans, tomatoes, corn, tobacco, cucumbers, peppers, plums and nuts. Prek Harusha, his wife Lule who stemmed from Nikaj Merturi on the banks of Lake Fierza and their five children all pitched in to do the farm work. On that autumn morning, Prek and his youngest son Francesco were busy with the beehives. His son Nikolla was tending to the sheep grazing up in the higher mountain pastures and his son Paulin was feeding the chickens. The daughters Pashkë and Sofia were helping their mother with the meals.

Prek's brother, Gjergj Harusha, was married to Age ("old Age") from the village of Lekaj, and had seven children. The eldest children were already married and no longer lived in Theth. His son Sokol lived and worked in Greece with his family, and the two daughters, Lena and Maria, were married and lived in Shkodra. His son Nika lived on the family farm in Theth with his wife Age ("young Age") and his boy Pëllumb. The youngest daughters Lina and Marasha were also still at home. Each member of the family, no matter how young they were, had his or her own chores to do in the household. The Harusha business was a well-oiled machine, and it was fascinating to see how well it worked. The tables set up in the courtyard reminded us of old times, of things we had seen in the schoolbooks of our grandparents' generation. This was the last year that the two families would be living together on the big farm.

We returned to Theth in May 2010, after a marvellous long trip through the snowy mountains. The Bun i Thorës Pass had only opened a couple of days before our arrival, when bulldozers serving as snowploughs made their way through. But there was still much snow in the mountains and it was bitterly cold. We stayed once again with the Harushas, but this time with Prek's family. The brothers had done well in the tourist trade and the money they had made was now enough for one of them to move to another house. Prek and his family remained on the old farm.

Gjergj and his large family now lived a few hundred metres down the road in a new house on the way to the church. Gjergj and some workmen were busy constructing a large new inn for visitors. Unfortunately, it was not built in the traditional style of the valley, i.e. grey stone houses with small windows and grey shingled roofs. It looked more like a modern bungalow.

We sat in Prek's garden while "young Age" Harusha brought us little cups of Turkish coffee. We had mixed feelings about the new construction work going on in Theth. Cement mixers were turning and constructions workers were busy building expansive guestrooms with comfortable baths. They were all in a hurry. Everything had to be ready for the coming summer season. We found that Prek Harusha's old farmhouse with the open fireplace was much more romantic, but were painfully aware that the future could not be held back.

The Koçeku Family (Theth Kolaj)

We already knew the Koçeku family. Herman and I had met them in September 2007 during the opening of the Vendetta Tower. Nikollë Zef Koçeku was the owner of the tower and posed proudly in front of the newly restored building. The tower was still empty at that time and there were vague plans for a museum in it, but they were still at the initial stage.

The home next to the Vendetta Tower was abandoned. The following day, I could not resist the temptation of peeking into another traditional Albanian farmhouse. I opened one of the rotting windows and clambered inside. It was no great difficulty. To my surprise and great embarrassment, the house was not abandoned at all. There were clothes hanging on the wall, a dressing table, a coffee table and a bed with sheets and blankets in it. The old vats used for making cheese were still there, too. Everything was just as it had been on the day the family left the house and went to Shkodra to spend the winter. It looked as if they had not been back for several years.

In May 2010, we visited the Vendetta Tower again and were given a tour by the owner's son, Sokol Koçeku. Sokol, his wife and children had returned to Theth for the summer and were staying for the time being in a rather basic summer cottage behind the tower. The family understood the importance of the Vendetta Tower as a tourist attraction and had invested their modest funds to this end. They had set up a little café where they served coffee and cold drinks. There were benches outside to sit on, and everything was buzzing with activity.

Construction workers were redoing the house next to the tower, the one I had broken into. Beams lay about on the ground as they were replacing the old roof.

In the summer of 2011, we took a large group of Dutch, Norwegian and Albanian friends with us to go hiking in the mountains around Theth. This time, we could see the other side of the coin – the drawbacks that the rise of tourism had brought to the valley. We wanted to stay with the Harusha family once again and had phoned months in advance to reserve the rooms, but when we arrived with a twenty-man group, Prek was busy renovating and extending his guesthouse and Gjergj had already promised all of his rooms to a group from Kosovo. The "booking system" was obviously not functioning at its best. The alternative, a newly constructed guesthouse located next to the Shala River owned by the Kola family had been swept away in good part during the spring runoff and had still not been rebuilt. In addition to this, it was quite a ways away and the bathroom facilities were very basic. Fortunately, just when it was getting dark out, we were able to find another place, the newly constructed guesthouse belonging to the Koçeku family, and after a long walk in the dark over the fields, we managed to find the family of Mark Koçeku, the brother of the owner of the famous Vendetta Tower.

Nikollë and Mark Koçeku had lived in Shkodra for many years and were not, like the Harushas, among the first to invest in tourism in Theth. Recently, they had begun spending their summers in the valley once again, with their families. In 2010 the brothers renovated Mark's old abandoned, two-storey house. The bedrooms were each furnished with four beds and a bathroom was added with a hot-water boiler. The rotting but beautiful old grey shingles on the roof had been replaced by ugly plastic tiles in bright red, and a covered terrace had been added. Alas, while we were there, there was no power or running water. This was due to problems at the two decrepit hydroelectric plants – one in Theth Gjegaj and the other farther away in Theth Nдёrlysa. Both of them broke down regularly. In the evening, they hooked up a generator which was enough to provide light but not strong enough for warm water. There was no more hope of a shower, and certainly not of a warm shower, but we were at least able to charge our i-phones and laptops, and there was light!

Mark and his wife Maria lived in the old house in the summertime with their grown son and the latter's wife and two children. They slept in a little room on the main floor, and all pitched in to ensure that we got three hearty Albanian meals a day. With the help of a tiny kitchen in the house and a large stove outside, the family was able to get spaghetti and tomato sauce ready within half an hour, together with cucumbers, peppers, cheese, fresh yoghurt and homemade bread for twenty people. There were also bowls full of apples and plums. We had brought several bottles of wine with us from Tirana, but we did not need them. The tables were decked with big jugs of fermented, freshly pressed grape juice from their own vineyard and bottles of raki.

There was not enough room in the house to accommodate the whole group, so five of us set off in the night over the fields to the home of Pavlin and Vlora Polia that had also been renovated and recently converted into a guesthouse. We slept two nights in brand new beds, all of us in one room together with the sisters of Pavlin and a baby in a wooden cradle. There was no electricity or tap water here either. In the morning, the sisters brought us large pitchers of warm water to wash in the bathroom. We made do and found it all quite an adventure. It reminded me a little bit of the hardship that Edith Durham and Rose Wilder Lane had endured. Of course there was no real comparison to the harsh life they had experienced in the mountains in the cold and rain, hiking over the hills in drenched clothes and soggy boots.

The grandparents of Mark Koceku had also lived in his house. In the kitchen there was a photo of two young couples, one in traditional costume and the other in clothing dating from the 1960s. Mark explained that his parents were on the left and he and his wife Maria were on the right. We could see his parents as young people in costume thirty years ago standing beside Mark and Maria today. Something was wrong in the photo. Mark then explained that he had taken the picture of his parents to a photographer in Shkodra and asked him to make a new one with all of them together. Photoshop in action!

The picture from 1940 was duly combined with the one from the 1970s, showing both couples, one in costume and the other in modern clothes. I had never seen anything like it.

The Pisha Family (Theth Ulaj)

We met Martin Pjetër Pisha on our expedition to Theth in the autumn of 2007 when we expressed our wish to visit the Ethnographic Museum. His house had once belonged to the oldest man in the village, Lulash Keq Boshi, who had welcomed Rose Wilder Lane there. Herman, Flutura Açka, Sofia Harusha and I stood in front of the impressive building on a stone cliff base, but it was closed. A young boy playing nearby told us that he would get the caretaker who had the key and who lived a little bit farther down the road.

A quarter of an hour later, we were greeting by the imposing figure of Martin Pisha, now in his seventies. He gave us the key so that we could get into the building and visit it. We were fascinated to see the house and the living quarters on the upper floor in which Rose Wilder Lane had stayed in 1921, and conversed with its former owner. Sofia Harusha informed us that Martin Pisha was the village bard and could sing old warrior songs accompanied by traditional Albanian instruments that he played himself, so we asked him if he would play for us. The elderly gentleman sent someone home to get his instruments - a *lahuta*, a *gajde* and a *çifteli*, and improvised a concert for us in the museum garden. Aside from us, the audience consisted entirely of goats.

In the spring of 2010 we once again visited Martin Pisha and his wife Pashkë Pisha, taking the children of our host, Francesco and Sofia Harusha, with us as interpreters. They could both speak English quite well now. Their house was located higher up above the village. Dogs barked, announcing our arrival long in advance.

Martin spread his collection of traps and wolf pelts out on the grass for us to see. He had been a hunter all his life and laid traps for wolves in the harsh winter months in Theth. His wife Pashkë waited in the house with refreshments and sweets. Pashkë originally came from the village of Kir and had moved the Theth as a young girl. She was a shepherdess and cared for all of the family's sheep and goats.

Of the couple's seven children, three sons had emigrated to Italy. Two sons and two daughters were living in Albania, but no longer in the mountains. Present in the house with us were the granddaughter Afërdita and her girlfriend Fatmira, the youngest daughter of Martin's brother Okol. Afërdita did the housekeeping for her grandparents and lived all year round with them in Theth.

The Pisha family was not originally involved in tourism and had not renovated their house to add bathrooms and sleeping quarters for visitors. As such, it was an authentic old Albanian home. In the living-room there was a wall of black-and-white photos of Pashkë and Martin's parents and grandparents in the splendid heavy traditional costumes of the region. The wall was also decorated with typical northern Albanian embroidery of dyed wool. Martin's instruments were hanging on a hook in a corner and, of course, he sang a few songs for us. We were highly impressed, but Afërdita and Fatmira giggled all the time at grandpa's funny music and gestures.

Okol Pisha then came in. He was Martin's brother and the father of Fatmira. He was not drunk but visibly a bit tipsy. The conversation in the room suddenly took a serious turn. Okol was married to Pren who had been betrothed to him when she was a young girl.

Pren had been interviewed for the Shala Valley Project by the student Nadia Al Hashimi who was conducting research for a thesis on the life of women in Theth (*Keepers of the Pass: Gender Roles of Women in Northern Albanian*, 2010). In the interview, Pren noted that life had been hardest under communism, when she earned very little money and there was little to eat. She also mentioned that her marriage to Okol had not been a happy one. Okol drank too much and was not nice to Pren when he was drunk. Fortunately, she had received a lot of support over the years from her sister-in-law, Pashkë, and her friend Shkurte Gumnari.

In the summer of 2011 we visited Martin Pisha once again and of course asked him to sing us some more songs. That evening, the aging bard came around, dressed in a colourful suit and vest, and with a traditional Albanian white felt cap on his head, bringing all of his instruments with him. The concert he gave for our group was a great success.

The repertory consisted of old songs. Those in our group who knew Albanian and English translated the texts for us. What we noticed in particular was that all of the songs, without exception, dealt with the Albanian struggle against the Serbs. Not one song had anything to do with the struggle against the Turks!

The Gumnari Family (Theth Gjecaj)

It was September 2007. In the cornfields was an old man with a splendid turban wrapped around his head. Our young interpreters, Francesco and Sofia Harusha, told us that he was extremely old, but spent every day out in the fields. We approached to say hello. His name was Nue Keq Gumnari. Herman took his picture that turned out to be a wonderful portrait of the aged gentleman, and got a tremendous shot of his weathered hands, too. When we went back three years later, we took copies of the photos with us, hoping that he was still alive. He was indeed there, living at the home of his daughter-in-law, Shkurte Gumnari.

After a long walk through the village, we met Shkurte at home. She had arrived from Shkodra where she had spent the winter with her husband and daughter of fifteen, and where her father-in-law lived. Shkurte returned to Theth every summer without her husband. She had three daughters, but only the youngest of them, Maria, went back with her every summer. Her oldest daughter was studying in Tirana and the two others were married with the loves of their lives and lived in Italy. Shkurte and Maria spent the summers taking care of her father-in-law, who was happy to be in a familiar environment.

Shkurte grew fruit and vegetable in her garden, took care of her dog and cow, and had a lot of social contacts with neighbouring families that had returned to Theth for the summer. Without hesitation, she invited us into her traditional stone house. On the main floor, there was a large living-room with an open fire. It also served as a kitchen and dining room. There was a bed in one corner that was used by her father-in-law who was now dying.

Upstairs, reached by an open ladder-like staircase, was the bedroom, above which hung sides of smoked ham drying, and all around, there were vats of homemade cheese that were aging. On one wall, the daughter had pinned English translations of the Albanian words and expressions she needed whenever foreign tourists came to stay. However, we thought it rather unlikely that any foreigners would stay there.

There were now many functioning and well-equipped guesthouses and even a campsite in Theth. We felt that even hardy backpackers would be unlikely to stay in a two-room house with no bath or toilet, and with hardly any comfort at all.

The daughter Maria had worked as an interpreter in 2005-2009 for the Shala Valley Project and knew English well enough. During her interview, her mother Shkurte told Nadia Al Hashimi that what she liked most was the great freedom she had in Theth during the summer months. She could decide things for herself and talk to anyone in the village she wanted to, mostly the women, but occasionally even the men. As a woman, she did not go to any of the little bars or cafes, but she could visit homes and receive visitors herself. Everywhere we went, we came across her, either alone or with her friend Pren Pisha, the sister-in-law of Martin Pisha.

The Grunas Family (Theth Grunas)
All the hikers who go down to see the waterfall at Grunas, one of the village's main attractions, pass by the house of the Grunas family. We went down that way in the autumn of 2007, too. The house was the best situated of all in Theth, with a splendid view of the river and the mountains. The Grunas family consisted of the father, the mother, a son and two daughters. They lived in Shkodra in the winter and spent their summers in Theth.

The daughters were very shy and did not say much, spending most of their time doing the laundry. We had met the son Eddi at the hydroelectric power plant when they were attempting to repair it. He spoke good English because he had spent some time in England. He had enjoyed a brief career with an English football club, but had had to abandon it because of an injury, and had recently returned to Albania.

We sat on the grass in the garden, where we ate grapes and drank cup after cup of strong Albanian coffee. The Grunas family told us about their lives in the summer in Theth, what the home there meant to them, and why they did not want to get involved in the tourist trade. The family house was finely situated on a hill, but was quite a distance from the road. It would be quite a struggle to get construction material up to it. They were willing to invest, but they felt that there was no sense in opening a guesthouse and trying to rent out rooms at that location.

Herman took several photos of the family in front of the house while the two sisters where hanging the washing out on the line. A few days later, they left for Shkodra, taking their things with them, and charging a neighbour with looking after the dog, the animals and the house.

The Deda Family (Theth Okol)
In the autumn of 2007, on the day of the opening of the Vendetta Tower, we lunched with a group of travellers and embassy staff at the home of the Deda family. Like many other families, Gjon and Marija Deda only spent the summer in Theth and returned

to Shkodra in the winter. They, too, had transformed their home into a guesthouse.

The Deda family lived in the famed old house of Sadri Luka (a rich merchant), which Rose Wilder Lane had visited in 1921. It was a huge building, much larger than anything else we had seen in the valley. We climbed the stairs up to the first floor and had a true Albanian meal where Rose Wilder Lane had eaten.

Not much was left of the impressive interior that Rose had described in great detail during her stay. The furnishings were just as basic as those in other homes. The beds of the guesthouse that had stood in the one-time living-room, had now been stowed into a corner, and we sat at a long table that was put together for us. The meal was served on plastic plates. Two elderly ladies, Dile Ndoja and Shuke Rama, who were relatives of the family, cooked for the group and served, too.

The local specialities they prepared for us were round loaves of cornbread, roasted vegetables including cabbage and pickles (typical of food from the communist period), sheep cheese, mutton, baked potatoes and fresh yoghurt.

This house was used to distribute the sixty copies of the Albanian translation of Den Doolaard's novel, The Horseshoe Inn, that a Dutch tourleader, Dolf Went, had brought with him. The local prefect, Gjergj Harusha, received them on behalf of the inhabitants. Each house got a copy of the well-known Dutch novel about Albanian blood feuding.

It was not easy to reach the house of Gjon and Maria Deda in Theth Okol when we went back in May 2013. The last winter had been severe. There was still a lot of deep snow and the spring runoff had caused much flooding. The bridge was washed out and brought our four-wheel drive to a merciless stop. As such, we had to walk for about an hour until we could find a place to get across the river.

I was saddened to see how the raging river had washed out the power lines that had once brought electricity from the hydropower station in Theth to the isolated homes of Okol. They had snapped like proverbial matchsticks amidst the huge boulders. The violence of nature here made me shiver. There was no more electricity anywhere in the valley. We were told that people from other villages further down the valley had stolen the power lines for their copper. The issue now was how to get the power back on before the tourist season started up. The local people would have to find some sort of solution quick.

We passed by many abandoned homes – once proud domiciles in stone, now all locked up and in various states of disrepair. It was the middle of May and many of the people would soon be returning from Shkodra to spend the summer in the valley. All of the families that owned guesthouses were already back from the city and were busy getting their accommodation ready for the season. Kitchens and pantries were brimming with large sacks of corn, beans and potatoes, and the four and five-bed guestrooms had been spruced up with fresh bedding and towels.

Maria Deda was back in her old home, too, together with her mother-in-law, Dila Ndoja, dressed as always in black. Maria was a cheerful, talkative woman in her forties, full of enthusiasm. She already had reservations from British, Bulgarian and German travellers and groups, though no Dutch people yet.

I asked Maria about Sadri Luka, the famed warrior who had once owned the house. As a dauntless *bajraktar*, he was well known in his day, and his name comes up in the texts of many of the foreign writers who visited the region: from Karl Steinmetz in 1905 to Jan and Cora Gordon in 1925. Some of them even stayed at his house.

Sadri Luka can be seen in a photo dating from 1940, taken by the Italian photographer Giuseppe Massani. Maria explained to me that Sadri Luka's only son, Prek Luka, escaped to Yugoslavia in 1948. His large house in Okol, which in its day had opened its doors to 70 people, was confiscated and given to the Deda family in 1950. It was a sad period in the long history of that venerable house.

In 1959, the head of the Deda family then fell into disfavour with the communist authorities himself, and ended up in prison in Tepelena, together with two fellow villagers, Gjelosh and Ded Ndoja. After that, the house was inhabited solely by the womenfolk, eight of them in all. It was no easy life for them without a man in the house, and their annual trips to visit the men in prison were arduous indeed. Maria's mother-in-law had suffered greatly as a young woman.

Like all the rest of the women of Theth, Maria Deda herself was from elsewhere. She was one of the eleven daughters of Kolë Pal Gjimaj from Precimaj in the lower part of the Shala Valley and married Gjon Deda in 1981. After the wedding, she moved to Okol to live with him and his parents.

For Maria and her family – she now had three children – the end of the communist dictatorship meant the start of a new life. They all moved to the town of Shkodra, and two of her children – her twenty-seven-year-old son Artan and her twenty-four-year-old daughter Liliana – now live in Turin, in Italy. Only her eldest son, the thirty-year-old Vladimir, is still in Albania. He lives in Shkodra.

It was in 2005 that the Deda family joined the tourist development project organised by the German development organization, the GIZ. With the funds made available, they equipped their guestrooms with bathrooms. The GIZ has recently provided a number of guesthouses, including that of Maria, with solar panels. The energy they produce is a godsend when the tourists come in the summer.

Next to Maria's house stands a kitchen shed with a firewood oven for baking bread. In the shed is a magnificently carved wooden chest for flour, with cross-shaped patterns painted on it. Beside the oven are piles of firewood. It is here that the meals are prepared for guests.

Maria's neighbour, Shuke Rama, heard that visitors had arrived and came over to see us. She was eighty-four-years-old and was never married. The white woollen socks she wears are a symbol of her unmarried state. Shuke was not a Sworn Virgin, who are born as women but dress and behave as men. She simply rejected the suitor that her parents had chosen for her as a young girl. Under tribal law, the *Kanun* of Lekë Dukagjini, she was allowed to remain unmarried on condition that she do so for life. She later moved in with her brother and sister-in-law and, since her brother's death, she has lived with his widow.

There was one Sworn Virgin in Okol, however. Her name was Pashkë Sokoli. She was interviewed extensively by the British anthropologist Antonia Young, who met her in 1993. A description of their encounter is given in Antonia's book, the standard reference work on the subject: *Women Who Become Men: Albanian Sworn Virgins*, published in 2000.

We were soon given coffee and a large glass of raki, and we all drank to the success of the coming tourist season.

The Nika Family (Theth Ndërlysa)

In the summer of 2011, we went on a long hike from the centre of Theth down to the waterfall, taking the bridge over the Shala River near the ravine where the Grunas family lived and continued all the way to Theth Ndërlysa.

Theth Ndërlysa is about ten kilometres south of the centre of Theth. As in most of the other parts of Theth, the people of Ndërlysa only stay here in the summer months, and prefer to spend the winter in Shkodra. As a result, this part of the village is virtually abandoned in the wintertime. It boasts of a hydropower station that does not function, an empty school building and a lot of abandoned homes that are mostly in ruins. However, it does have one must-see tourist attraction in the summer, the ravine and rapids in the river. They can be viewed from a bridge that spans the river at a modestly spectacular height. Behind it is a rock formation in stunning hues of pink and brown through which the waterfall squeezes its way, leaving several pools of water for bathing.

I am almost sure, from the precise description of the hues and colours in the rock that she left in her book, that Rose Wilder Lane was here in 1921, saw the river and walked the ten kilometres back to the centre of Theth.

There are two simple guesthouses here. One of them is an impressive two-storey building with a large garden and much pastureland around it. It is right near the river. This is the property of a young couple with four small children. The family, consisting of father Deda Nika and mother Shpresa Nika, with their sons Kristian and Albert and their daughters Denise and Daniela, lives off the money they make in the summer by providing meals and lodging to foreign visitors.

The Nika family served us a scrumptious meal outdoors, with fresh fish they had caught themselves in the river, sheep cheese, yoghurt also made from the milk of their sheep, vegetables, tomatoes and fresh spring onions from their garden.

Before we departed, we bought some white woollen socks from Deda's mother Prena, that she had knitted in the winter months in Shkodra.

As soon as the Buni i Thorës Pass is cleared of snow at the end of April or in early May, the Nika family packs their suitcases in Shkodra and sets off for Theth. Deda Nika is the first to go on foot with his flock of about hundred sheep, a tour that takes him several days, and the rest of the family follows by car.

The Nika family is self-sufficient in the summer. They manage this with the help of their sheep, from which they get milk, wool and meat. Shpresa and her mother-in-law, Prena, milk the sheep every day. She then takes her son Kristian with her up into the high mountain pastures that surround the valley.

Anyone, like the Nika family that owns more than one hundred animals is considered rich because sheep here are life insurance against poverty and hunger.

"If you need money to visit a doctor or to go into town to buy salt and flour, you sell a sheep". The animals are the major source of food during the long winter months of heavy snowfall. Not only do the sheep have to be milked and shorn, they also need new pastureland to graze on every day, and such land is rare in the steep mountain valleys on the border with Montenegro. In the autumn, it takes several hours to get up into the highest of the green pastures.

In May 2013 we visited the Nika family again.

The Deda Nika family now had become rather famous; all the members were interviewed and filmed in their daily life in their mountain village by German Arte TV in 2012 for the program "Zu Tisch...in Albanien".[29]

In the documentary film you can see Farmer Deda opening a water channel at the edge of his farmstead to irrigate his fields. He grows almost everything that his family needs: plums, apples, tomatoes, zucchini, beans, potatoes, grapes, nuts and corn. The fields are irrigated by a complex system of channels. "I learned to farm when I was a small boy," he tells Arte TV. "We have been farming all our lives. We more or less inherited the job. Everyone who lives here knows how to keep animals and to grow crops." He shovels manure into the water to turn it into fertilizer for the crops, while his wife, Shpresa, picks peas and gathers onions and zucchini in the garden for dinner. Like the generations before him, Ded does all his farming without the help of machinery, chemicals and artificial fertilizers. Ded started also keeping bees, together with an old friend from Theth to produce an excellent quality honey of spring flowers.

In the summer, Shpresa cooks not only for her own family, but also for the many hikers who visit the region and stay at her house. Potatoes and beans are the basic ingredients of most meals. To them are added vegetables, onions, salad and sheep cheese. Shpresa often makes lamb or fresh trout, the latter being caught in the torrent flowing right behind the house. She and Ded are among the many families in the valley making a living from the tourists who have found their way into the northern Albanian Alps. Their life in the mountains, which used to be characterised by ceaseless work and deprivation, is now much easier. Some of the farmers who left the region and emigrated during the unrest in 1997 are now returning to this remote valley in northern Albania. Ded, for his part, stayed put when chaos reigned throughout the country. "We have a saying: stones weigh heavier on their own land," he tells Arte TV confidently. "You have more importance and enjoy more respect in your own country. And as you have probably heard, there are not enough jobs abroad, so many people are coming back."

The Rupa Family

Roza Rupa (35), who is the daughter of the proprietor of the Rupa Guesthouse, happened to be with us on our way from Shkodra to Theth in May 2013. She was busy

[29] youtube.com/watch?v=kVEwuj4q7So

remodelling her house to get it ready for the first foreign tourists of the year who were scheduled to arrive in June.

Before we left, we stopped to get some food at a small grocery store on the outskirts of Shkodra because, for the next six or seven hours, there would be no stores or restaurants or cafés on the bumpy road to Theth. Roza bought groceries not only for herself but for us, too, because we decided to stay at her place. It was funny to see her coming out of the store, loaded down and balancing a tray of eggs in one hand. In the old days, the Rupa family had chickens of their own in Theth and eggs galore, but that age had passed.

When got to Theth in early evening we were greeted by Roza's brother, Alfred, who was a student of law in Shkodra. In his spare time, he was busy with repairs to the family house, to get it ready for the many groups that would be coming.

The Rupa Guesthouse is splendidly located. It is a detached stone house in the simple classic style of the valley, the kind of house that children draw. It has two storeys, a red gabled roof, and chimneys for the two fireplaces. It is situated in the middle of the village, between the school and the church, and is surrounded by a large, fenced plot of land, suitable for campers. Right behind the house begin the lofty mountains.

It was in this house, which her father, Pal Rupa, had built with this own hands, that Roza lived from the age of fourth to sixteen. It was here that the Danish travel writer, Nina Rasmussen, stayed on her motorcycle journey through the Shala Valley in 1994 (see Chapter 2: Travel Writers). Roza's eldest brother, Fatmir, spoke French, something quite rare for the people of the valley at the time, and was able to communicate with Nina on her gruelling trek through the mountains and he offered to accommodate her at his place.

In the nearby school building, Roza attended elementary school and the first two years of her secondary education. Three years after Nina's visit, the whole Rupa family then left for the big city, Shkodra.

Pal and Pashkë and their seven children (Fatmir, Valbona, Diana, Sokol, Mirela, Roza and Alfred) lived and worked in Shkodra. They now only go back to Theth in the summer months. All of the Rupa children studied in the city - Roza, too. After completing secondary school, she did a specialized training course in tourism and learned German and English.

When in 2005, the German development organization, the GIZ, prepared a project, in collaboration with about a dozen local families, to transform some of the traditional houses in the valley into accommodation for tourists. Roza immediately applied on behalf of her family to take part in the experiment.

To participate, the Rupa family had to come up with a substantial amount of money of its own, which was not easy for them to do. Fortunately, they received backing from a Dutch tour guide called Dolf Went, who had organised group tours to Albania from the 1960s on, and who knew how enchanting the northern Albanian mountains were. He was enthusiastic about the stunning valley and about the village of Theth, and was willing to play a role in developing tourism in this remote region. As such, he kindly provided a sum of money to renovate the bathrooms and redo the plumbing. During our first visit in 2007, Roza Rupa proudly showed us the results. The living room with an open fireplace also served as a guestroom sleeping four, and upstairs there was a new bathroom. There was only room for four guests at the time. Alfred and a fellow villager then worked on building two more rooms and by late May, everything was ready. They now had enough room to accommodate twelve guests in all. There was even a double room with its own private bath, and a large window extending to the floor that provided a fantastic view of the mountains. I was allowed to sleep there when it was being furbished and had to promise not to step out onto the non-existent balcony. The new bathroom had a nice shower and toilet, but there was no hot water or electricity at the time, and Roza had no generator.

The fireplace was now blazing in the living room, our original bedroom. Roza vanished into the kitchen, not yet renovated and certainly authentic, to make us some pitch-black Turkish coffee. This time, we spent three nights at the guesthouse of Roza and Alfred Rupa, and enjoyed an impressive breakfast every morning on the terrace outside. There was homemade jam and wheat bread, coffee and fresh sheep cheese. Roza also made us her speciality - deep-fried fritters made of flour, water and eggs. While we were having breakfast, she and her brother were busy getting the house in order and tending to the garden.

That evening, we had dinner at the house of Roza's neighbours. This guesthouse, next to the church, was run by Pavlin Polia and his Kosovar wife Vlora, who cooked fantastic meals for their own guests and visitors alike. Pavlin had a generator so there was enough electricity in the evening for lighting and hot water. Vlora made various dishes consisting of peppers, eggplant, beans and cornbread.

As he poured us a glass of light red wine, made in Theth, Pavlin told us tall tales of their Spartan existence in the valley during the winter months, when they were often snowbound for weeks and would hunt wolves.

It was pitch dark when we made our way back to our guesthouse. We managed to keep to the path with light from the screens of our cell phones and with the occasional flashlight. Roza had kindly put candles in the windows to guide us back.

The next day, I asked Roza how her family was doing in Shkodra. Her father Pal had been a farmer and the part-time mayor of the village of Precaj. Her mother Pashka not only did the housework and cared for the seven children, but worked on the side as a midwife. In fact, she served as a country doctor, performing simple medical procedures for the surrounding population whenever need arose. Both of her parents were now retired. They had paid great attention to their children getting a proper education, and the results paid off. Two of the children lived abroad. With help from Nina Rasmussen, the eldest brother Fatmir was able to move to Scandinavia and now has a job in Sweden. His sister Diana is studying medicine in Italy, and the other four children live in Shkodra.

Tourism in the Shala Valley

Herman and I undertook the long and arduous journey into the northern Albanian mountains, from Shkodra to Theth, for a very special reason – to revive the atmosphere we had encountered in the novel 'The Horseshoe Inn' by Dutch writer A. den Doolaard. In and around Theth we found all the locations mentioned by the author, though it took us a full three days to do so. The picturesque surroundings were still there, unchanged, although things were not quite as pristine as they had been during Den Doolaard's visit in 1932.

The Beginnings of Tourism
But a few years ago, the village of Theth had no experience with tourism whatsoever. The Shala Valley had always been isolated, surrounded as it is by high impenetrable mountains. It was nothing unusual for the inhabitants of Theth to walk for days to get anywhere, be it to get goods in a nearby market town or to drive their herds and flocks up into the high mountain pastures.

Between 1900 and the start of the Second World War, a few foreign visitors did manage to get over into the valley for a visit. Most of them were explorers, writers and photographers who were interested in the tribal society preserved there and seeing what the warring clans of the north were up to. After the Balkan Wars and the declaration of Albanian independence in 1912, the region began attracting more scholars, and a flurry of publications arose about the region.

In the early days, foreign visitors who wanted to get to Theth had a long walk before them, or at least a long ride on a horse or mule over the mountain pass. In 1936, a road was constructed from Shkodra to Theth via Boga which made it much easier to reach the valley, but after the Second World War and the rise of the communist regime, Albania's borders were closed.

One of the direct consequences of the break in relations with Yugoslavia in 1948 was that large swathes of northern Albania were declared to be military border zones and were sealed off hermetically. All the mountain passes to Montenegro, Macedonia and Kosovo were strictly guarded by the military. As a result, the Shala Valley became more and more isolated.

Few Albanians from other parts of the country had any interest in going up into the poor and backward mountains, and foreign visitors became extremely rare.

During the communist period, Albanian was virtually sealed off from the rest of the world. Tourism was restricted to a few hundred visitors per year. Most of these people were "fellow travellers", i.e. western admirers of the communist regime. They were put up in hotels at the beach in Durrës and were only able to travel through the country by bus in organized groups, going from one Albturist hotel to the next. They normally visited the archaeological excavations in Butrint and various factories and agricultural co-operatives. I was able to visit Albania myself several times in the seventies and eighties as a fellow traveller.

The tourist groups of the period travelled in old Czech buses that were not entirely suitable for the hairpin turns of the narrow road to Theth. Nor was there any hotel in Theth to accommodate larger groups. Some privileged individuals with good connections were able to visit Theth in the summer when the pass was open and get away from the stifling heat on the coast. Because it was cooler in the mountains, Theth was, even at that time, a very special place for families to spend their holidays. From 1968 onwards Albanians were able to stay in the new hotel or in small wooden huts at the campsite higher up in the valley.

Early Alpine Tourism Nipped in the Bud
The communist dictatorship collapsed in 1990-1991 and things got better in Albania by the mid 1990s. The economy was recovering and the many Albanians who had found jobs abroad were sending their money back home. Foreign investors were also arriving to see what they could do with their capital. Tourism began to flourish, but only along the coastline. The newly created Ministry of Tourism concentrated all of its efforts on stimulating tourism around Durrës and on the southern coast, with its spectacular beaches.

Somewhat later, western tourist agencies came to realise that the mountains had something to offer, too. They began organising tours into the wild and untouched nature reserves in the Albanian mountains.

Once such agency, the Netherlands Development Organisation (*Stichting Nederlandse Vrijwilligers* - SNV), agreed to finance a small tourism project in the Shala Valley. Sustainable regional development was the motto. In co-operation with the impoverished farmers of the valley, the SNV organised hiking and climbing tours for Dutch tourists on well-marked paths in and around Theth. Arrangements were made for hearty meals and cheap accommodation with about ten local families. Setting things up was not easy at the start because the local people were desperately poor and did not know quite what western standards of comfort were. With time, however, everything was arranged: group transport from Shkodra, a Shala Valley Information Centre in Theth and an enthusiastic Albanian SNV representative in Tirana called Ani Dhima.

"Welcome to the breathtaking Albanian Alps. The impressive limestone mountains, the lush beech forests, the pastureland, the icy mountain springs and a hospitable populace will make your stay unforgettable. The farmers of the Shala Valley are waiting to introduce their region to you. Their traditional farmhouses are situated in a rugged landscape – the narrow valley of the Shala River. They will take you over stunning mountain passes covered in alpine flowers, passes that offer spectacular views of the whole valley at the foot of Mount Jezerca, one of the highest peaks in Albania (2,695 m.). Local guides can also take you on various shorter and longer hikes and, if you wish, your luggage can be transported on mules. They can take you to the Arapi Cavern or up to the caves above Vuksanaj that offer an impressive collection of stalactites and stalagmites. Or you can tour the village of Theth on foot and visit the two large stone towers – fortified buildings where men caught up in blood feuds could take refuge. They now serve as little museums. For accommodation, you can stay with local families. They offer rooms in their homes and will provide you with simple but delicious meals."[30]

The SNP (*Stichting Natuur Producties*) travel agency in the Netherlands soon got interested in northern Albania and at the national tourism fair in Amsterdam in January 1997, it offered group tours there. Bookings were made for four groups, ready to go in June, July and August 1997.

Unfortunately, one month after the tourism fair in the Netherlands, the Albanian economy collapsed under the infamous pyramid investment schemes. Many Albanians had sold their homes and property to invest cash in these 'get rich quick" schemes that promised extremely high profits – ten to twenty percent per year. These high interest rates could only be sustained as long as more and more people invested. Those who got in early, actually did make a lot of money but latecomers saw their life's saving go up in smoke. Such pyramid investment schemes, also known as Ponzi schemes, had made their appearance in western countries, but in Albania, where the population and its rulers had little experience with a free-market economy, they proved to be a national catastrophe. For months, there was complete anarchy in Albania. Many people died. Prisoners in all the jails escaped and arms caches were plundered. I witnessed an Albturist hotel in Vlora, where I had stayed, being looted. Armed men were running in and out, carrying off beds, lamps and tables. It was not a pleasant sight for a country that was in the early stages of building up a tourist industry.

The pyramid investment schemes signified the abrupt end to Albanian tourism and, in particular, an end to the project supported by the SNV and the SNP travel agency in the north. The collaboration was called off, and other foreign investors who had invested money in tourism projects fled the country. Albania was the last place on earth where a tourist would want to go.

At the same time, more and more inhabitants of the mountain valleys in the north were abandoning their homes and settling in Shodra and on the coast. Most people left Theth and those who remained behind lived in isolation and under appalling conditions.

About ten years later, the German development organisation GIZ (*Gesellschaft für Internationale Zusammenarbeit*) revived the old tourism project. And it was high time. Two Albanian representatives of the GIZ in Tirana, Ismail Beka and Edlira Kruja, set up an Association of Family Tourism with some of the inhabitants of Theth, to be run by the mayor, Prek Harusha. Ismail and Edlira provided the members of the as-

---

30 From *De Albanese Alpen: de Himalayas van Europa*, brochure of the Netherlands Development Organisation, 1996.

sociation with support to renovate their farmhouses for accommodating guests and organised training courses in communicating with foreign guests (none of the farmers spoke any English). They also had the trails marked for hikers.

Two experienced Swiss mountain climbers, Christian Zindel and Barbara Hausammann, provided tremendous impetus with the publication of an excellent hiking map (scale 1 : 50,000) of the region and a guidebook with a total of 17 hikes from Theth to Valbona and Kelmendi. All of the routes and hiking paths are well marked with red and white stones and the GPS coordinates are given. Anyone going to Theth for hiking should definitely get a copy of their hiking guide to northern Albania.

The families in Theth only had wooden outdoor toilets and no showers. This was a bit of a drawback for most tourists. The GIZ therefore invested two thousand Euros per family to build modern bathrooms. The members of the association had to provide some funds, too, for furnishings. Most of the managed to save up to buy simple beds with mattresses and western-style bedding, and clothes closets. Eight families were ready by the start of the project in 2005, and this provided a new accommodation capacity in Theth of sixty beds. Accommodation in the rest of the homes was rather Spartan, as we discovered when we first spent the night there. We slept in very basic four-bed rooms with one simple clothes closet for everyone, very basic bedding and a primitive bedside table. We had to share the bathroom and toilet with other guests. Fortunately there was light because the hydropower station was still working at the time.

In the early years of the project, many problems arose because none of the families could speak or read English. In the morning, the first time we visited Theth, we filled out a bilingual (Albanian/English) checklist of what we wanted to have for dinner in the evening. This way, Lule and Age Harusha could see if we wanted a vegetarian meal or any of the regional specialities, such as maize porridge with butter, or cheese, cornbread and mutton. Nowadays there is usually no more need for such lists because the children speak English and the women who do the cooking know enough about what tourists like and do not like.

Mountain Climbing

In principle, Theth is an excellent point of departure for mountaineers. The first foreign mountain climber to visit the region and scale lofty Mount Jezerca was the Hungarian scholar Baron Franz Nopcsa in 1907.

The mountains became popular after the Second World War, and Eastern European climbing groups soon discovered the Theth region and the nearby peaks of Radohima (2568 m.), Jezerca (2692 m.) and Arapi (2217 m.). But Albania fell out with these countries (it broke off ties with Yugoslavia in 1948 and with the Soviet Union in 1961), so that there were no more foreign climbers. In addition, the passes were not far from the border with Yugoslavia. The whole border area and all the passes northwards were closed and strictly guarded for 45 years.

When the borders were finally opened, the climbers lost no time getting back into the region and its exotic, unexplored mountains. The Dutch mountain climber Ronald Naar (1955-2011) visited the region in 1995, following in the tracks of Den Doolaard. He and his guide, the geologist Kujtim Onuzi, climbed the Arapi, Jezerca and Radohima, the highest peaks of the Accursed Mountains. He was extremely enthusiastic about Albania's potential for mountain climbing.

Theth is indeed an excellent location for experienced mountain climbers. Most of them now come from the Czech Republic, Poland and Hungary. It must be noted that it can be dangerous to climb in this region because basic equipment is lacking. You have to get your maps, prepare your journey and bring everything with you. And there is no helicopter available for emergencies.

Winter Sports

There are no winter sports facilities in Theth as yet. It could be a great ski area, but for this, the Albanian government would have to invest in paving the road and improving the basic infrastructure. Theth is simply too remote, and the current road used to get there is in an appalling state. No commercial ski operator would invest in lifts, slopes or hotels here at the moment.

The region on the other side of the Valbona Pass has great potential, too. Valbona is much easier to reach with the new highway from Tirana to Kosovo, and quite a number of new guesthouses have sprung up there recently.

The Rise in Tourism Brings New Problems

The village of Theth has experienced a modest economic boom from tourism. In 2007 there were 7.000 overnight stays. In 2011 there were twice that number. The first pioneers to venture into Theth did so to climb the mountains. Ninety percent of them were from Eastern Europe, from Albania's one-time socialist allies – the Czech Republic, Poland and Hungary. They did not bring much money into the valley because they camped out in the farmers' fields rather than spending the night in the guesthouses. Many of them also brought their own food and cooked it outdoors on cookers. When we were staying with the Harusha family, there were still a couple of tents of Czech mountain climbers in the garden, yet they paid for the privilege and the local people were happy to have them.

More important for the native inhabitants, however, are tourists who stay in the guesthouses. And there are more and more of them. Several travel agencies now specialise in group tours to Theth as they have discovered that northern Albania is an ideal and inexpensive destination for hikers. Travel agencies from all European countries and from the USA organise hiking tours to northern Albania. The number of visitors to the Shala Valley and Theth is rising very fast. Transnational hiking tours across the mountains of Albania, Kosovo and Montenegro are also gaining in popularity (Peaks of the Balkans trail: www.peaksofthebalkans.com).

Tourism is now vitally important to the economy of Theth. Otherwise, the village would most certainly have been abandoned by now. More and more tourists are staying with the original five families who, with the help of the GIZ, invested their money in 2005 and transformed their homes into guesthouses. It turned out to be a very good investment for them, and they have since expanded. Other people in the village soon realised what was going on and were sorry they had not taken part in the project. There are now fourteen families in Theth that offer accommodation and the beginning of some real competition. A certain amount of envy arose within the village community of those families who had access to capital from relatives abroad and could invest. They were able to renovate and extend their homes and now live better than the families who started later or who had no relatives abroad. Other people have remained very poor.

As a result of recent developments, a new but understandable problem has arisen. What is to be done with all the refuse left over by the tourists? Rubbish bins are needed, and have to be set up throughout the village. But there is no garbage collection in the valley and no garbage dump. The local inhabitants did not produce much waste. They were wont to recycle everything or to burn it. Beer cans and plastic bags were unknown. Garbage is now an enormous problem on the Albanian coast and in particular in the larger towns which are drowning in their own waste. The GIZ has discussed the issue with the inhabitants of the valley and plans have been made, for the moment, for waste to be transported to Shkodra.

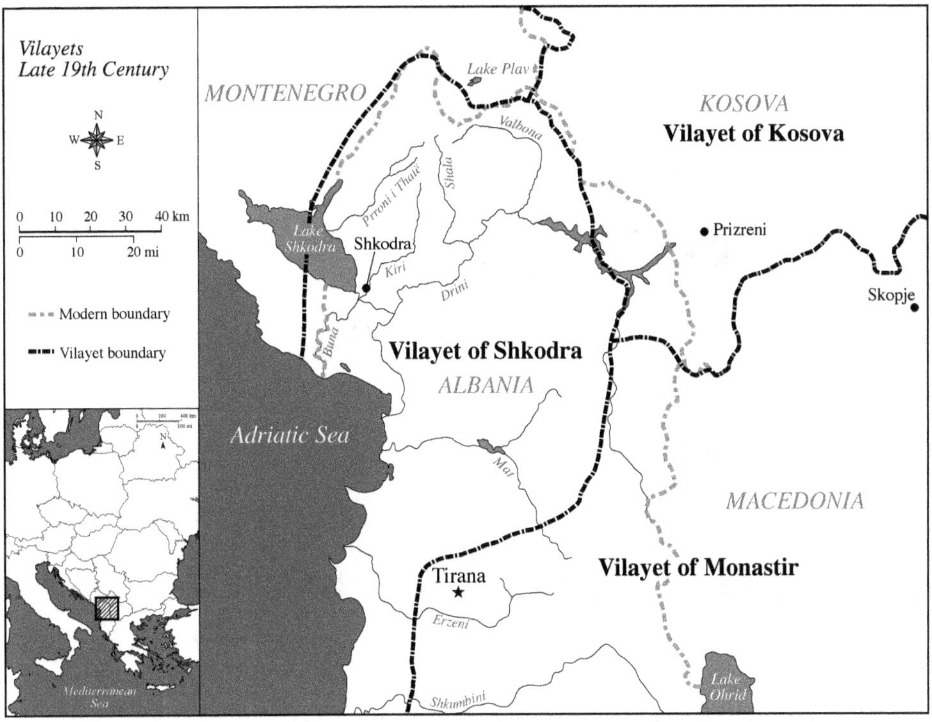

Map of Ottoman provincial boundaries in northern Albania; late nineteenth-century vilayets (based on Pitcher 1972 and Malcolm 1999). Jill Seagard

Map of northern Albania tribal territories (derived in large part from the Admiralty War Staff Map of Northern Albania showing Distribution of Tribes, 1916 and Durham 1985 (1909). Jill Seagard

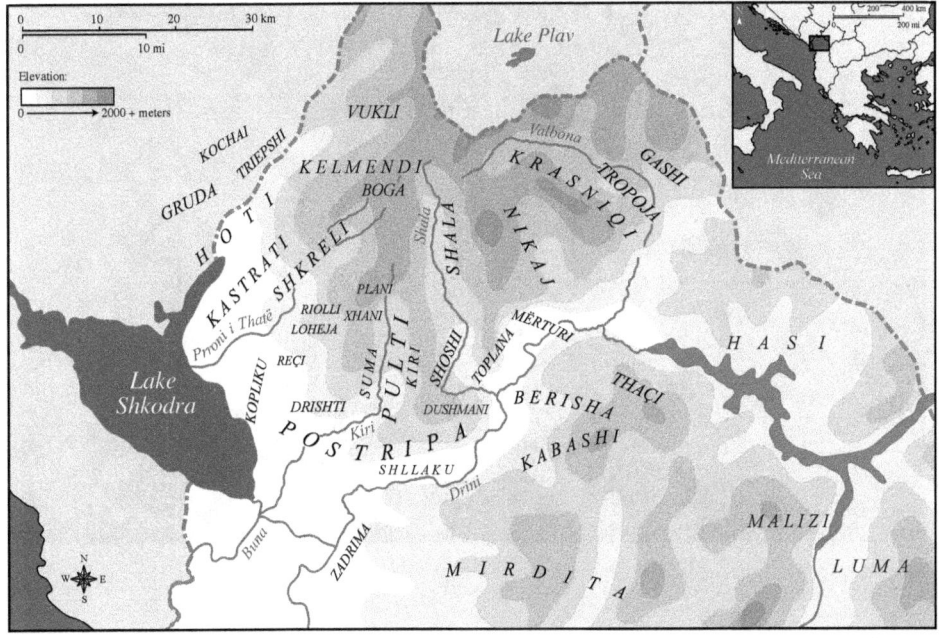

Map of modern northern Albania and surrounding countries showing major cities, rivers and lakes.
Jill Seagard

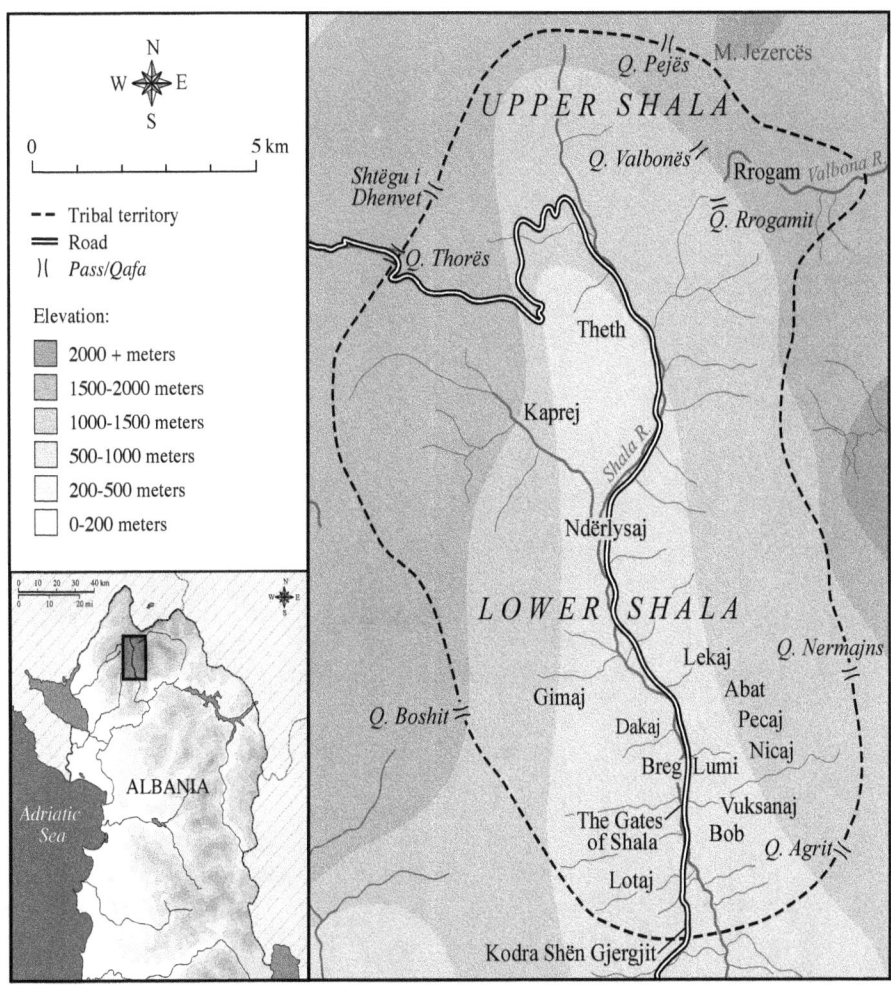

Map of the Shala Valley showing villages, roads, rivers, mountains and passes. Jill Seagard

Left: Theth overview of the village, 2011.

On the northerly road from Boga to Theth, near the Sheep Trail Pass, 2007

The southerly road, from Kir to Theth, 2013

Cafe owner in Boga, 2010

Cafe owner in Kir, 2013

The monument to Edith Durham on the Buni i Thorës Pass, 2010

Interior of the church of Theth, 2011

The church of Theth, 2007

Wooden crosses in the graveyard, 2007

The Vendetta Tower, 2010

Nicollë Koçeku in front of his tower, 2007

Repairing the hydropower station, 2007

The refurbished school in the village, 2007

Sofia Harusha as the only child in her class, 2007

The Kola mill, 2010

Entrance to the Ethnographic Museum, 2007

House and fence, 2007

Fence of branches marking the edge of a property, 2007

Bunker near Okol, 2013

Gjergj Harusha, 2007

'Old' Agé Harusha, 2007

Prek Harusha, 2007

Lulë Harusha, 2007

'Young' Agé Harusha, 2007

Nikë Harusha, 2007

Pëllumb Harusha, 2007

Pashkë Harusha, 2007

Marasha Harusha, 2007

Sofia Harusha, 2007

'Old' Agé Harusha, 2007

Paulin Harusha, 2007

Prek Harusha and his beehives, 2010

The Harusha family cow, 2010

House of the Grunasi family, 2007

The Grunasi family standing in front of their house, 2007

Father Grunasi, 2007

Mother Grunasi, 2007

Shkurte Gumnari, 2010

Nikë Gumnari at work in the fields, 2007

Cross and horseshoe above the door at the Gumnari family residence, 2010

The Gumnari family learns to communicate in English, 2010

Nikollë Koçeku, 2011

Pashkë Koçeku, 2011

Mark Koçeku, 2011

Sokol Koçeku, 2011

Pashkë Pisha, 2010

Martin Pisha with a goat skin, 2010

Martin Pisha, 2010

House of the Rupa family, 2007

Roza Rupa, 2013

Maria Deda sifting flour at the old wooden chest in the storeroom, Okol, 2013

Shuke Rama, Okol, 2013

Dile Ndoja, Okol, 2013

Dedë Nika, Ndërlysa, 2013

Dedë's mother, Prena Nika, with freshly baked cornbread, Ndërlysa, 2013

Denise Nika, Ndërlysa, 2013

Labouring in Ndërlysa, 2013

File Shkafi in front of the church, 2011

A farming woman, 2007

Shepherdess Zefja Polia, 2007

Leze Gërla with her grandchildren, Kristofer and Elizabeta, 2007

Shepherdess, 2010

Martin Pisha's grandson beside the cauldron for distilling raki in the attic of the ethnographic museum, 2007

Drane Gjergji, 2007

Man on the field in front of the church, 2007

Woman knitting on the field in front of the church, 2007

Couple harvesting corn, 2007

Lindita Koçeku, 2011

Ndoc Deda, 2013

Man in Ndërlysa, 2013

Man in Ndërlysa bringing home maize stalks, 2013

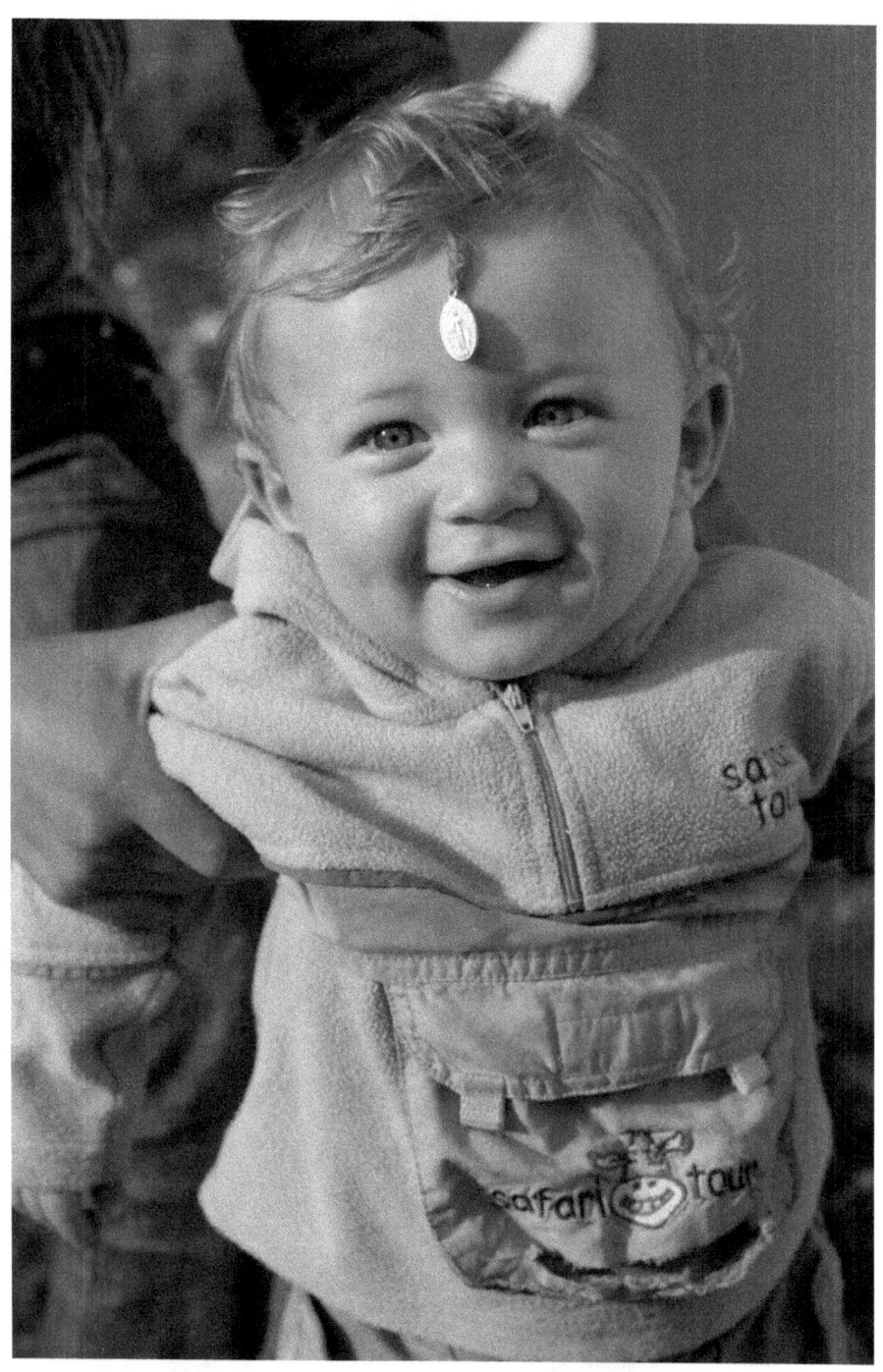

Grandson of Gjergj Harusha with amulet against evil, 2013

Farmer ploughing, 2010

A woman hoeing between the maize, 2011

Sheep on their way to summer pasture, 2010

Making hay near the cemetery, 2011.

Haystacks, 2007

The valley, 2011

The Grunas ravine, 2007

Mount Arapi, 2010

The valley in the mist, 2011

Houses in Okol during the spring runoff, 2013

Rock formations carved out by water, near Ndërlysa, 2013

Waterfall at the Blue Eye, near Ndërlysa, 2013

The Vendetta Tower and the house of the Koçeku family in winter, 2012

Church in winter, 2012

Graveyard in winter, 2012

Winter landscape, 2012

Old house in the winter, 2012

Bibliography

AL HASHIMI, Nadia, *Keepers of the Pass: Gender Roles of Women in Northern Albania*. Thesis Honors Program, Shala Valley Project. Jackson MS, Millsaps College, 2010. 92 pp.

ALLCOCK, John B. and YOUNG, Antonia, *Black Lambs and Grey Falcons: Women Travellers in the Balkans*. Bradford: Bradford University Press, 1991. 216 pp

BEILMAN, Georgia Ellen, *Albania: Religion, Identity and Solidarity*. Thesis Honors Program. Shala Valley Project. Jackson MS, Millsaps College, 2005. 82 pp.

BELLUSCIO, Giovanni and GENESIN, Monica, Thethi e la sua parlata: osservazione di carattere linguistico e culturale dopo un'indagine sul campo [Theth and its Dialect: Linguistic and Cultural Observations Following Field Research]. in: Demiraj, Bardhyl (ed.) *Wir sind die Deinen: Studien zur albanischen Sprache, Literatur und Kulturgeschichte dem Gedenken an Martin Camaj (1825-1992) gewidmet*. Wiesbaden: Harrassowitz, 2010. p. 199-230.

DOOLAARD, A. den, *De Herberg met het Hoefijzer* [The Horseshoe Inn]. Novel. Amsterdam: Querido, 1933. 156 pp.

DOOLAARD, A. den, *Van vrijheid en dood* [Of Freedom and Death] Amsterdam: Querido, 1935. 251 pp.

DOOLAARD, A. den, *Het leven van een landloper: Autobiografie* [A Vagrant's Life: Autobiography]. Amsterdam: Querido, 1958. 367 pp.

DOOLAARD, A. den, *Bujtina me potkua* [The Horseshoe Inn]. Novel. Albanian translation by Sherefedin Mustafa. Utrecht & Tirana: Skanderbeg Books, 2005. 88 pp.

DURHAM, Mary Edith, *Through the Land of the Serb*. London: Edward Arnold, 1904. 345 pp.

DURHAM, Mary Edith, *The Burden of the Balkans*. London: Thomas Nelson and Sons, 1905. 384 pp.

DURHAM, Mary Edith, *High Albania*. London: Edward Arnold, 1909 reprint London: Virago Press, 1985. 352 pp.

DURHAM, Mary Edith, *The Struggle for Scutari*. London: Edward Arnold, 1914. 320 pp.

DURHAM, Mary Edith, *Twenty Years of Balkan Tangle*. London: Allen & Unwin, 1920. 295 pp.

DURHAM, Mary Edith, *Some Tribal Origins, Laws and Customs of the Balkans*. London: Allen & Unwin, 1928, reprint AMS 1979. 318 pp.

DURHAM, Mary Edith, *Albania and the Albanians. Selected Articles and Letters, 1903-1944*. Introduction by Harry Hodgkinson. London: The Centre for Albanian Studies, 2001. 261 pp.

DURHAM, Mary Edith, *Letters from Albania: the Unpublished Correspondence of Edith Durham, 1908-1914*. Edited by Bejtullah Destani. London: I. B. Tauris, 2014. 352 pp.

DURHAM, Mary Edith, *The Blaze of the Balkans: Selected Writings, 1903-1941*. Edited by Robert Elsie and Bejtullah Destani. With an introduction by Elizabeth Gowing. London: I. B. Tauris, 2014. 224 pp.

EBERHART, Helmut, KASER, Karl (Hg), *Albanien, Stammesleben zwischen Tradition und Moderne*. Wien, Koln, Weimar: Bohlau Verlag 1995. 200 pp.

ELSIE, Robert, *A Dictionary of Albanian Religion, Mythology and Folk Culture*. London: Hurst & Company, 2001. 357 pp.

ELSIE, Robert, *Historical Dictionary of Albania*. Second Edition. Historical Dictionaries of Europe, No. 75. Lanham, Toronto and Plymouth: Scarecrow Press, 2010. LXXIII + 587 pp.

ELSIE, Robert. *Biographical Dictionary of Albanian History*. London: I. B. Tauris, in association with The Centre for Albanian Studies, 2013. ix + 541 pp.

ELSIE, Robert & MATHIE-HECK, Janice (ed.) Songs of the Frontier Warriors: Këngë Kreshnikësh. Albanian Epic Verse in a Bilingual English-Albanian Edition. Edited introduced and translated from the Albanian by Robert Elsie and Janice Mathie-Heck. Wauconda: Bolchazy-Carducci, 2004. XVIII + 414 pp www.elsie.de

FISHTA, Gjergj, *The Highland Lute (Lahuta e Malcís): the Albanian National Epic*. Translated from the Albanian by Robert Elsie & Janice Mathie-Heck. London: I. B. Tauris in association with the Centre for Albanian Studies, 2005. XVIII + 487 pp.

GALATY, Michael, LAFE, Ols, LEE, Wayne E., TAFILICA, Zamir (editors). *Light and Shadow, Isolation and Interaction in the Shala Valley of Northern Albania*; Monumenta Archeologica 28, Cotzen institute of Archaelogical press.Los Angeles: University of California, 2013. XXVI + 274 pp.

GJEÇOV, Shtjefën, *Kanuni i Leke Dukagjinit / The Code of Lek Dukagjinit*. Albanian text collected and arranged by Shtjefën Gjeçov. Translated with an introduction by Leonard Fox. New York: Gjonlekaj Publishing Company, 1989. 269 pp.

GORDON, Jan and Cora, *Two Vagabonds in Albania*. London: John Lane, 1927. 304 pp.

GOWING, Elizabeth, *Edith and I. On the trail of an Edwardian traveller in Kosovo*. Cornwall: Elbow Publishing, 2013. 280 pp. www.elizabethgowing.com

GRIMM, Hans, "Einige Ergebnisse anthropologischer Untersuchungen von Dr. Reimer Schulz in Nordalbanien" [Some Results of the Anthropological Research of Dr. Reimer Schulz in Northern Albania]. in: *Anthropologischer Anzeiger*, Jahrgang 19, Heft 1-2 (1943-1944), p. 54-58.

HANBURY-TENISON, Robin, *Land of Eagles: Riding through Europe's Forgotten Country*. London: I.B. Tauris, 2009. 224 pp. Website www.robinsbooks.co.uk

HASLUCK, Margaret, *The Unwritten Law in Albania: A Record of the Customary Law of the Albanian Tribes*. Cambridge: Cambridge University Press, 1954. 285 pp.

HOLTZ, William, *Travels with Zenobia: Paris to Albania in a Model T Ford. A Journal by Rose Wilder Lane and Helen Dore Boylston*. Columbia: University of Missouri Press, 1983. 117 pp.

HOLTZ, William, *The Ghost in the Little House: a Life of Rose Wilder Lane*. Missouri Biography Series. Columbia: University of Missouri Press, 1993. 425 pp.

KADARE, Ismail, *The Palace of Dreams*. A Novel Written in Albanian and Translated from the French of Jusuf Vrioni by Barbara Bray. New York: William Morrow & Co., 1993. 205 pp.

KADARE, Ismail, *Broken April*. Translated from the Albanian. New York: New Amsterdam, & London: Saqi, 1990. 216 pp.

LIEBERT, Erich, *Aus dem Nordalbanischen Hochgebirge* [From the Northern Albanian Highlands], Zur Kunde der Balkanhalbinsel, Heft 10. Sarajevo: Daniel A. Kujon, 1909. 74 pp.

LUCKWALD, Erich von, *Albanien: Land zwischen Gestern und Morgen* [Albania: Country between Yesterday and Tomorrow]. Munich: F. Bruckmann, 1942. 128 pp.

MACBRIDE, Roger Lea, *Rose Wilder Lane: Her Story*. New York: Stein & Day, 1977. 236 pp.

MULDER, Gerda and ORDEMAN, Piet, *Albanië: Een Reisgids, geografie, geschiedenis, politiek, economie, beschrijving van reisroutes, praktische informatie voor toeristen*. [Albania: A Travel Guide, Geography, History, Politics, Economy, Travel Routes, Practical Information for Tourists]. Rotterdam: Ordeman. First edition 1984, 308 pp. Second edition 1988, 376 pp.

MULDER, Gerda and ZONDERLAND, Herman, *Een fascinatie voor Theth: het Albanese bergdorp van A. den Doolaard* [A Passion for Theth: The Albanian Mountain Village of A. Den Doolaard]. Gerda Mulder, tekst en samenstelling. Herman Zonderland, foto's. Utrecht & Tirana: Skanderbeg Books, 2012. 229 pp.

NOPCSA, Franz, Baron, *Das Katholische Nordalbanien* [Catholic Northern Albania]. Vienna: Gerold, 1907. 56 pp.

NOPCSA, Franz, Baron, *Aus Šala und Klementi: Albanische Wanderungen* [From Shala and Kelmendi: Albanian Wanderings]. Sarajevo: Daniel A. Kajon, 1910. 115 pp.

NOPCSA, Franz, Baron, *Haus und Hausrat im katholischen Nordalbanien* [House and Household Equipment in Catholic Northern Albania]. Sarajevo: Bosnisch-Herzegowinisches Institut für Balkanforschung, 1912. 92 pp.

NOPCSA, Franz, Baron, *Beiträge zur Vorgeschichte und Ethnologie Nordalbaniens* [Contributions to the Prehistory and Ethnology of Northern Albania], Sarajevo 1912, NOPCSA, Franz, Baron, *Bauten, Trachten und Geräte Nordalbaniens* [Buildings, Costumes and Tools of Northern Albania], Berlin: De Gruyter, 1925. VIII + 257 pp.

NOPCSA, Franz, Baron, *Geologie und Geographie Nordalbaniens* [Geology and Geography of Northern Albania], Öhrlingen 1932.

NOPCSA, Franz, Baron, *Reisen in den Balkan: die Lebenserinnerungen des Franz Baron Nopcsa* [Travels in the Balkans: Memoirs of Baron Franz Nopcsa]. Eingeleitet, herausgegeben und mit Anhang versehen von Robert Elsie. Peja (Kosovo): Dukagjini Balkan Books, Dukagjini, 2001. XII + 527 pp.

NOPCSA, Franz, Baron. *Traveler, Scholar, Political Adventurer, a Transylvanian Baron at the Birth of Albanian Independence: the Memoirs of Franz Nopcsa*. Edited and translated from the German by Robert Elsie. Budapest, New York: Central European University Press, 2013. 240 pp.

OLINK, Hans, *Dronken van het leven: A. den Doolaard, zwerver, schrijver, journalist. Biografie* [Drunk with Life: A. Den Doolaard, Wanderer, Writer and Journalist]. Amsterdam: Atlas, 2011. 500 pp.

RASMUSSEN, Nina, *Som en albansk jomfru: en rejse gennem et ukendt land i Europa* [Like an Albanian Sworn Virgin: A Journey Through an Unknown Country]. Copenhagen: Gyldendal, 1995. 231 pp. www.ninaoghjalte.dk

RYALL, Anka, *Odysseus i skjørt: kvinners erobring av reiselitteraturen* [Ulysses in a Dress: Women's Conquest of Travel Literature]. Oslo: Pax, 2004. 350 pp.

SCHULZ, Reimer, "Leichenbegräbnis und Totenkult bei den Malisoren" [Burial and the Cult of the Dead among the Northern Albanian Highlanders]. in: *Atlantis, Länder, Völker, Reisen*, Leipzig, vol. 10 (1938), p. 257-259.

SELIGER, Kurt, *Albanien. Land der Adlersöhne. Ein Reisebuch in Wort und Bild* [Albania: Land of the Songs of the Eagle. A Travel Book in Words and Pictures]. Vienna: Globus, 1958. 237 pp.

SENECHAL, Marjorie, *Long Life to your Children: A Portrait of High Albania*. Photographed by Stan Sherer. Boston: University of Massachusetts Press, Boston, 1997. 240 pp

SHALA VALLEY PROJECT. *Archeological and Ethnographic Reports*. Jackson MS, Millsaps College, 2005-2009.

STEINMETZ, Karl, *Eine Reise durch die Hochländergaue Nordalbaniens* [A Trip through the Highlands of Northern Albania], Zur Kunde der Balkanhalbinsel, Heft 1. Vienna: A. Hartleben, 1904. 68 pp.

STEINMETZ, Karl, *Ein Vorstoß in die nordalbanischen Alpen* [A Venture into the Northern Albanian Alps], Zur Kunde der Balkanhalbinsel, Heft 3. Vienna: A. Hartleben, 1905. 60 pp.

STEINMETZ, Karl, *Von der Adria zum Schwarzen Drin* [From the Adriatic to the Black Drin], Zur Kunde der Balkanhalbinsel, Heft 6. Sarajevo: Daniel A. Kajon, 1908. 78 pp.

TALANI, Rifat (ed.), *Razëm-Bogë-Theth: veçori fiziko-gjeografike, hartografike dhe turistike* [Razëm-Bogë-Theth: Geographical, Cartographic and Touristic Characteristics]. Shkodra: Camaj-Pipa, 2000. 102 pp.

TANNER, Marcus, *Albania's Mountain Queen: Edith Durham and the Balkans*, London: .B. Tauris, 2014. 293 pp.

TRETHOWEN, Gill, *Kralica e malësorëvet: Brenga e Ballkanit dhe Edith Durham. Queen of the Mountains: The Balkan Adventures of Edith Durham*. London: The British Council, 1996. 28 pp.

WILDER LANE, Rose, *Peaks of Shala, Being a Record of Certain Wanderings Among the Hill-tribes of Albania*. London: Chapman & Dodd, 1923, 224 pp.

WILDER LANE, Rose, *Majat e Shalës* [Peaks of Shala]. Përktheu Avni Spahiu. Prishtina: Rilindja, 1997. 333 pp.

YOUNG, Antonia, *Women who Become Men: Albanian Sworn Virgins*. Oxford & New York: Berg Publishers, 2000. 168 pp.

YOUNG, Antonia, *Gratë që u bënë burra*. Utrecht/Tirana: Skanderbeg Books, 2014. 168 pp.

ZINDEL, Christian & HAUSAMMANN, Barbara, *Shqipëria e Veriut: Thethi dhe Kelmendi, guide për ecje malore* [Northern Albania: Theth and Kelmendi, a Hiking Guide]. Tirana: Toena, 2010. 142 pp.

ZINDEL, Christian & HAUSAMMANN, Barbara, *Wanderführer Nordalbanien: Thethi und Kelmend*. Munich: Huber Verlag, 2008. 142 pp.

ZINDEL, Christian & HAUSAMMANN, Barbara, *Hiking Guide Northern Albania. Thethi and Kelmendi*. Munich: Huber Verlag, 2008. 142 pp.

ZINDEL, Christian & HAUSAMMANN, Barbara, *Wanderkarte Nord Albanien*, Thethi und Kelmendi. Map. Scale 1 : 50.000. Munich: Huber Verlag, 2009. www.kartographie.de

Photo Credits

Part I and II
Pjetër and Kel Marubi © Fototeka Marubi, Shkodra (Pjetër p. 34, 43, 48, 49; Kel p. 37, 58, 102 and 109)
Shan Pici © Fototeka Marubi, Shkodra (p. 39, 40, 52, 146, 153, 159, 165, 177, 178)
Franz Nopcsa © Hungarian Natural History Museum, Hungary (p. 61)
Carl Pietzner © Derszi Elekes Andor, Budapest (p. 56)
Kurt Steinmetz © A. Hartleben, Vienna 1904 (p. 45)
Edith Durham © Royal Anthropological Institute, London (p. 69, 71, 79, 82, 84, 85, 86 and 87)
Annette Marquis © Harper & Brothers, New York 1923 (p. 90, 93, 95, 110 and 114)
A. den Doolaard © Erven Spoelstra, Sint Anthonis (p. 148, 149, 150, 152, 154, 155 and 156)
Erich von Luckwald © F. Bruckmann, Munich 1942 (p. 122, 147, 158, 160, 162 and 172)
Giuseppe Massani © Il Rubicone, Rome 1940 (p. 41, 120, 128, 130, 132, 133, 161, 162, 163 and 164)
Reimer Schulz © Zeitschrift *Atlantis, Länder, Völker, Reisen*, Leipzig 1938 (p. 166 and 167)
Kurt & Fritzi Seliger © Veb F. A. Brockhaus, Leipzig 1960 (p. 170 and 174)
© American Red Cross, Library of Congress Prints and Photographs Online Catalog (PPOC Washington DC) (p. 97 and 99)
© Spaarnestad Archives, Amsterdam (p. 145)
© Nina Rasmussen, Copenhagen (p. 183, 186, 188 and 191)
© Artur Metani, The Hague (p. 12)
© Richard van den Brink, Utrecht (p. 23)
© Herman Zonderland, Delft (p. 26, 29 and 30)
© Roger Sorel, Giethoorn (p. 31)

Part III
All the photos were taken by Herman Zonderland
© Herman Zonderland, Delft, www.zonderland.nl
with the exceptions of:
© Freek Zonderland, Delft (p. 232)
© Roger Sorel, Giethoorn (p. 239)
© Ricardo Fahrig, Tirana (p. 315, 316, 317, 318 and 319)

www.ingramcontent.com/pod-product-compliance
Lightning Source LLC
Chambersburg PA
CBHW071653160426
43195CB00012B/1457